MW00534548

Guns, Guerillas, and the Great Leader

Tom,

I am really happy to be able to send you a copy of my book. This was a long time in the making – 8 years to be exact! Thanks for continuously being a source of support and friendship during the past few years. I look back on my time at NWC with great fondness and appreciation. You and I sure did create some nice and unique memories! This book is a small token of my gratitude for all your help you've given me over the past few years. You may even find a little S&P influence in here!

Best,
Ben Young

COLD WAR
INTERNATIONAL HISTORY
PROJECT SERIES

Edited by James G. Hershberg

Wilson Center

Published in collaboration with the Woodrow Wilson International Center for Scholars

GUNS, GUERILLAS, AND THE GREAT LEADER

NORTH KOREA AND THE THIRD WORLD

Benjamin R. Young

STANFORD UNIVERSITY PRESS
Stanford, California

STANFORD UNIVERSITY PRESS
Stanford, California

©2021 by the Board of Trustees of the Leland Stanford Junior University.
All rights reserved.

No part of this book may be reproduced or transmitted in any form or by any means, electronic or mechanical, including photocopying and recording, or in any information storage or retrieval system without the prior written permission of Stanford University Press.

Printed in the United States of America on acid-free, archival-quality paper

Library of Congress Cataloging-in-Publication Data
Names: Young, Benjamin R., author.
Title: Guns, guerillas, and the great leader : North Korea and the Third World / Benjamin R. Young.
Other titles: Cold War International History Project series.
Description: Stanford, California : Stanford University Press, 2021. | Series: Cold War International History Project | Includes bibliographical references and index.
Identifiers: LCCN 2020041443 (print) | LCCN 2020041444 (ebook) | ISBN 9781503613294 (cloth) | ISBN 9781503627635 (paperback) | ISBN 9781503627642 (epub)
Subjects: LCSH: Korea (North)—Foreign relations—Developing countries. | Developing countries—Foreign relations—Korea (North)
Classification: LCC DS935.7.D44 Y68 2021 (print) | LCC DS935.7.D44 (ebook) | DDC 327.51930172/4—dc23
LC record available at https://lccn.loc.gov/2020041443
LC ebook record available at https://lccn.loc.gov/2020041444

Cover design: Derek Thornton / Notch Design

Typeset by Kevin Barrett Kane in 10/13.5 Adobe Garamond Pro

I dedicate this book to my wonderful and loving parents,
Ted and Annette Young.

Contents

Acknowledgments

First and foremost, I want to thank my partner, Susan Kim, my family (Mom, Dad, Sara, and Tom), and my grandmothers, aunts, uncles, and cousins for supporting me during the process of writing this book. Without their help and support, I would not have been able to complete it. I also want to thank my mentors Gregg Brazinsky, Jim Hershberg, Jisoo Kim, Mitch Lerner, and Ed McCord.

My journey into the historical discipline began at my alma mater, SUNY Brockport. The history department at Brockport, especially Professors Meredith Roman and Anne Macpherson, always encouraged me in my pursuit of a higher degree in history and a career in education or public policy. I also want to thank my group of lifelong friends back home in Rochester, New York, for providing much needed levity and humor during the course of writing my book. My colleagues at the U.S. Naval War College, especially Commander Tom Baldwin and Professors Jason Kelly, Michelle Getchell, Rob Hutchinson, and Dave Stone, were incredibly helpful and supportive during my one-year postdoctoral fellowship in Newport. I also want to thank my colleagues at Dakota State University, especially Joe Bottum, Judy Dittman, Pete Hoesing, Viki Johnson, Kurt Kemper, and Will Sewell, for helping me adjust to teaching and doing research at a small public university in South Dakota. Finally, I want to thank Victor Cha, David Kang, and my CSIS/USC Korea #NextGen cohort for their camaraderie and sense of community. I also want to express appreciation to all the individuals who have helped me obtain files from foreign archives for this project, such as Tycho Van Der Hoog, Christian Ostermann, Chuck Kraus, Sergey Radchenko, and George Roberts. Additional thanks go to my colleagues in North

Korean studies and Cold War international history who have supported me during this research, most notably Adam Cathcart, Steven Denney, Chris Green, Oliver Hotham, Cheehyung Harrison Kim, Andrei Lankov, Chad O'Carroll, Andrei Schmid, Alek Sigley, and Peter Ward.

I also want to express gratitude to the many institutions that provided me with research support for this project, including SUNY Brockport's History Department, the Fulbright Foundation, the Cosmos Club, George Washington University's History Department, GWU's Korean Studies Institute, GWU's East Asian Languages & Cultures Department, the GWU Sigur Center, the U.S. Department of Education's Foreign Language and Area Studies (FLAS), and the Harvard University Yenching Library. The U.S. Naval War College provided me with additional funding during my postdoctoral fellowship. Dakota State University has also been highly supportive of this research project with a faculty research initiative grant. This publication was supported by the 2020 Korean Studies Grant Program of the Academy of Korean Studies (AKS-2020-P03).

I also want to take a moment to appreciate the dogs in my life, Luna and now Benji, for their cuteness and ability to make things better during the doldrums of finishing a book manuscript amid a global pandemic. Our beloved Luna passed away during the final completion stages of this book. My partner and I will always remember Luna's funny quirks and adorable attitude. As a dog lover and someone who believes animals can also be family members, I feel that dogs need a shout-out in acknowledgments too.

From moving halfway across the country to supporting my seminomadic academic lifestyle, I could not ask for a better partner in life. Susan's sense of humor and appreciation for the small joys of life have helped me in the writing of this book. Most importantly, she is a wonderful person who helps others around her with her kindness and compassion. To my partner in life, may we have many more laughs and dog-related fun in our lives together!

Guns, Guerillas, and the Great Leader

Introduction

IF SOMEONE WALKS into the Mamelles district of Senegal's capital city Dakar, they will quickly be confronted by a large monument depicting a large, bare-chested, muscular African man looking into the beyond while holding a baby in one arm and guiding a virtuous woman in the other. This socialist-realist monument is anything but African in aesthetics. Built in 2011, Dakar's African Renaissance Monument is just one of the many commemorative projects built by North Korea's state-run construction company, Mansudae Overseas Projects, in Africa.[1] Known for their relatively cheap price tag and artistic achievements, Mansudae construction projects have left a quintessentially North Korean architectural footprint in at least fifteen African nations. As a Mansudae promotional booklet proclaims, the company "helped to splendidly build many statues, monuments, and other structures of lasting value, demonstrating the vitality of ever-developing Juche-based fine arts."[2] These projects are only one part of a long and complex history of North Korea–Third World relations. This book investigates this history and North Korea's place within the Third World.

First coined by French demographer Alfred Sauvy in 1952, the term *Third World* referred to nonaligned countries and was analogous to the Third Estate, the common people, of the French ancien régime.[3] In 1955, the Bandung Conference in Indonesia brought together for the first time heads of state from the decolonizing Afro-Asian world.[4] With this historic event, the Third World started to take shape as a real political force, and the term was further plunged into global revolutionary discourse with the 1961 publication of Frantz Fanon's famous book, *The Wretched of the Earth*.[5] As Vijay Prashad explains, the Third World was not a geographic area but a global project or movement that prioritized anti-imperialism and anti-colonialism.[6] As a postcolonial Communist state, the Democratic People's Republic of Korea (DPRK; the official title of North Korea) used the term "Third World peoples" (*chezsegye inmindŭl*) or "emerging countries" (*shinhŭngseryŏng naradŭl*) in its own propaganda as it had one foot in the anti-colonial Third World and the other in the socialist Soviet-led Second World.[7]

Third Worldism was a reaction to Cold War bipolarity, the rise of revolutionary nationalisms, and the sudden overthrow of imperialist regimes by national liberation movements in Africa, Asia, and Latin America. Unlike the negative connotation associated with the term *Third World* today, those in the decolonizing world that sought an alternative system different from U.S.-style liberal democracy and Soviet-style socialism used the word proudly during the Cold War era. The contemporary Western imagination of the "Third World" as a mass of nonwhite nations suffering from immense poverty is in steep contrast to the radical vision of the Third World that the North Korean leadership held during the Cold War era. Third Worldism was a global movement that opposed white supremacy, capitalism, and Western cultural domination. It promoted national sovereignty, popular revolution, and transnational solidarity. To borrow Lenin's phrasing, Third Worldism was the amalgamation of all anti-colonial nations in the higher unity of global revolution.[8]

North Korea's Third Worldist sensibilities originated during the Japanese colonial period. Under the leadership of Korean nationalist Kim Il Sung, a band of revolutionary guerillas fought Japanese colonialists in Manchuria during the 1930s. In his autobiography, *Reminiscences: With the Century*, North Korea's founder, Kim Il Sung, recalls the early days of his life fighting Japanese colonialists in the rough-and-tumble Manchurian landscape. Born and raised in a time of great turmoil on the Korean peninsula, Kim Il Sung endured hardships and struggles that few twentieth-century leaders could relate to. He said, "I was born at an uneasy time of upheaval and passed my boyhood in unfortunate circumstances. This situation naturally influenced my development."[9] While *With the Century* remains a highly propagandized work published by the North Korean state apparatus, it nonetheless provides a window into Kim's early life and signifies the importance of the anti-colonial struggle to North Korean political culture. These early anti-colonial fighting experiences undeniably molded the later North Korean regime's worldview since Kim Il Sung's band of Manchurian partisans later became the political elite of the DPRK.[10] This Manchurian tradition fashioned North Korea into a staunchly anti-colonial state that sympathized with the national liberation struggles of many Third World peoples. As former guerillas themselves, the North Korean leadership understood the heroism and sacrifice required for anti-colonial rebellions and thus later did their part to further global decolonization during the Cold War era.

The anti-colonial legacy of the Manchurian generation is encapsulated in North Korea's concept of Juche (also transliterated as chuch'e), which was expressed as national autonomy during the Cold War era. North Korea expert B. C. Koh's foundational 1965 article on Juche explains, "If there is a single Korean word which sums up North Korea's national preoccupation today, it is probably chuch'e—a word which has been variously translated as 'autonomy,' 'independence,' 'theme,' and 'subjective entity.'"[11] Etymologically, *ju* refers to "master," and *che* means "body." Thus, Juche can be directly translated as "master of one's body." Scholar Jiyoung Song explains that it can be interpreted as "sovereign autonomy," "self-determination," or "self-reliance."[12] Juche, with its emphasis on national independence and sovereignty, was Kim Il Sung's theoretical contribution to the international revolutionary movement. As the classic texts of Communism were minimally read in the DPRK, Kim Il Sung essentially owned the Marxist intellectual universe within the country.[13] In other words, with the promotion of Juche, Kim Il Sung did not merely join the pantheon of Communist heroes: Marx, Engels, and Lenin. He supplanted them. Juche allowed the North Korean regime to claim Kim Il Sung as a world revolutionary leader and thus reinforced his absolute power domestically.

Kim Il Sung's personality cult went beyond North Korean borders as the regime disseminated Juche throughout the Third World. By funding and sponsoring conferences, study groups, and books, the North Korean government represented Juche as a viable path to rapid postcolonial development. As a developmental guide, the Juche idea advocated national independence and self-sufficiency. North Korea's autonomous stance in foreign affairs under the rubric of the Juche idea appealed to a wide range of decolonizing nations in Africa, Latin America, and Asia. The DPRK's independent streak naturally meshed with the anti-colonial rebellions of the Third World and the various liberation philosophies that circulated throughout the decolonizing world. There was a tension within North Korea's exportation of Juche. On the one hand, it genuinely represented a socialist modernity rooted in autonomy and anti-colonialism, but on the other hand it was a pragmatic strategy used by the North Korean leadership to bolster its international status and prestige.

Due to their anti-colonial mentality and commitment to autonomy, the North Korean leadership tended to view the international community as being divided between big and small countries. According to this worldview, big countries (especially Western capitalist ones) naturally tended to dominate small countries. Thus, the DPRK treated small Third World nations with a spirit of friendliness and solidarity. On the other hand, the leadership in Pyongyang treated large nations, especially those with colonialist pasts such as Britain and Japan, with suspicion and distrust. To put this into international relations terminology, the North Koreans were and still remain classical realists who believe "international politics, like all politics, is a struggle for power."[14] North Korea adhered to a foreign policy of anti–Great Powerism. In 2014, North Korea expert Rudiger Frank explained, "The desire to be regarded as an equal is still a driving force of North Korea's foreign policy. . . . In its international relations, behind a smokescreen of bellicose rhetoric, a thoroughly pragmatic North Korea focuses on interest and power."[15]

The size difference between North Korea and the two Communist superpowers mattered a great deal to newly independent governments that worried about neo-colonialism.[16] North Korea's small geographic size and inability to dominate a foreign country's socioeconomic life earned it support in the Third World. Juche influenced North Korea's foreign policy since it functioned as a way to distance Pyongyang from the Soviet or Chinese brands of communism, which earned the Kim family regime a status in the Third World as a great defender of national autonomy. The North Korean leadership viewed the world spatially and prescribed "national autonomy" under the rubric of Juche to decolonizing nations as a solution to the international problem of domineering superpowers. These two strains of radical thought, autonomy and anti-colonialism, undergirded Pyongyang's diplomatic efforts in the Third World.

In this book, I argue that Third Worldism formed a fundamental part of North Korea's national identity during the Cold War era. In defining Third Worldism as a global commitment to anti-imperialism and anti-colonialism, I examine North Korea's internationalism and broad engagement with the decolonizing world. I borrow the concept of "national identity" from political theorist Francis Fukuyama's book *Identity: The Demand for Dignity and the Politics of Resentment*: "National identity begins with a shared belief in the legitimacy of the country's political system, whether that system is democratic or not. . . . But national identity also extends into the realm of culture and values. It consists of the stories that people tell about themselves: where they came from, what they celebrate, their shared historical memories, what it takes to be a genuine member of the community."[17] In establishing close ties with the Third World, North Korea forged a national identity as a member of a global community of anti-imperialism and anti-colonialism. Resistance to imperialism worked across national borders, and these hardships created a sense of transnational solidarity and comradeship. Additionally, the North Korean regime exported its value system, centered on the principle of national autonomy, to the Third World as a way to enhance its international prestige and recognition. Engagement with the Third World not only bolstered the global status of the Kim family regime but also boosted the DPRK's internal legitimacy as the truly sovereign Korean government.

The autonomous anti-colonial features of North Korea's national identity resulted in a foreign policy that irritated superpowers in both the Western and Eastern blocs during the Cold War era. Pyongyang's stubbornly independent stance and flexible take on Marxism-Leninism meant the DPRK was an outlier in the Communist world.

Although Kim Il Sung was just one person in a large political apparatus, his domination in the North Korean system is obvious and his influence on North Korean policymaking carried far more weight than that of any other Politburo member.[18] Kim Il Sung was a charismatic and brutal leader that used Marxism-Leninism as a vehicle for his anti-colonial agenda. Autonomous anti-colonialism was at the core of Kim Il Sung's foreign policymaking decisions. While China's anti-colonial agenda was full of contradictions due to its internal suppression of ethnic minorities and Soviet anti-colonialism was steeped in a historical tradition of Russian chauvinism, Kim Il Sung's brand of anti-colonialism fiercely promoted self-determination and armed struggle. "The oppressed peoples can liberate themselves only through struggle," he wrote in a 1967 treatise for the Organization of Solidarity of the Peoples of Asia, Africa, and Latin America. "This is a simple and clear truth confirmed by history."[19]

The conceptualization of North Korea's national identity as autonomous anti-colonialism is the analytical framework running throughout this book. According to the Korean-language scholarship of historian Wada Haruki and the English-language scholarship of linguist Adrian Buzo, North Korea was a "guerilla state" during the Cold War era as Kim Il Sung's band of Manchurian partisans became his closest allies within the North Korean government.[20] Both scholars neglect the more malleable category of national identity and how the leadership's anti-colonial heritage shaped the regime's Third World diplomacy. The North Korean leadership, which understood the rigors and sacrifices of guerilla warfare, never abandoned its revolutionary duty and continued to support other anti-colonial rebellions during the Cold War era. Economic incentives did not drive North Korea's Third World policy. Rather, inter-Korean competition with Seoul for international legitimacy and a desire to rid the world of imperialist forces, most importantly the U.S. military presence in South Korea, was at the heart of Pyongyang's Third World policy. These dual factors, which often reinforced one another, shaped and molded North Korea's Third World diplomacy.

In this book, I investigate the four main themes of North Korea's Third World policy. First, I examine the idea of North Korea as a developmental model. Today, the DPRK is a poor country struggling in the face of international sanctions. During the Cold War era, North Korea was a wealthier country as its economy quickly recovered after the Korean War. *New York Times* reporter Harrison Salisbury said in 1973 that the DPRK had accomplished "tremendous technical and industrial achievement" and that the country was "on a per capita basis . . . the most intensively industrialized country in Asia, with the exception of Japan."[21] Historian Jon Halliday said in 1981 that the DPRK "has achieved remarkable economic growth and advances in social services. It raises important issues concerning industrialization and self-reliant high growth for a medium-sized Third World country."[22] Contrary to the contemporary notion of the DPRK as impoverished, North Korea during the Cold War era was regarded by some Western scholars and Third World leaders as a developmental model worthy of emulation and adoration. This book attempts to place the DPRK within its proper historical context and resists the urge to rip the regime from its spatial and temporal Cold War world.

Unbeknownst to most Third World admirers of the DPRK model, North Korea's rapid postcolonial development was heavily subsidized by China and the Soviet Union. According to the U.S. Library of Congress's official book *North Korea: A Country Study*, "Estimates vary, but it is likely that the equivalent of U.S. $4.75 billion of aid was accepted [by North Korea] between 1946 and 1984. Almost 46 percent of the assistance came from the Soviet Union, followed by China with about 18 percent, and the rest from East European Communist countries."[23] Liudmila Zakharova explains, "By the early 1990s, the facilities built in the DPRK with Soviet help produced up to 70% of electricity, 50% of chemical fertilisers, and about 40% of ferrous metals. The aluminum industry was created entirely by Soviet specialists. Approximately 70 large industrial enterprises in North Korea were built with the assistance of the USSR."[24] Predictably, as a revolutionary nationalist and international champion of self-reliance, Kim Il Sung downplayed the massive amounts of economic assistance provided to the DPRK by the Eastern bloc. In 1965, during a visit to Indonesia, Kim admitted in a speech, "During the period of postwar rehabilitation, our country received from fraternal countries economic and technical aid amounting to some 550 million dollars, and this, of course, was a great help to our revolution and construction." He concluded, "In actual fact, it was our own efforts that played the decisive role in the postwar rehabilitation and construction."[25] Rhetorically, the North Korean government promoted the concept of national self-reliance, but in reality, Pyongyang depended heavily on foreign aid and assistance.

To many Third World supporters of the North Korean sociopolitical system, Juche was a political discourse that signaled aspirations for national self-sufficiency, anti-capitalist development, and self-defense. Juche was a utopian concept that symbolized a future-oriented commitment to autarky and revolutionary socialism. As with most Marxist states, utopianism was a central component of the state's future-oriented political culture. Lenin wrote in *What Is To Be Done?* that Communists "should dream."[26] Utopian thought was a way to construct a shared value system, revolutionary society, and new collective consciousness. Robert Winstanley-Chesters writes, "Juche has been the vessel through which utopian possibility has filtered into the more conventional forms of developmental and institutional approach and governmental function in North Korea as well as in its narratives of presentation, support, and legitimacy."[27] Juche was a kind of Third World utopianism that did not reflect the lived realities of North Korean governance but put forth a future-oriented goal of absolute sovereignty.

Rhetorically, Juche upheld the dignity of national unity and patriotism in the midst of Great Power competition and the Sino-Soviet split. Some North Korea watchers view Juche as shallow humanistic gibberish and a sham doctrine. However, a philosophy does not need to be complicated in order to function as a developmental goal and value system. Juche's utopian motivations and ideological simplicity, with its emphasis on national autonomy, was precisely what appealed to many Third World peoples and operated as an effective form of soft power for the North Korean regime. One of the connective tissues between North Korea and the Third World was this discourse of speaking Juche.[28] This sociopolitical affinity, stated under the rhetoric of Juche, was articulated in many Third World governments' expressions of solidarity with North Korea. Juche established a linguistic terrain for both Pyongyang and its Third World supporters in which both sides could articulate ambitions for national self-reliance.

This inherent contradiction between North Korea's official policy of national self-reliance and dependency on Communist bloc aid does not diminish the importance of Juche. Similar to Maoism, Juche-style socialism was full of ideological illogicalities and inconsistencies. Both were also revolutionary and utopian in nature. As Julia Lovell explains in *Maoism: A Global History*, Mao's "perplexing, inconsistent mutability . . . has given the political line which carries his name its potency, persuasiveness and mobility." Lovell adds, "Somehow, Maoism is the creed of winners and insiders, of losers and outsiders, of leaders and underdogs, of absolute rulers, of vast, disciplined bureaucracies, and oppressed masses." She quotes Christophe Bourseiller, stating that "Maoism doesn't exist. It never has done. That, without doubt, explains its success."[29] North Korea's Juche operated in a similar manner as China's Maoism. Nevertheless, unlike Maoism's multifaceted emphasis on chaotic insurrection and rural revolution, Juche focused almost exclusively on the principles of national autonomy and sovereignty.

As a small, nonwhite industrialized nation that straddled the line between the socialist Second World and the anti-colonial Third World, the idea of North Korea as a developmental model gained traction throughout Africa, Asia, and Latin America. Both Maoist China and North Korea based their political systems on one-party rule, cultish leader worship, and social mobilization. However, Maoist China's development during the Cultural Revolution emitted overtones of chaos and violence. Mao preached that "it is right to rebel," and Chinese Red Guards unleashed a brutal campaign against wayward intellectuals and party officials.[30] On the other hand, North Korea's development strategy appeared disciplined, highly organized, and efficient.[31] Kim Il Sung's regime was built on absolute loyalty and regimentation. Insurrectionary youth, such as the Red Guards, were not tolerated in the DPRK. This key difference made North Korea into a Third World model of law and order.[32]

Meanwhile, the Soviet Union's influence on the DPRK was palpable. Due to his name recognition among the Korean masses as an anti-Japanese resistance leader, Soviet leader Joseph Stalin chose guerilla fighter Kim Il Sung after liberation to rule the DPRK. From the implementation of a centrally planned economy to a Stalinist political structure, Moscow guided Pyongyang in its party-building measures and economic expansion.[33] Nevertheless, the two nations differed in a number of important ways. If the Soviet Union, as Soviet historian Stephen Kotkin explains, "was a violent experiment in an avowedly noncapitalist modernity," the DPRK was a postcolonial experiment in a rapidly constructed and highly autocratic noncapitalist modernity.[34] Unlike the Soviet Union, North Korea emerged out of a harsh colonial experience under Japanese rule that deeply shaped the worldviews of its leaders. "Instead of emphasizing the study of Marx-Leninism," noted the Czechoslovak embassy in Pyongyang on April 18, 1961, "they base ideological education on experiences of anti-Japanese guerillas."[35] Secondly, as the Soviet Union underwent de-Stalinization in the mid-1950s, the DPRK leadership adhered to a pervasive personality cult and massive surveillance system built on anti-Americanism, militarism, and religious-like devotion to the "Great Leader."

The North Korean leadership also instituted hereditary succession as Kim Il Sung cultivated his son, Kim Jong Il, to become the next ruler of the DPRK. Many Communist parties around the world, including that in the Soviet Union, criticized this Marxist-Leninist heresy. Hereditary succession arguably made the DPRK more stable after the death of Kim Il Sung in 1994 and allowed the so-called Korean Revolution to continue after the collapse of the Communist bloc. These disparities made the DPRK into a crueler and far more autocratic regime than the post-Stalinist Soviet Union, which may help explain why the Kim family regime persists today under its third-generation dictator, Kim Jong Un.

Thus, North Korea was no miniature China or Soviet Union because its political culture had a unique style of mass surveillance and social control. Paradoxically, this oppressive sociopolitical system attracted many Third World leaders, government officials, and intellectuals who sought quick postcolonial solutions. Many came to Pyongyang to marvel at and learn from North Korea's modernization projects, such as its educational system, industrialization, and agricultural collectivization. After visiting the DPRK in the mid-1960s, left-leaning British economist Joan Robinson published an article entitled "Korean Miracle." She wrote, "Eleven years ago in Pyongyang there was not one stone standing upon another. Now a modern city of a million inhabitants stands on two sides of the wide river, with broad tree-lined streets of five-story blocks, public buildings, a stadium, theaters, and a super-deluxe hotel."[36] A couple decades later, South African political activist Karrim Essack wrote that the North Korean people "have a wealth of experience not only of armed struggle, not only of revolution but also of construction. This the Third World countries appreciate. The number of heads of states, ministers from Third World countries visiting the DPRK shows the eagerness of the people to learn from this rich and varied experience."[37] Although observers today often describe the DPRK as frozen in time, North Korea during the Cold War era often represented an advanced version of postcolonial development that was based on national autonomy and socialist modernity.[38] Unlike Western-style liberal democracy, North Korea's brand of postcolonial development carried no vestiges of colonialism and promoted national self-reliance. This unique model gained North Korea prestige and status within the decolonizing world.

The second theme of North Korea's Third World policy that I investigate is Pyongyang's support of national liberation movements and newly independent governments. Due to its rapid postcolonial and postwar development, the Kim family regime was able to send materials (construction materials, military equipment, arms, ammunition) and people (military advisors, agricultural specialists, cadres, gymnasts, artists, teachers, doctors, technical workers, and engineers) often free of charge to the Third World as acts of solidarity with postcolonial peoples. As former non-state actors themselves, the North Korean leadership often sympathized with the struggles of anti-colonial movements, such as the Palestinian Liberation Organization (PLO) and Namibia's South West Africa People's Organization (SWAPO). North Korea's state-run media formed a discourse that promoted solidarity with colonized peoples and at times mobilized the domestic population to support wars of national liberation, such as the Vietnam War.

The third theme I examine is the role of inter-Korean competition in North Korea's Third World policy. As a divided nation that saw the southern half of Korea as illegally occupied by the "U.S. imperialists," the DPRK pursued recognition from foreign governments as the true representative of the Korean people in international forums. During the Cold War era, the Third World became the site of many newly independent countries and thus fertile ground for the inter-Korean conflict. The DPRK leadership pushed its political positions in the Third World as a way to improve its international status as the truly independent Korean government and thus subvert its South Korean "puppet" rivals. Pyongyang's competition for international recognition vis-à-vis Seoul largely informed the DPRK's presence in the Third World.

Finally, I examine Kim Il Sung's personal relationships with Third World leaders and the ways in which the North Korean dictator navigated the complexities of the Communist world. Kim Il Sung was raised as an anti-colonial guerilla fighter in rough-and-tumble Manchuria, and this unique experience in exile inevitably gave the North Korean system a nationalistic character. The East German ambassador to the DPRK explained in 1968, "The internal development of the guerilla movement during World War II amounts to further and deeper separation of the guerilla movement and its leaders from the Korean people. . . . This factor began to take effect in several stages from the very origins of the DPRK onwards and is to a certain extent one of the reasons why the Korean Workers' Party today maintains 'independent' positions precisely in the fundamental questions of war and peace, the international communist movement, and so on."[39] In one-person management systems such as Stalin's Soviet Union or Kim Il Sung's North Korea, the leader's personality and background deeply influenced the state's institutions and national identity. Kim Il Sung also formed some of his closest relationships with former guerillas-turned-autocrats, such as Fidel Castro. Thus, Kim Il Sung's foreign policy came with a heavy dosage of anti-colonial sentiment and sympathy for fellow guerilla fighters.

During the Cold War era, Kim Il Sung's foreign policy included a tension between striving to be independent of its more powerful Communist neighbors, the Soviet Union and China, and participating in the socialist world order that Moscow and Beijing shaped. This book investigates this tension as it traces Kim Il Sung's desire to not only benefit from his contacts with the socialist world but to also be independent and self-reliant in his foreign policy. One of the ways in which Kim Il Sung's regime navigated this complex Cold War landscape was by carving out niches in the Third World and providing expertise in unique developmental spaces, such as exporting mass gymnastics instructors, building palaces for foreign leaders, and providing cheap arms. These niches earned praise from many around the world and allowed Kim Il Sung to distinguish himself as not a mere Soviet or Chinese puppet but an autonomous leader that offered specialized services and skills that neither Communist superpower could match.

The DPRK's promotion of national autonomy within the Third World project stands as one of the great contradictions of Pyongyang's foreign policy. In promoting the idea of the nation-state as the nucleus of all revolutionary consciousness, North Korea's Third World policy paradoxically reconfirmed the centrality of the nation-state in the transnational space of decolonization. As historian Jeffrey Byrne explains, decolonization signaled a "dramatically more state-centric world order."[40] It was specifically North Korea's status as a proudly independent nation-state and promoter of national autonomy that earned it accolades and recognition from many in the decolonizing world. In a December 28, 1955, speech to North Korean propagandists, Kim Il Sung announced, "He who does not love his own country cannot be loyal to internationalism, and he who is unfaithful to internationalism cannot be faithful to his own country and people. A true patriot is precisely an internationalist and vice versa."[41] The DPRK's identity was and still remains very much tied to the nation-state framework.

This book does not investigate the history of North Korea's industrialization or the degree to which the regime depended on Soviet and Chinese aid. Nor does it examine the Kim family regime's long history of human rights abuses. Rather, this book analyzes the political, ideological, and cultural ties between the DPRK and the decolonizing world. In doing so, it elucidates the ways in which Third Worldism shaped and molded North Korea's national identity. By becoming active in the Third World, North Korea based its national identity around the core principles of autonomy and anti-colonialism. Pyongyang articulated its national identity via speaking Juche with its Third World supporters.

Kim Il Sung's foreign policy, specifically his relations with Communist leaders in Moscow and Beijing, has received much scholarly attention.[42] However, Pyongyang's policy towards recently decolonized Third World nations from the 1960s to the 1980s has received relatively little attention in Korean- or English-language scholarship.[43] While recent journal articles by Ji Hyung Kim, Sangsook Lee, and Jean Do focus on various elements of North Korea's Third World policy, there is still no comprehensive study on North Korea's extensive ties with African, Asian, and Latin American nations in the Korean language.[44]

My book fits into a recent trend in Cold War historiography that emphasizes the agency of small nations during the Cold War.[45] While Soviets and Chinese engaged in a struggle for dominance in the Eastern bloc, smaller Communist nations such as North Korea pursued foreign policies distinct from that of their chief patron states. My study builds off this recent scholarship as it positions North Korea as an agent of its own history and creator of an independent foreign policy during the Cold War. Although the Soviet Union did largely subsidize the DPRK's postwar reconstruction and rapid industrial development, the North Koreans were not Soviet proxies, nor did they solely pursue Moscow's foreign policy objectives. While I hope to restore agency to the history of North Korean foreign policy, I also acknowledge the important effect that the global Cold War had on Pyongyang.[46] The Sino-Soviet Split worked to North Korea's advantage as Pyongyang forged a unique role in the Communist bloc as a more nationalistic and militant Third World–oriented actor.

Because North Korean archives remain closed to all outsiders, the sources that I use in this book primarily come from publications produced by the North Korean government and archival materials from the United States, Mexico, South Korea, the United Kingdom, Canada, Australia, Sweden, and the former Eastern bloc. The U.S. National Archives from 1968 to 1979, specifically Record Group 59, are particularly fruitful as the State Department closely monitored the activities of North Korean officials and diplomats in the Third World. U.S. State Department materials from the 1980s onwards are still classified so I used primarily the UK National Archives (UKNA in the endnotes) and the Republic of Korea's (ROK) Diplomatic Archives for that decade. ROK's Diplomatic Archives (SKDA) are particularly insightful with regard to the analysis of Third World local newspapers. South Korean diplomats regularly perused the print media of their respective host nations and reported any mention of North Korea back to Seoul. Reports of North Korean activities in the Third World press often proved to be more intuitive and perceptive than archival documents from the Eastern bloc and the West.

Cited throughout this book are documents from Canada, Sweden, France, the United Kingdom, Australia, and Mexico, which were Washington's closest Western allies during the Cold War. Their embassies regularly confronted North Korean influence in the Third World and reported these events back to their home offices. British documents were particularly useful because the foreign ministries and embassies kept a close eye on former British colonies in the decolonizing world. I also used sources from the infallible Woodrow Wilson Center's History and Public Policy Program Digital Archive (WCDA in the endnotes), which collects documents from the archives of former Eastern bloc nations, such as Bulgaria, Hungary, Romania, East Germany, Poland, and the Soviet Union; these sources provide critical information on North Korean activity in the Third World from the perspective of its Eastern bloc allies.

North Korean propaganda also provides a window into Kim Il Sung's Third World policy. Domestic-oriented Korean-language propaganda, especially the Korean Workers' Party's (KWP) official organ *Rodong Sinmun*, provides valuable information on DPRK ties to Third World nations. I also examine North Korea's English-language propaganda designed for foreign consumption, such as the *Pyongyang Times*, *Korea Today*, *Korean Central News Agency*, and the *People's Korea*, as a way to understand the "socialist paradise" image that the DPRK tried to project to foreigners. I utilize North Korean propaganda as primary sources in order to trace the intersection between the foreign and domestic policies of the DPRK government.

Chapter 1 investigates the start of North Korea's Third World policy from 1956 to 1967, which began with Kim Il Sung's domestic power consolidation and subsequent purges. As the DPRK reached out to the world and advocated a self-reliant path to socialist construction, Pyongyang found natural allies in Jakarta, Havana, and Hanoi. These alliances were based on a shared militant stand towards Western imperialism and a belief in revolutionary socialism.[47] Since all four Third World nations had recently defended themselves against imperialist forces, the DPRK, Indonesia, Cuba, and Vietnam found much in common ideologically, militarily, and politically. North Korea demonstrated its material commitment to Third Worldism by assisting the Vietnamese Communists during the Vietnam War. Although Hanoi did not permit Kim Il Sung to send ground forces to Southeast Asia, the North Korean leader mobilized his citizens to defend North Vietnam and called for volunteers to help fight the Americans. This Vietnam War mobilization campaign also reinforced Kim Il Sung's authority domestically.

Chapter 2 investigates the globalization of Kim Il Sung's personality cult and the quixotic dissemination of his sycophantic ideology, Kimilsungism, throughout the Third World during the late 1960s and early 1970s. While Cuba's, China's, and the Soviet Union's roles in fomenting world revolution are well known, North Korea's assistance is lesser known. As a former anti-colonial guerilla fighter, Kim Il Sung assisted Third World rebels and insurgents as a way to advance the cause of world revolution. In an attempt to bolster the personality cult of Kim Il Sung, North Korea invested heavily in a public diplomacy campaign during the late 1960s and early 1970s. Pyongyang disseminated Kimilsungism throughout the Third World in the form of newspaper advertisements, photo exhibits, film screenings, free trips to the DPRK, and the establishment of friendship societies.

Chapter 3 focuses on one of the most successful periods of North Korea's Third World policy, from 1972 to 1979. Rather than focus on disseminating its propaganda of Kim Il Sung as a world revolutionary leader, North Korea exported its value system of Juche to the Third World in order to improve the image of the DPRK abroad and promote its version of socialist modernity. When the North Korean government focused on disseminating its core values of national autonomy and anti-colonialism, the image of the DPRK in the Third World improved. North Korea used its improved international status to enter the Non-Aligned Movement, an international body that sought to represent the political interests of the Third World.

Chapter 4 largely deals with the emergence of Kim Jong Il as the central player in the North Korean leadership during the early 1980s. Kim Jong Il's rise gave Pyongyang's Third World policy a more violent character. Rather than foster transnational solidarity, Kim Jong Il used the Third World as a space to undermine his South Korean and American enemies. He also advanced his father's long-sought-after goal of reunification under the DPRK's terms. North Korea's 1983 assassination attempt on South Korean president Chun-Doo Hwan in Burma devastated the DPRK's reputation in the Third World. Prior to this event, many Third World governments saw North Korea as an anti-imperialist stalwart and a modern industrialized state, if somewhat strange and belligerent at times. The Burma bombing revealed that the DPRK was reckless, violent, and terroristic. As a result, some Third World governments cut all diplomatic ties with Pyongyang. The DPRK increasingly looked at the Third World as a relatively easy place to sell weapons, test its military capabilities, and engage in other nefarious activities.

Chapter 5 examines North Korea's Africa policy in the 1980s and Pyongyang's hosting of the 1989 World Festival of Youth and Students. As North Korea's economy stagnated, the need for hard currency increased and the façade of self-reliant development was quickly falling apart in this supposed "socialist paradise." As newly established governments in postcolonial Africa looked for arms dealers, cash-hungry Pyongyang was all too willing to send weapons, ammunition, and military equipment to these nations. Sometimes, Pyongyang would send military trainers to instruct foreign troops on how to use their North Korean–made materials. In addition, as South Korea surpassed North Korea in international prestige and economic power during the late 1980s, Pyongyang faced an identity crisis. As a weakening and divided nation that claimed the other half, North Korea made one last-ditch effort to gain legitimacy by hosting the 1989 World Festival of Youth and Students. During this festival, the North Korean government did not permit a genuine exchange of ideas between locals and foreigners and many participants left disappointed at their lack of access within the DPRK. This festival also cost the North Korean government millions of dollars, which may have hastened the downfall of the DPRK economy.

My conclusion looks at the post–Cold War period and North Korea's legacy in the Third World. The perception of the DPRK as an economic basket case has replaced its once-vaunted status in the Third World as modern and industrialized. Recently, North Korea's few remaining allies in the Third World have come under fire from the United Nations and the U.S. government for continuing to trade and interact with Pyongyang. My book roughly follows a chronological timeline and aims to present new details on North Korean activities in the Third World that are based largely on previously underutilized primary sources.

1

Building a Reputation
1956–1967

THE KOREAN WAR, specifically the U.S. air bombing campaign, had left North Korea in ruins.[1] According to Bruce Cumings, more napalm was dropped by the United States during the Korean War than during the Vietnam War.[2] The devastation of the Korean War made the North Korean leadership focus on reconstruction efforts from the mid-1950s to the late 1950s. As Shen Zhihua and Yafeng Xia explain, China more than any other socialist country, even the USSR, assisted the DPRK in the postwar period.[3] Along with economic difficulties and the presence of foreign advisors and troops on its soil, Kim Il Sung encountered domestic political challenges in the mid-1950s. Faced with opposition from pro-Soviet and pro-Chinese factions, Kim's band of former anti-Japanese partisans rallied around their "Great Leader" and purged their political rivals in 1956.[4] Kim's aspirations for power did not stop at the borders of the DPRK. In the late 1950s and 1960s, Kim Il Sung aspired to be a leader of the Third World and an internationally renowned figure that championed a unique brand of revolutionary socialism. This global prestige would then reinforce his power consolidation within the DPRK and bolster his nascent personality cult.

In his worldwide anti-imperialist struggle, Kim Il Sung initially found no better friends than Indonesia's Ahmed Sukarno and Cuba's Fidel Castro. Kim and Sukarno based their relationship around the concept of self-reliance as both championed indigenous versions of national autonomy. However, the close relationship between the two leaders was short-lived as Sukarno was ousted in 1965 during a military coup. Meanwhile, North Korea's presence in Latin America primarily grew out of its initial

Cuban contacts. Although the North Korean and Cuban socialist systems differed, both filled a role in the Third World as small anti-imperialist nations that assisted national liberation movements and promoted guerilla-based armed struggle.

During the 1960s, the Vietnam War captured the international spotlight. Despite North Korea's geographical distance from this conflict, Kim Il Sung felt a special connection to the Vietnamese struggle and often voiced his support for the Vietnamese Communists. The Vietnam War also allowed Kim Il Sung to improve his stature abroad as a committed internationalist revolutionary leader in the Third World. By directly assisting the Vietnamese struggle, Kim enhanced his credentials as a notable Communist leader uninhibited by the petty divisions of the Communist bloc. Kim also used the Vietnam War for domestic reasons and presented the image of an embattled Vietnam as an increasingly likely future for the North Korean people if they did not rally around their leadership in Pyongyang and send military forces to stop U.S. aggression in Southeast Asia. To borrow Toni Weis's phrasing, the DPRK government's solidarity with Vietnam became a means for North Koreans to affirm their support for the political system.[5] Kim saw the war in Vietnam as a mirror image of the Korean situation and pragmatically used the conflict to gain intelligence on the South Korean military and test his pilots in wartime combat for a future conflict on Korean soil.

From 1956 to 1967, the DPRK's Third World policy focused primarily on building up Kim Il Sung's international reputation as a revolutionary who prioritized relationships with small anti-colonial nations, especially Cuba and Vietnam, over big power alliances with Beijing or Moscow. Thus, an alliance between the leaderships in Pyongyang, Havana, and Hanoi naturally formed as a result of the Sino-Soviet split and shared political values. The leaders of these three small Communist governments understood the necessity of forming a unified internationalist front of Third Worldism as the great Communist powers could not always be relied upon as protectors of the world revolution. Like the great colonial powers that came before them, large, powerful nations regardless of their common ideology naturally tended to dominate and subjugate rather than empower smaller nations. Kim Il Sung most likely witnessed this phenomenon when Soviet troops rolled into Hungary in 1956 and suppressed uprisings in this satellite state.[6] These three revolutionary countries had recently experienced varying forms of colonialism and did not seek to entrust their national security, independence, and ambitions to large imperialistic powers once again. All three spoke the language of Juche and articulated a socialist vision of anti–Great Powerism.

This chapter begins with an explanation of the imagination of Third Worldism that was promoted in the DPRK. It then shifts to the development of the DPRK government's alliances with Sukarno's Indonesia and Castro's Cuba amid the burgeoning Sino-Soviet split. In the early 1960s, the Cuban Missile Crisis brought the world to the brink of a nuclear war. The safety of the world was at stake and despite their geographical remoteness, the leadership in Pyongyang paid close attention to these events in the Caribbean and drew important conclusions from the crisis, which would continue to inform Kim Il Sung's foreign policy during the Cold War era. Kim Il Sung also used lessons from the Vietnam War to improve his positions at home and abroad. Although 1956 to 1967 was one of the least active periods of North Korean involvement in the Third World, it provided valuable lessons to the North Korean leadership and shaped its Third World policy for the rest of the Cold War era.

Imagining the Third World

As part of its efforts to bolster Kim Il Sung's international status, the North Korean government began to educate its citizens on the various histories and cultures of the Third World. Beginning in the early 1960s, various North Korean publications featured informational sections on Third World nations. Kim Il Sung's regime wanted the North Korean public to see themselves as part of a global anti-colonial community that resisted all forms of Western imperialism and promoted national autonomy. In its propaganda, the North Korean government emphasized public awareness of the Third World's struggle for independence and sovereignty.

In 1964, *Chollima*, the North Korean cultural magazine named after a Pegasus-like mythic horse, published a short article detailing the relationship between colonialists and African ivory. This article serves as a useful case study for exploring the strategic messaging that the North Korean government conveyed to its citizens about the Third World. The section begins, "In Africa, with its hot weather and vegetation, there are many wild elephants with long, extending tusks." The article continues, "The tearful history of the African people and colonialist invasion can be told through these tusks. Greedy colonialists who set their foot in Africa have been so crazy searching and running around for ivory and gold." The article then delves into the long history of slavery and European exploitation of African resources. The unnamed North Korean author illustrates extraordinary knowledge of Western literature by citing late-1800s European explorer Henry M. Stanley's travelogue, *In Darkest Africa*. The article explains, "Stanley, who had been loyal to the king of Belgium during the 1890s, wrote the following in his book: 'One gram of ivory is the same as the life of one child or male adult or female adult. In order to get five kilograms of ivory, you need to burn a house. To get twenty kilograms, you need to burn a village.' " The article ends with a question for its North Korean readers: "Considering the fact that more than ninety percent of ivory is used mostly by European people, how many African people must give their lives for ivory?"[7] This illustration of Western imperialist brutality surely resonated with a North Korean audience accustomed to anti-Western themes in their propaganda.

Depictions of the Third World in *Chollima* often included overtly anti-imperialist messaging and expressions of revolutionary solidarity. For example, a Ceylonese poem translated in *Chollima* proclaimed, "Wake up Sinhalese youths," and described the imperialist onslaught facing Ceylon.[8] A November 1963 *Chollima* article announced that "the flames of anti-imperialist national liberation struggles are spreading on the African continent" and that "the solidarity movement in countries which have already won independence gives enormous inspiration to peoples fighting colonialism."[9] In a 1964 *Chollima* article on Portuguese Guinea's fight for independence, the North Korean author Kyongsik Kim stated, "The Portuguese colonialists' fascist controlling policy has been completely supported by the U.S. imperialists. However, they could not extinguish the burning flame of the Guinean people."[10] *Chollima* also portrayed the people of the Third World as unified under the banner of national self-reliance. For example, a 1967 *Chollima* article on Tanzanian president Julius Nyerere's revolutionary policies explained, "The Tanzanian people will continue to vigorously follow the path of self-reliance and anti-imperialist struggle, with a hoe in one hand and a gun in the other hand."[11] North Korean propaganda portrayed the Third World as a unified front in its efforts to defeat Western imperialism and combat U.S. aggression.

There were also real attempts to educate North Koreans on the geography, history, and culture of various Third World nations. For example, *Chollima* in the early 1960s had a section entitled "International Knowledge," which spotlighted a different Third World nation each issue. For example, in the second issue of 1963, this section focused on Somalia and described the nation's history of European colonialism and current agricultural and drought problems. Complete with a map of Somalia, this section, although tinged with an anti-Western theme, told a mostly fact-based history of the East African nation.[12] The back page of the *Rodong Sinmun* also regularly published news regarding the Third World. From celebrating Zanzibar's anti-imperialist revolution to reprinting a Malian president's speech on building a Marxist society, the *Rodong Sinmun* presented an image of a unified anti-colonial community with the DPRK at its center. This North Korean–produced "imagined community" of Third Worldism naturally presented Kim Il Sung as the leader and Pyongyang as the capital of world revolution.

Third World diplomats were often bewildered by the overtly political nature of their interactions with North Koreans. For example, South Yemeni officials in the Ministry of Agriculture who spent considerable time with visiting North Korean agricultural specialists told the U.S. embassy in Aden, "The [North] Koreans adhered very much to the Chinese style in emphasizing the 'glorious thoughts of Kim Il Sung.' A Korean embassy official told them that he had worked as a furnace man in the factory in North Korea and when Kim Il Sung had visited the plant he had felt 'physically stronger' merely in the presence of 'that glorious leader.'" The South Yemeni officials observed that this sort of Asian mentality seemed ludicrous even to the most ignorant Arab. However, following the same lines, the Koreans asked on a number of occasions why more signs and posters were not erected glorifying [South Yemeni] President Qahtan.[13]

This sentiment regarding North Korean ignorance was not isolated to South Yemen. In Botswana, "the [North] Korean delegation left an unfavorable impression on government officials. They pressed too hard, were here too long, refused to hear what was being said to them, misrepresented statements made by various government officials and in general made a nuisance of themselves."[14] While DPRK propaganda bolstered the autocratic rule of Kim Il Sung domestically, it often created political hardships for its diplomats in the Third World who had to toe the party line of cultish leader worship.

From Bandung to Pyongyang

Due to its postwar reconstruction efforts, North Korea did not attend the famous 1955 Bandung Conference, which brought heads of state together from the Afro-Asian world for the first time and paved the way for Third Worldism and the Non-Aligned Movement. Nonetheless, the North Korean government subscribed to the principles of national independence and anti-imperialism set forth by this conference, held in the Indonesian city of Bandung. As a powerful and emerging radical force in the decolonizing world, Indonesia under the leadership of President Sukarno looked for allies abroad and perceived North Korea to be in a similarly precarious position as a divided nation that was geographically located between two larger and more powerful East Asian neighbors. Soon, a series of trade ties and diplomatic exchanges began between the two governments. Sukarno and Kim bonded over their shared promotion of national self-reliance, and both spoke the political discourse of Juche. Most importantly, both leaders aspired to be key figures in the decolonizing world and the international revolutionary movement.

Desperate for foreign trade partners outside the Communist bloc, a North Korean trade delegation visited Jakarta for the first time in the spring of 1957 and signed an agreement that stated the DPRK government would sell to Indonesia electrolytic zinc, lead, cement, window glass, silk fiber, and mineral fertilizer. In return, the North Koreans would buy rubber, tea, vegetable oil, coconut products, coffee, quinine, and other goods from Indonesia.[15] According to a December 10, 1957, report from the East German embassy in Pyongyang, "Indonesia wants to trade with the DPRK. It is considered a first step towards the establishment of contacts. Only then agreements should be signed on [the] government level."[16] Thus, it seems that both sides actively sought a close economic and diplomatic relationship in the late 1950s.

As a developing Asian leftist state that struggled to affirm its nonalignment in international affairs, the Indonesian government gravitated to the proudly independent and socialist North Koreans. On November 29, 1957, the DPRK's deputy foreign minister Pak Seong-cheol told his East German counterparts, "In Indonesia, large masses of underclass people have a strong interest in Korean issues. There is massive pressure on government ministers from these people." Pak added, "There is only one party not interested in establishing a good relationship with the DPRK. This is the Masyumi Party, which represents the middle classes."[17] Despite the supposed favorability towards the DPRK from Indonesia's working classes, the pluralism and instability of Indonesian politics slightly worried North Korean officials. For example, on March 15, 1958, North Korea's foreign minister Nam Il told the Soviet ambassador to the DPRK, "The Communist Party and trade unions of Indonesia are helping us establish closer ties between the DPRK and Indonesia. True, the situation in Indonesia is complex and tense, but we think that conditions are favorable for ties."[18]

Pyongyang's closeness to the government in Jakarta also stemmed from South Korean president Syngman Rhee's public support of an anti-government rebellion, known as the PRRI/Permesta Rebellion, in late 1950s Indonesia. Rhee gave a speech on June 7, 1958, at the Fourth National Assembly in Seoul that mentioned the danger of Indonesia falling to Communism under Sukarno's left-leaning government. Rhee said, "The situation in Indonesia is not so promising. Freedom fighters are continuing their determined effort to save the country and its eighty million people from Communism, but they need help, and need it desperately. You know the strong feelings of the Korean people in this regard." Rhee continued, "Thousands of them have volunteered to go to Indonesia and fight the Communists. Such unselfish willingness to risk life itself in the cause of freedom for others is, I think, a measure of the strength and sincerity of our own democracy."[19] This public declaration of support for anti-government forces and the desire to be involved in Indonesia's internal affairs deeply angered Sukarno. After Rhee's speech, Seoul struggled to distance itself from his inflammatory remarks, which made Jakarta gravitate even further into Pyongyang's orbit of diplomacy.

Predictably, the North Korean state-run media jumped on Rhee's provocative remarks and alleged that South Korea was preparing to send soldiers to Indonesia to crush Sukarno's left-wing government in the late 1950s. The *Pyongyang Times* said, "The South Korean regime ballyhooed about the dispatch of volunteers to help the Indonesian rebels when they staged a counter-revolutionary revolt in 1957 at the instigation of the imperialists." It added, "The puppet South Korean government launched a campaign against the Indonesian revolution. It sponsored, with the help of the police, what it called 'rallies for dispatch of volunteers to Indonesia' in all parts of South Korea."[20] The North Korean press used Rhee's speech as evidence that the ROK government was imperialistic in its affairs with other Asian nations.

During the late 1950s, Pyongyang focused on strengthening its cultural ties with the government in Jakarta. In 1957, an Indonesian photo and handicraft exhibition was held in the DPRK, which "provided a good opportunity for the Korean people to learn more about the life and arts of the diligent and peace-loving people of Indonesia."[21] In addition, on November 10, 1958, a (North) Korean-Indonesian Friendship Society was founded in Pyongyang, which the *Korea Today* magazine deemed "another decisive blow to the Western colonialists who are scheming to attain their aggressive purposes by creating discord and strife among the Asian peoples." The *Korea Today* article congratulated the Indonesian government "in suppressing the rebellious clique" during the 1958 PRRI/Permesta Rebellion and noted, "Despite the different social and political systems, the peoples of Korea and Indonesia are firmly united for the maintenance of peace and national independence against imperialist aggression."[22]

Cultural ties between Indonesia and the DPRK were also strengthened by the visit of an Indonesian art troupe in 1959. Collaborating with North Korean writers and artists, members of the Indonesian art troupe learned "The Song of General Kim Il Sung" and the Korean folk song "Arirang." In addition, North Korean singers learned Indonesian songs, such as "Sing Sing So!" Visiting a North Korean factory, Mount Keumgang, and the beachside city of Wonsan, the Indonesian art troupe also met Kim Il Sung, and both parties declared, "Long live Korean-Indonesian friendship and solidarity."[23]

Official governmental delegations from the DPRK kept traveling to Indonesia in the early 1960s. For example, North Korea's minister for foreign trade Li Jo Yun visited Indonesia from June 4 to June 17, 1961, when both sides agreed to expand trade with each other and establish a consular office in each other's country at the level of consulate general.[24] As the birthplace of the "Bandung spirit," Indonesia prioritized neutralism and noninterference in the international system. Thus, it is no surprise that the Indonesian government disapproved of the presence of foreign troops south of the Korean DMZ and in Vietnam.[25] From the standpoint of national sovereignty, the Indonesian government favored Pyongyang over Seoul and spoke the discourse of Juche.

Within the regional context of close ties between Pyongyang and Jakarta in the late 1950s and early 1960s, Sukarno's foreign policy was decidedly more pro-Beijing in its orientation. As historian Hong Liu describes, Sukarno viewed China as a positive example of postcolonial development and incorporated some of Mao's revolutionary programs into his own statecraft. "In reformulating his agendas for Indonesia," Liu explains, "Sukarno consistently drew upon his positive impressions of the success of the China example. His notion of what was wrong with Indonesia was constantly set against his perception of what was going right in the PRC."[26]

Sukarno romanticized Mao's socialist project and depicted China as a land of genuine people's revolution. While North Korea's agenda of national self-reliance resonated with Sukarno's nationalist sensibilities, the PRC dominated his worldview and revolutionary consciousness.

Not all Indonesian government officials preferred China to North Korea. An Indonesia Communist Party (also known as the Partai Komunis Indonesia, or PKI) delegation, led by Chairman D. N. Aidit, took a tour of Communist Asia in 1963. After touring both China and North Korea, Aidit came back to Indonesia proclaiming that the DPRK was "the model Asian communist state."[27] Aidit deeply admired North Korea's Juche ideology and participated in the discourse of speaking Juche. For example, Aidit encouraged a "Banteng spirit" in Indonesia, which emphasized the same self-sufficiency concepts as North Korea's Juche ideology. In a December 1963 political report to the PKI's Central Committee, Aidit said, "The 'Banteng spirit' is burning in the breasts of the Indonesian communists and people, a spirit of confidence in our own strength, a spirit of the courage to stand on our own two feet, [and] a spirit of resolutely upholding the revolutionary standpoint and the resolve, 'Ever forward, No retreat.' "[28] Despite Sukarno's preference for Maoism, the revolutionary discourse of Juche strongly resonated with PKI chairman D. N. Aidit.

The establishment of the Malaysian government by the British government reinforced anti-Western sentiments in both Pyongyang and Jakarta. In the early 1960s, Sukarno's government believed the British creation of a Malaysian state in Southeast Asian was an illegal act and infringed upon Indonesia's sovereignty because the government in Jakarta claimed parts of Malaysian territory. North Korea followed Indonesia's lead and soon put quotes around "Malaysia" in its press, which implied the new state was a puppet akin to South Korea. North Korean officials claimed Malaysia was "a product of the imperialists" and therefore illegitimate.[29] On April 5, 1964, a delegation from the DPRK's Supreme People's Assembly traveled to Jakarta and met with Indonesian officials. During their meetings, the North Korean delegation told Arudji Kartawinata, the minister of the House of Representatives and chairman of the United Indonesian Islamic Party, "Two North Korean [military] divisions are being made ready to 'crush Malaysia.' "[30] According to a report in the Indonesian press, "All members of the North Korean parliamentary delegation stated immediately after their arrival in Indonesia last week that they [themselves] wanted to become volunteers to crush the neo-colonialist project of Malaysia."[31] The "illegal" creation of Malaysia became a touchstone of the anti-colonial worldview shared by the Indonesian and North Korean governments.

Volunteer fighters, including the delegation members themselves, from the DPRK were allegedly ready "to fight shoulder to shoulder" with Indonesians against Malaysia. Kartawinata said, "This was an historical demonstration" of solidarity by the

North Koreans. The delegation also brought a message to President Sukarno from the Great Leader Kim Il Sung himself that stated, "I am convinced that the anti-Malaysia struggle waged by the Indonesian people under your leadership will be greatly conducive to the preservation of peace in Asia and in the world." Kim added, "The entire Korean people express once again their firm solidarity with the Indonesian people who have courageously risen up in the just struggle to smash Malaysia."[32]

Two North Korean military divisions were probably not being prepared to fight in Indonesia. The delegation members, some of whom were elderly, were unlikely, as the British Embassy in Jakarta said, "to be found shouldering a rifle in Borneo."[33] Nonetheless, this type of rhetorical support implies that the DPRK government saw Indonesia as a trustworthy and dignified ally that was worth some degree of self-sacrifice and heroism. Despite having a different political system, the DPRK perceived Indonesia as a vital revolutionary partner in Asia and a supporter of the Juche idea. In turn, Kartawinata said, "The Indonesia people would never forget the sympathy and moral support given by the North Koreans to Indonesia during times of stress."[34]

In early November 1964, President Sukarno visited North Korea and met with Kim Il Sung on a formal state visit. The *Rodong Sinmun* welcomed Sukarno to the DPRK and announced, "President Sukarno and the Indonesian government stand firm and unshakeable in its anti-imperialist struggle while also carrying out a peaceful foreign policy that is constantly raising the international status and prestige of Indonesia today and raising its influence day by day."[35] A mass gymnastics event honoring Indonesian–North Korean friendship, with students holding placards stating "Welcome Comrade [Su]Karno," was held in Pyongyang. The two leaders also gave speeches at a state dinner in which both announced their support for anti-imperialism and Korean reunification, and their opposition to the "British neo-colonial project of Malaysia." Sukarno was apparently "in awe" of North Korea's Juche ideology.[36] The Indonesia-DPRK relationship continued to revolve around matters of sovereignty and national independence. Thus, it is no surprise that when Kim Il Sung visited Indonesia in April 1965 to celebrate the tenth anniversary of the Bandung Conference, he gave a speech that laid out the framework of the Juche ideology. During Sukarno's reign, Juche was the shared political language of the Indonesia-DPRK relationship.

During his visit to Indonesia, Kim Il Sung, who was accompanied by his son and successor Kim Jong Il, gave a relatively famous speech on Juche at the Ali Archam Academy of Social Sciences, which explained the three main principles of the ideology.[37] In this speech, Kim said that Juche emphasizes independence in politics (*chaju*), self-reliance in the economy (*charip*), and self-defense in the military (*chawi*).[38] Kim noted, "We by no means oppose economic cooperation between states or advocate building socialism in isolation." He added, "What we do reject is the great-power chauvinist tendency to check the independent and comprehensive development of the economy of other countries and, furthermore, to subordinate their economy to one's own on the pretext of 'economic cooperation' and 'international division of labor.' " He ended his speech by stating, "The anti-imperialist, anti-colonialist struggle of the communists and people of Indonesia is conducive to this common struggle of the Asian peoples. The Korean people attach great value on their ties and solidarity with the communists and people of Indonesia, and actively support their revolutionary struggle."[39] During Kim's visit to Indonesia, Sukarno said in a speech at the Provisional People's Consultative Assembly of Indonesia that "a new society should be built under the banner of self-reliance and self-supporting economy." He noted, "His Respected Excellency Premier Kim Il Sung, the author of the famous doctrine of self-reliance [Juche] and the daring and successful builder of a self-supporting economy is present here!"[40] This Juche discourse was a joint anti-colonial vernacular that strengthened the DPRK-Indonesia relationship during Sukarno's rule and boosted Kim Il Sung's prestige in the Third World as a revolutionary theorist.

During Kim Il Sung's trip to Indonesia, Sukarno took the North Korean leader on a tour of the Bogor Botanical Garden. According to North Korean folklore, Kim Il Sung was particularly impressed with a new species of orchid. Sukarno told Kim that this orchid would be hereafter named "Kimilsungia," after the North Korean leader. Kim initially declined this offer, but Sukarno insisted because the North Korean leader had "rendered enormous services to mankind." North Korean propaganda said, "Kimilsungia is not simply a beautiful flower of nature; it is a flower that symbolizes the greatness of President Kim Il Sung, who illuminated the road ahead for the world by means of his Juche idea, and a flower that has bloomed in the hearts of the people in the era of independence in honor of a great man."[41] With his naming of the Kimilsungia flower, Sukarno bolstered Kim's personality cult and reinforced his global propaganda campaign.

During the early 1960s, Sukarno had adopted a Maoist-style anti-imperialist philosophy that divided the world into two blocs: New Emerging Forces and Old Established Forces. Sukarno hoped to decenter the United Nations and construct an international system that rejected the hegemonic powers of the Soviet Union, United States, and other Western countries.[42] Thus, Kim's selection of Indonesia as the location for his Juche speech was an attempt to ride Sukarno's wave of radical nonalignment as both Third World leaders applied similar independent lines to their foreign policies. In his Independence Day speech on August 17, 1965, Sukarno advocated a Jakarta–Phnom Penh–Hanoi–Beijing–Pyongyang axis.[43] Sukarno's attempt to reconstruct the Cold War world along the lines of imperialists and anti-imperialists undoubtedly resonated with the staunchly anti-imperialist North Korean leadership.

Starting the evening of September 30 and continuing into October 1, 1965, a faction within Indonesia's military, led by Major General Suharto and Lieutenant Colonel Untung, overthrew a number of key military leaders and unleashed a nationwide campaign of terror against Communists, who were used as scapegoats for the coup. Weakened by the demise of the Indonesian Communist Party, Sukarno turned power over to Suharto, who was formally announced president of Indonesia in March 1967. Suharto reversed the radical foreign policy of his predecessor and quickly formed close ties with anti-Communist Western powers.[44]

The North Korean government lamented the fall of Sukarno's regime. However, Kim Il Sung and the North Korean leadership learned a number of valuable revolutionary lessons from the Indonesian coup d'état. Namely, Kim believed that the "guided democracy" system under Sukarno, which had given equal governmental powers to the military, the Communist Party, and religious Islamic leaders, was unsustainable and volatile. In other words, political pluralism was a recipe for disaster if one's ultimate goal was a truly revolutionary society and, more importantly, the retention of political power. The coup proved Kim's interpretation to be correct. Thus, when a Chinese government delegation met with the North Korean leader on October 9, 1965, Kim said, "The occurrence of this kind of incident was a necessity; it is the rule of revolutionary developments. We have to be cautious regarding the Indonesian situation [because] there have been no concrete sources of information since the Indonesian communists went underground." He added, "There has been information from the West, but we cannot issue articles on that. Temporarily we can only observe [the situation]. . . . The Americans will not leave the development of the Indonesian Communist Party alone, in this world there are no such kindhearted enemies." Kim concluded, "The Indonesian [Communist] Party is a large party; we believe they will not keep silent like this; of course, they cannot publicly issue statements and articles like before. However, it will slowly gather strength and continue the struggle."[45] The military coup in Indonesia may have demonstrated to Kim Il Sung that absolute autocracy and one-party rule was the key to power consolidation and longevity. The party, not the military, had to be at the center of the state's affairs.

The North Korean leadership believed only armed struggle and dictatorial control would resurrect the possibility of a Communist revolution in Indonesia.[46] In November 1965, North Korean vice premier Ri Ju-yeon told Chinese leader Zhou Enlai, "It is Indonesia's political system, society, and economic setting that made Untung and others turn to revolution. It has nothing to do with Untung as an individual, but the background producing a revolution."[47] Guk-hyeon Choe, a North Korean diplomat in Budapest, told his Hungarian counterparts, "The Indonesian Communist Party used wrong tactics by making all its leaders and members known [i.e., by not maintaining an underground organization]. Following the start of the uprising, as soon as it encountered the first signs of opposition, [the party], counting on Sukarno, wanted to solve the conflict by peaceful means."[48] The overthrow of Sukarno in Indonesia may have reinforced Kim Il Sung's commitment to absolute autocracy.

Prior to the military coup, the Indonesia–North Korea relationship was based around shared values of national autonomy, self-sufficiency, and nonalignment. Both leaderships spoke the political language of Juche and saw their role as a vanguard in a new international order that prioritized national liberation and global decolonization. Despite their different political systems, the two governments' shared emphasis on self-reliance made them natural partners. After the military coup, Kim Il Sung lost a valuable revolutionary partner in Sukarno but pushed ahead in building his reputation as a Third World leader.

The Cuban Alliance

On August 29, 1960, the governments of Cuba and North Korea signed a cultural cooperation agreement, which stipulated that the two countries would exchange scientists, educators, writers, artists, and athletes. On September 24, less than a month after signing this agreement, the two countries formally established diplomatic relations.[49] Thus, a long and enduring friendship was formed between these two revolutionary governments. Led by former guerilla fighters and predisposed to despising the U.S. government based on violent historical experiences with U.S. armed forces, the two leaderships became natural allies. Shortly after establishing diplomatic ties, the most well-known guerilla fighter in the world and Cuba's minister of industry Che Guevara traveled to Communist Asia. Guevara's visit to the DPRK paved the way to a strong and mutually beneficial relationship between the two countries. Although an incident in 1965 nearly disrupted this nascent alliance, international events such as the Cuban Missile Crisis and the Sino-Soviet split led both leaderships to understand the benefits of having a like-minded anti-American ally on the other side of the world.

In November 1960, a high-level Cuban delegation, including notable revolutionary Che Guevara, visited the People's Republic of China and met Vice Chairman Zhou Enlai. During the course of their conversation, Zhou recommended that the Cubans get in touch with the North Koreans in order to fortify their defenses against a future U.S. invasion. Zhou told Guevara, "When you visit Korea, you could even talk to them, to see what secret defensive works could be constructed in mountainous areas. It's these defensive works that the Chinese Volunteer Army and Korean People's Army relied on." Zhou continued, "The U.S. spent several ten thousand tons of explosives, [only to find] that they couldn't take even one mountaintop. With these defensive works, he [the U.S.] was on the hilltop, while we were within the hill. They couldn't capture [our positions] in any way."[50] Zhou's recommendation to Guevara speaks volumes about the rugged and militaristic image that North Korea projected to other

Third World revolutionary states. As a small, mountainous nation that successfully fought off the Americans during the Korean War, Kim Il Sung's nascent state appeared bold and resilient to other Third World leaders.

Shortly after visiting China, Guevara traveled to Pyongyang and met with Kim Il Sung. Guevara later told American journalist I. F. Stone that the most impressive part of his tour of the Eastern bloc was his trip to the DPRK. Guevara, who wrote a famous guidebook for guerilla fighting in 1961, boasted that North Korea "was a tiny country resurrected from the ashes of American bombardment and invasion" and had successfully industrialized.[51] The close Cuban–North Korean relationship, which began with Guevara's 1960 visit to Pyongyang, continued during the Cold War era as Havana became an important part of Pyongyang's international network.

Situated on the other side of the world, North Korea saw Cuba as also standing on the front line of the global battle against the "U.S. imperialists." A January 6, 1969, article in the *Pyongyang Times* commemorating the tenth anniversary of the Cuban Revolution said, "The Korean people deem it as a great pride that they have a heroic and strong-willed, revolutionary people like the Cuban people as their comrades-in-arms and brothers."[52] Although their revolutions and ideological approaches differed, both Havana and North Korea proved to be thorns in the side of Washington for much of the Cold War. Both were small, non-domineering nations that successfully repelled U.S. armed forces and promoted guerilla-based revolutions around the world. Due to their relative sizes, the fact that these two small countries could never colonize or economically dominate a foreign nation helped their international reputations as genuine anti-imperialists.

On April 17, 1961, around 1,500 U.S.-armed Cuban exiles landed in the Bay of Pigs on the southern coast of Cuba in an attempt to overthrow the Castro-led government. These U.S.-trained Cuban exiles were quickly defeated by Castro's armed forces, which proved to be a great embarrassment for the U.S. government and would strain U.S.-Cuba relations for years to come.[53] As both nations experienced U.S. imperialistic maneuvers, the DPRK and Cuba bonded over shared anti-Americanism after the Bay of Pigs incident. The front-page headline of the April 19, 1961, issue of the *Rodong Sinmun* declared, "Stop the U.S. imperialists' armed invasion of Cuba."[54] The *Rodong Sinmun* translated reports from the Soviet Union's state-run media agency, TASS, on the Bay of Pigs incident. For example, one translated TASS article in the *Rodong Sinmun* said, "The Cuban people guard their combat posts. Some of the people are fighting off the invasion, some keep a vigilant guard of the island's coastline, while others are raising production results in factories and sugar cane plantations."[55]

In late April 1961, the *Rodong Sinmun* continued to promote solidarity with Cuba by publishing articles on the Cuban peoples' successful struggle to repel the U.S.-aided invaders. On April 22, 1961, headlines in the *Rodong Sinmun* proclaimed,

"The world is congratulating the Cuban people."[56] The Bay of Pigs incident made a psychological impact on one young North Korean. Kim Hyŏn-hŭi, a North Korea agent who would plant a bomb on Korean Airlines flight 858 in 1987, later told investigators that she grew up terrified of Americans. Raised in Cuba during the 1960s as the daughter of a North Korean diplomat, she recalled her father taking her to the beaches at the Bay of Pigs and telling her that the U.S. imperialists might come again to try to invade the small Caribbean island.[57]

Another event in Cuba also helped to shape the North Korean government's paranoid militarism. The Cuban Missile Crisis confirmed Kim Il Sung's supposition that great powers, especially the Soviet Union, could not be counted on during times of national crisis. The effects of the Cuban Missile Crisis were felt around the world, even in faraway Pyongyang. Based on the events surrounding the Castro regime and what Kim Il Sung perceived was Soviet abandonment of its Cuban allies, the Cuban Missile Crisis serves as a meaningful starting point in explaining the DPRK's militarization. Kim Il Sung felt that Soviet leader Nikita Khrushchev "was buddy-buddy with Eisenhower and Kennedy" and "had betrayed Cuba at the time of the Caribbean crisis," which signaled to the North Korean leader that self-defense was the only way to guarantee his nation's security.[58] During this same conversation, Kim Il Sung also criticized his perceived lack of Soviet support for anti-colonial fighters and told Soviet Premier Alexei Kosygin that he felt Moscow "did not support the national liberation struggle of the Asian and African peoples."[59] Kim Il Sung's linking of the Cuban Missile Crisis with the Third World movement suggests that he saw the two events as intertwined. Kim Il Sung felt an obligation to assist national liberation struggles and downplayed Soviet involvement in the Third World. He partially used crises in the Third World as a means to build up his own international prestige and revolutionary credentials.

In the fall of 1963, Kim Il Sung's regime sent flood aid to Cuba, which had suffered substantial damage as a result of Hurricane Flora. The North Korean government officially sent five thousand tons of rice, five tractors, and axes, saws, hammers, and drugs. The North Koreans proudly showed Cuba's ambassador to the DPRK their ship full of aid supplies bound for Havana from the Nampo port.[60] The North Koreans also sent around seven hundred "volunteer" fighters in the mid-1960s to assist the Cubans against U.S. imperialism.[61] Although Havana was quite far from Pyongyang, Kim Il Sung saw the value of having another committed ally directly opposing the U.S. imperialists on an imagined global front line and supporting socialist revolutions in the Western hemisphere.

In order to signify the importance of the Cuban Revolution to the North Korean people, the DPRK government established domestic measures celebrating solidarity between the two nations. For example, the week of July 10 in North Korea was announced as "Korea-Cuba Friendship Week." The week was marked in Pyongyang by lectures, meetings, photo exhibitions, and a documentary film on Cuban history. A "Korea-Cuba Friendship" cooperative farm and a "Korea-Cuba Friendship" textile machine factory were also established in North Korea.[62] These solidarity measures with Cuba were part of the North Korean government's efforts to make its citizens imagine another small anti-American nation in a similar precarious position and globalize North Koreans without their leaving the borders of the DPRK.

While the DPRK and Cuban governments enjoyed close ties for much of the Cold War, an incident involving the Cuban ambassador in Pyongyang in 1965 nearly derailed the relationship. On March 28, 1965, the Cuban ambassador to the DPRK, Lazaro Vigoa, his family, and a delegation of visiting Cuban physicians were touring Pyongyang when they stopped to take photos of a building that had been destroyed during the Korean War. North Koreans living near the structure took offense to this and started crowding around the Cubans' vehicle. Soon, a very large crowd developed, which included around one hundred children, and the situation quickly turned violent. The residents allegedly pounded their fists on the Cubans' vehicle and yelled racial slurs at the ambassador's Afro-Cuban wife. Vigoa tried to calm the crowd and spoke in Korean to them. A report from the East German embassy in Pyongyang explains, "This had no effect on the crowd's actions, . . . [and] the militia in the vicinity took no action at all." When the Cubans tried to exit their car, the mob of angry North Koreans took away the delegation's cameras.[63]

The East German report continues, "At about this time a member of the security service arrived, and when he realized what was going on, he put his hands in front of his face, and, as the Cuban ambassador said, groaned." Soon, a large unit of North Korea's armed security service arrived and "proceeded to exercise extraordinary brutality against the crowd, including the children. They struck these people, including the children, with the butts of their weapons." After driving away from the crowd, Vigoa realized the Cuban flag on his vehicle had been torn off. He told the leader of the North Korean security service, who then ordered his unit to unleash even worse brutality on the North Korean residents. The Cuban ambassador told the East German diplomat that the actions of the DPRK's security service "were so brutal that if he had been Korean and had had the flag, he would have preferred to eat it rather than to give it back."[64] This incident demonstrated to the Cuban government that the North Korean people lacked proper political education on the benefits of multicultural Third Worldism.

Although North Korean officials tried to contain the fallout from this incident, Vigoa asked to speak to the "Supreme Leader" of the DPRK. Kim Il Sung met with Vigoa and "asked the ambassador to express his regret for the incident to Fidel Castro and the Cuban leadership, and made assurances that the guilty parties would be punished and measures would be taken to prevent similar incidents in the future." Ri Hyo-sun, KWP Politburo member and deputy chairman of the Ministers' Council, then met with Vigoa and told him, "The level of training of the masses is extremely low. They cannot differentiate between friends and foes. They completely misinterpret our call for revolutionary vigilance." The East German embassy agreed in their report and said, "The incident is indicative of the difficult internal situation and of how little influence the leadership really has on the Korean masses."[65] While the North Korean government preached the benefits of socialist internationalism, the North Korean people lacked the outside information necessary to make the distinction between enemy and ally. The DPRK's political education relied so heavily on the notion that the outside world was inherently evil that when faced with a real life situation, North Koreans could not make the distinction between "good" and "bad" foreigners. Despite their official declarations of antiracism and solidarity with the anti-colonial Third World, the DPRK government struggled to instill the values of international multiculturalism in its population.

In March 1967, Kim Il Sung hosted a farewell luncheon for Vigoa, who was ending his diplomatic post in Pyongyang. During this dinner, there was no mention of the 1965 incident that Vigoa had been involved in. Instead, Kim praised the great friendship of the Cuban and North Korean peoples. A report from the Hungarian embassy recounted that Kim said that "the KWP fully supported the standpoint of the Cuban Communist Party. As an example, he noted that the KWP supported only those Latin American revolutionary movements which the Cubans also agreed with and which they supported."[66] Fortunately for Kim Il Sung, the 1965 incident did not derail the close Cuban–North Korean relationship. The two small Communist states continued to value the revolutionary foreign policies of each other and thus formed a close comradeship.

In the early to mid-1960s, North Korean propaganda regularly celebrated the revolutionary feats of their Cuban comrades. From reprinting Fidel Castro's speeches to publishing pro-Cuba poems in the *Rodong Sinmun,* North Korea depicted Cuba as a vital anti-imperialist partner. For example, a pro-Cuba poem by a North Korean propagandist in the January 1, 1963, issue stated, "Cuba! Even though we are separated by tens of thousands of *ri* [a traditional Korean unit of measurement equal to around four hundred meters], we stand shoulder to shoulder as one beating heart in our sacred joint struggle."[67] The January 6, 1963, issue of the *Rodong Sinmun* reprinted a speech by Fidel Castro that commemorated the fourth anniversary of the Cuban Revolution. The article was entitled "Even if the U.S. invasion is repeated fifty and hundred times, the Cuban people will instantly defeat all invasions."[68] In July 1965, two Cuban journalists traveled to Pyongyang to interview Kim Il Sung. The North Korean leader told them, "The Korean and Cuban people are comrades-in-arms and intimate brothers who are fighting shoulder to shoulder on the front of the struggle for the revolutionary cause of the international working class and of the struggle against U.S. imperialism, our common enemy."[69] The two governments bonded over shared adoration for guerilla warfare, one-party rule, and anti-colonial rebellion. Both leaderships also aspired to be key players in the international revolutionary movement.

The feelings of solidarity and comradeship seemed to have been mutual as the North Korean and Cuban leaderships lauded each other's brilliance. For example, a 1967 Soviet embassy report stated, "The Korean leadership calls Fidel Castro 'the great leader of the Cuban revolution and the Cuban people.' For his part, Fidel Castro characterized Kim Il Sung as 'one of the most eminent, outstanding, heroic leaders of socialism.' "[70] By 1968, diplomatic relations between the two countries were so close that Cuban deputy premier Raul Castro said, "If someone is interested in what the Cubans' opinion is on certain questions, he should ask the [North] Koreans." He continued, "And if someone asks what [North] Korea's standpoint may be in certain cases, he can safely ask the Cubans about that. Our views are completely identical in everything."[71] Meanwhile, in a speech at a 1968 North Korean industrial exhibition in Havana, Cuba's minister of foreign trade Marcelo Fernandez "referred to [North] Korea as the sole country besides Cuba where there was a spirit of real internationalism."[72] Rhetorically, North Korea and Cuba formed an anti-colonial brotherhood built on shared values of armed struggle and revolutionary socialism.

At the height of China's Cultural Revolution, Kim Il Sung spoke about the political climate of the international Communist movement at Cuban ambassador Vigoa's farewell luncheon. Kim said that relations with China during Mao's Cultural Revolution were "very problematic" and that the Chinese embassy in Pyongyang disseminated anti-DPRK propaganda among the ethnic Chinese living in North Korea. In addition, Kim criticized Chinese provocations in front of the DPRK's embassy in Beijing. Kim fretted to Vigoa that "the behavior of the Chinese was not compatible with the principles of proletarian internationalism and one should instead declare it a bourgeois nationalist action." Kim also mocked Mao Zedong by pointing out that the sixty-seven-year-old chairman of the DPRK's Supreme People's Assembly, Choe Yong-gon, was the same age as the Chinese leader but "his state of health was better and his mind was also livelier."[73] By the mid-1960s, Kim Il Sung depicted himself as the top Asian revolutionary leader.

During the Cultural Revolution, which Kim Il Sung called "unbelievable idiocy," Chinese Red Guards accused the North Korean leader of being a "fat revisionist."[74] The Chinese Red Guards' slander against North Korea's Great Leader naturally pushed the leadership in Pyongyang away from Beijing's orbit. In addition, the disorder and chaotic violence of China's Cultural Revolution appeared to run counter to the tenets of anti-imperialism and socialist internationalism. Kim Il Sung told the Soviet ambassador on June 21, 1968, "Lawlessness and chaos reign in China. Everything that the Chinese are doing is scandalous. This is also a great misfortune for Vietnam, both for you and us, and for the Chinese people themselves." Six months later, Kim Il Sung repeated similarly negative messages about the PRC to the Soviet ambassador: "Right now the Chinese are not waging any fight against imperialism, they just babble."[75] As a small, divided nation, Kim Il Sung's North Korea depended on regimentation, centralization, and national unity. Maoist extremism was seen as threatening and ideologically corrosive to the leadership in Pyongyang. In other words, the Cultural Revolution threatened the national security of the DPRK.

In a 1969 report for the celebration of the twentieth anniversary of the founding of the DPRK, Kim Il Sung "unambiguously criticized a number of aspects of the policy of the Chinese leaders." Kim "spoke of the 'mistakes of leftist excesses,'" reported the Soviet embassy in Pyongyang, "which appear in the event that 'reliance is placed on class struggle alone and overestimating its role, forgetting that the solidarity and cooperation of the working class, the peasantry, and the working intelligentsia comprise the basis of social relations in a socialist society.'"[76] In the late 1960s, the North Koreans also pushed to establish or improve relations with Third World nations, such as India, Singapore, and Malaysia, that had unfriendly relations with China.[77] During the Cultural Revolution in China, DPRK leadership used its presence in the Third World as a way to oppose Maoist extremism.

Although the Cuban press had organized a news blackout on China's border conflict with the Soviet Union, the Cubans allowed the DPRK's press corps in Havana to hold a press conference at its embassy in which they condemned Chinese accusations of revisionism against the DPRK. The Hungarian embassy in Cuba commented, "This fact sheds light upon the strength of the Cuban-Korean contacts."[78] The Sino-Soviet split had opened a space for small communist governments, such as those of the DPRK, Cuba, and North Vietnam, to strengthen their ties. "There existed a great triangle in world politics," said the Cuban foreign minister Raul Roa at a January 1968 Cuba-DPRK friendship rally, "and this was Cuba-Vietnam-Korea. These three countries were the sole true manifestations of armed revolution."[79] This new alliance of small, like-minded Third World states may explain the reason why the 1965 incident involving the Cuban ambassador did not spiral into a tense situation between the two governments. The DPRK, Cuba, and the Democratic Republic of Vietnam participated in "vanguard internationalism," to borrow political scientist Tuong Vu's term. With Beijing and Moscow quarreling, these three small nations took it upon themselves to blaze the revolutionary trail towards world communism.[80]

After Che Guevara's 1967 death in a Bolivian jungle, the North Korean leader commemorated the Latin American guerilla fighter as a revolutionary hero. In 1968, on the first anniversary of Guevara's death, the entire front page of the *Rodong Sinmun*

FIGURE 1. Artist name: Ro Ŭigŏn. "Long live militant unity between the people of Korea and the people of Cuba!" Source: Leiden University Libraries, digital collection.

featured a treatise by Kim Il Sung that said, "Che Guevara was a tireless revolutionary in battle and a true internationalist champion completely free of narrow nationalist sentiments. His whole life was a great example of being a committed revolutionary fighter and true internationalist." Kim added, "Che Guevara is not with us now. But the blood he shed will never be wasted. . . . Thousands, tens of thousands, of Che Guevaras will appear on the decisive battlegrounds of the revolutionary struggle in Asia, Africa and Latin America."[81] As an aspiring global revolutionary figure in his own right, Kim portrayed Guevara as a martyr for the world's oppressed masses.

The *Rodong Sinmun* continued to print articles on Guevara and celebrate his revolutionary legacy. On October 8, 1972, exactly five years after his death, the *Rodong Sinmun* published a commemorative article entitled "Che Guevara's Revolutionary Spirit Will Live Forever" that featured a large portrait of Guevara. The article announced, "Comrade Ernesto Che Guevara was a true internationalist fighter who devoted his whole life to the anti-imperialist revolutionary struggle for the freedom and liberation of the Latin American people."[82] On June 14, 1988, an article in the *Rodong Sinmun*, which also featured a portrait of Guevara, celebrated the deceased guerilla's sixtieth birthday. The article proclaimed, "The revolutionary cause that Che Guevara could not achieve will be accomplished by the struggle of Latin American revolutionaries and the world's revolutionary people." The International Culture Hall in Pyongyang also hosted a lecture and movie on June 13, 1988, about Guevara's life.[83] Although Guevara had died in 1967, the North Korean government's continued commemoration of his legacy signifies that the Latin American revolutionary fighter achieved almost heroic status in the DPRK. This heroic status was normally reserved for members of the ruling Kim family, but Guevara's selfless commitment to armed struggle strongly resonated with Pyongyang, which represented the deceased guerilla fighter as the revolutionary ideal that all Communists should strive to be like.

While North Korea's relations with the Soviet Union and China have been thoroughly researched, the North Korea–Cuba relationship remains regrettably underresearched.[84] During the course of the Cold War, the Pyongyang-Havana alliance remained close and was an anti-imperialist brotherhood. Although Castro shied away from establishing a pervasive personality cult of his own, unlike Kim Il Sung's North Korea, he nonetheless understood the value of having a similarly minded ally across the Pacific. As committed revolutionaries, both leaders would later assist guerilla fighters and national liberation movements in the Third World.

Vietnam War

Despite domestic political and economic struggles after the Korean War, Kim Il Sung remained dedicated to aiding the international revolutionary movement. When Soviet ambassador to the DPRK A. M. Puzanov met with Kim on August 1, 1957, he told the North Korean leader that Moscow had agreed to provide North Vietnam with one billion rubles for flood aid. Not wanting to be outdone by Moscow, Kim announced that the DPRK would also provide flood assistance to Hanoi. Although North Korea's amount of aid, five thousand rubles, paled in comparison to the large Soviet aid package, Kim showed that even during times of economic difficulty his government would assist allies, especially those in the Third World, during their times of need. Kim Il Sung told the Soviet ambassador "that the population of North Vietnam needed to be helped."[85] Kim remained dedicated to helping the Vietnamese Communists after 1957 and later offered North Vietnamese leader Ho Chi Minh military assistance during the Vietnam War.[86] Kim Il Sung's Vietnam War policy was not motivated purely by grand notions of world revolution. The Vietnam War proved useful in elevating Kim Il Sung's international and domestic prestige.

From November 28 to December 2, 1958, Kim Il Sung visited North Vietnam after a short trip to China. Ho Chi Minh welcomed Kim to Hanoi on a very warm day and said, "We give you the heat of our country as a gift because brotherly friendship is always warm." At a mass rally in Hanoi, Kim ended his speech with a few phrases in Vietnamese: "Long live the unification of Vietnam! Long live the unification of Korea! Long live socialism! Long live world peace!" The seemingly impressed Vietnamese crowd "responded at the top of their voices." During his trip to North Vietnam, Kim visited the Namdinh textile factory, an agricultural co-op on the outskirts of Hanoi, and the Vietnamese Military Officers' School.[87] Kim's visit to North Vietnam proved valuable for fostering close ties between the two Asian Communist states that both sought national reunification.

On March 27, 1965, the front page of the *Rodong Sinmun* featured the headline, "The Korean people will provide any kind of support, including weapons, to the Vietnamese comrades and upon request will send volunteer forces." This headline was labeled "Government Statement."[88] This was the first time that Kim Il Sung explicitly offered military support to a foreign leader, and it began a month-long series of articles in the *Rodong Sinmun* recruiting volunteers for the Vietnam War. This little-known episode of North Korean internationalism proved important for Kim's domestic and foreign policies. On one hand, Kim used the Vietnam War and the threat of a U.S. invasion as a way to mobilize his countrymen. The recruitment efforts for Vietnam War "volunteers" were reminiscent of the Chinese volunteers for the Korean War. Just as Mao had used the Korean War to push his strategy of "continuous revolution," Kim Il Sung used the Vietnam War in a similar vein.[89] On the other hand, Kim demonstrated his commitment to anti-colonial revolution by visibly offering Ho Chi Minh his military services. Ho covertly agreed to allow the North Korean air force to fight in the war, albeit disguised as Vietnamese aircraft.[90] Thus, the Vietnam War reflects the intersection between the domestic and foreign policies of Kim Il Sung's regime.

Pyongyang used the Vietnam War as a way to reaffirm the North Korean people's support for anti-colonialism. In April 1965, the North Korean press featured a barrage of letters from mass organizations, such as the Korean Unified Farm Workers' Association and the Korean Workers' Party, supporting the call to arms for their Vietnamese allies. The regime in Pyongyang brought the conflict in Vietnam to the front steps of North Korean factories, farms, and other workplaces via its print media. An April 6, 1965, headline in the *Rodong Sinmun* proclaimed, "Let's actively support the Vietnamese peoples' struggle!" while statements from North Korean steel mill workers and coal miners announced in the same section respectively, "Socialist countries have the right and duty to support the Vietnamese people" and "We are all prepared to run into South Vietnam at any time." A group of workers and students from Kaesong were even more fanatical in their support for their Vietnamese comrades as they signed a pledge to assist "the fighting Vietnamese people" as a volunteer fighting force.[91]

The DPRK's state-run media also brought the Vietnam War into the North Korean home. On April 7, 1965, the first vice chairman of the Korean Democratic Women's Union, Kim Ok-sun, declared in a *Rodong Sinmun* column, "Korean women will send their husbands, sons, and daughters, as volunteer forces to support the Vietnamese people."[92] She urged the North Korean leadership to send their "beloved husbands, sons, and daughters" to the Vietnamese front "in order to support the South Vietnamese people and women who are fighting the U.S. imperialists." A few months later, after ROK president Park Chung Hee decided to send another division of South Korean soldiers to Vietnam, Kim Ok-sun released a statement saying, "The more the U.S. aggressors step up their dirty war machinations in Vietnam, the firmer the Korean women will stand by the heroic Vietnamese people and women and give active support and encouragement to their struggle."[93] In this case, the North Korean mother, represented in the DPRK's propaganda as the most revolutionary female archetype, sacrifices for the collective well-being of the international revolutionary movement.[94] North Korean propaganda promoted soft femininity that was also revolutionary. Historian Suzy Kim explains that "a selfless militant mother as a universal model of revolutionary hero and a softer feminine maiden as an embodiment of the nation par excellence" represent the two sides of North Korean femininity.[95]

The Korean Democratic Women's Union proclaimed solidarity with Vietnamese women. The vice chairman of the Korean Democratic Women's Union, Choi Geum-ja, traveled to North Vietnam in the mid-1960s and visited factories, mills, farms, schools, and hospitals. Choi said she was particularly moved by the "heroic struggle of Vietnamese women." She explained, "The women of Vietnam are unfolding an extensive Three Ready's movement. It is a movement to engage themselves in productive labor in place of their husbands, brothers, and sons who have gone to fight, take good care of the family members of service members, and get themselves ready to fight when necessary." Choi proudly recalled stories of selfless Vietnamese women assisting the Vietnamese struggle. For example, she fondly remembered the female workers of the Namdinh textile factory raising their production quotas despite attacks from the "U.S. air pirates," and a fifty-three-year-old woman in Quảng Bình Province who secretly ferried munitions across a river forty-five times in three days despite heavy bombing.[96] The Korean Democratic Women's Union also sent telegrams to the South Vietnamese Liberation Women's Union and praised "the South Vietnamese women for taking an active part in the heroic anti-U.S. national salvation struggle with the entire people."[97] Despite their seemingly genuine attempt to promote the importance of women in the Vietnamese struggle for national liberation, the Korean Democratic Women's Union couched their support in language that emphasized the traditional maternal role of women during wartime. Rather than encourage Vietnamese women to take up arms, the North Koreans noted the significance of women in non-combat roles, such as in the home and the workplace.

This outpouring of support from the North Korean proletariat for the Vietnamese liberation struggle, as represented in the DPRK's state media, indigenized the threat of a U.S. invasion and propagated the notion that Washington was intent on destroying Third World socialism. The domestic mobilization campaign led up to a visit by a delegation of the South Vietnamese National Liberation Front in May 1965. According to the Czechoslovakian ambassador to the DPRK, the delegation "received a grandiose welcome . . . and huge gatherings were organized in Kaesong, Wonsan and Pyongyang in honor of the delegation."[98] The delegation's leader, National Liberation Front Central Committee member Nguyen Van Hieu, also gave a speech at the Third Supreme People's Assembly meeting in Pyongyang. In the speech, Nguyen said, "The entire South Vietnamese people and army always draw a lofty inspiration from the powerful, enthusiastic and active assistance, material and moral, that the government of the DPRK and the fraternal Korean people have rendered and will continue to render the South Vietnamese people in their just, patriotic struggle for driving out the U.S. imperialist aggressors, liberating South Vietnam, and achieving reunification of the fatherland." Nguyen added that the North Korean peoples' "lofty internationalist spirit of resolutely defending the world people's revolutionary struggle and national liberation" served as a valuable lesson for South Vietnam.[99] To encourage the Vietnamese struggle was an indirect way for the North Korean people to support their own country's socialist construction and self-reliant development.

The Czechoslovak ambassador to the DPRK commented on the domestic situation in North Korea during this period of close Vietnamese solidarity, saying, "Instead of mobilization to accomplish work goals, all attention is focused on foreign policy

FIGURE 2. Artist name: Pak Hŭngmo. "Let us do our utmost to help the people of Vietnam!" Source: Leiden University Libraries, digital collection.

issues, combat readiness and unity of Asian and African countries." He said that his "friends," most likely referring to other Eastern European diplomats stationed in Pyongyang, also noticed that this North Korean government-led campaign was intended "to distract people from pressing economic problems and to drown internal difficulties in similar actions."[100] Diplomats of Eastern bloc countries believed the DPRK's Vietnam War mobilization campaign was intended to distract North Koreans from domestic issues. "There is an increasing level of war psychosis among the [North Korean] people," the East German embassy in Pyongyang observed in June 1965. "For instance, one advises friends not to buy a table or a wardrobe since a war is imminent."[101] The DPRK government used the Vietnam War as a means to marshal public support for the Great Leader, Kim Il Sung, who supposedly protected North Koreans from Western imperialist aggression.

In the summer of 1965, Kim Il Sung met North Vietnamese deputy prime minister and Politburo member Le Thanh Nghi in Pyongyang. During their conversation, Kim offered large amounts of North Korean assistance to the Vietnamese and explained, "We are determined to provide aid to Vietnam and we do not view such aid as constituting a heavy burden on North Korea. We will strive to ensure that Vietnam will defeat the American imperialists, even if it means that North Korea's own economic plan will be delayed."[102] Kim's rhetoric was backed up by action; the East German embassy in Pyongyang reported in June 1965 that the DPRK government had started taking out 1,000 won from North Korean workers' wages in order to support the war in Vietnam.[103] Kim Il Sung also offered advice to his Vietnamese ally based on his experience fighting the Americans during the Korean War, and he stressed the importance of building underground facilities. He said, "Based on Korea's experience, you should build your important factories in the mountain jungle areas, half of the factories inside the mountains and half outside—dig caves and place the factories half inside the caves and half outside." Kim extrapolated on the process involved in building in caves and tunnels. He explained, "Building a factory in a cave, such as a machinery factory, will require a cave with an area of almost 10,000 square meters. It took North Korea from 1951 to 1955–1956 to finish building its factories in man-made caves, but today we can do the work faster."

Kim Il Sung offered Hanoi five hundred North Korean experts and workers to help the North Vietnamese build caves and tunnels. Kim noted that building caves for aircraft was far more cumbersome: "Building caves for aircraft (a regiment of thirty-two jet aircraft) is much more difficult, but we have good experience in this area, and our Chinese comrades who were sent here to learn how to do this have gone back home and have successfully built such caves." North Korea's expertise in cave and tunnel building earned it a niche within the Eastern bloc. Even large nations, such as China, sought North Korean assistance on these matters. After meeting with Kim,

Nghi concluded in his report, "The North Korean leaders were very honest and open; they expressed total agreement with us; and their support was very straightforward, honest, and selfless."[104] Although the Czechoslovak ambassador to the DPRK viewed the North Korean government's mobilization campaign as motivated by self-interest, Nghi relayed the message back to Hanoi that the North Koreans were entirely "selfless" and dedicated to aiding the Vietnamese struggle against the Americans. Kim used Vietnam as a way to bolster his revolutionary status in the Third World.

While it is unclear why the North Vietnamese leadership never took up Kim Il Sung's offer to send ground forces or tunnel-building experts, North Korea sent large amounts of construction materials, tools, and automobiles to North Vietnam via Chinese railways in Fall 1965.[105] North Korea's Foreign Economic Administration organized this arrangement with the assistance of the Chinese embassy in Pyongyang. Beijing sometimes did not charge for the use of its railways or would say the North Vietnamese needed to pay the shipping costs.[106] North Korea gave these materials, free of charge, to the North Vietnamese. Thus, Pyongyang may have felt that Beijing was not doing enough to support the North Vietnamese in their struggle against U.S. imperialism. This is confirmed in a 1967 Soviet report which notes that the North Korean leadership privately criticized the Chinese for their lack of cooperation in assisting the Vietnamese.[107]

North Korea also expressed frustration with the other large Communist power, the Soviet Union, in regard to assisting the Vietnamese struggle. On March 4, 1965, a large anti–Vietnam War protest, which had been organized by Asian, African, and Latin American students in Moscow, took place in front of the U.S. embassy in Moscow. During the protest, Soviet soldiers came and shut down the event. They beat and, according to a Chinese Foreign Ministry document, even killed some of the protesters.[108] Kim Byeong-jik, North Korea's ambassador to the Soviet Union, expressed outrage at this incident. He told the Chinese ambassador to the Soviet Union Pan Zili, "Our country's entire population is outraged at the Soviet side's unwarranted repression and has expressed condolences to the participants in the demonstrations and the injured students." He continued, "Despite Soviet repression of this demonstration, despite that there were casualties during this just struggle, the final victory will belong to us." Kim Byeong-jik then clarified to Pan Zili that no North Korean students participated in the protest. He also questioned why the Soviet authorities deployed the military and cavalry to brutally suppress the peaceful student protest. Pan Zili said simply, "It was meant to curry favor with the United States and out of fear of offending the U.S."[109] The North Korean leadership saw both the Chinese and Soviets as being uncommitted to aiding the Vietnamese revolution. As a way to play both Communist superpowers against each other and pave its own path to Third World leadership, Pyongyang privately criticized to Beijing and Moscow that the other insincerely supported the world revolutionary movement. As the U.S. embassy in Moscow aptly described in November 1967, Kim Il Sung felt "that one's position on Vietnam is [a] touchstone for judgment on whether one is resolutely combatting imperialism and actively supporting [the] liberation struggle."[110]

In a February 1966 letter to Władysław Gomułka, the first secretary of the Central Committee of the Polish Workers' Party, Kim Il Sung's increasing discontent with the two Communist superpowers clearly showed. The Polish suggested that a Vietnamese solidarity conference be organized among Communist nations and parties. Kim disagreed and told Gomułka that such a conference "without adequate advance preparation . . . would not bring benefit to the struggle of the Vietnamese people nor would it enhance the cohesion of the socialist camp; on the contrary, it would cause further damage to the unity of the international communist movement." This suggests that Kim felt each Communist nation could individually do its part to aid the Vietnamese struggle and that convening a conference for the sake of appearance only masked the disagreements between the USSR and China. Kim said in the letter, "At the same time, with regard to assisting the Vietnamese people in its struggle, all parties of the socialist countries and each one of them must first act in practice without waiting for the conference."[111] Kim Il Sung, a leader that prioritized armed struggle and militancy, became increasingly disillusioned with the lack of commitment to the Vietnamese struggle by both Moscow and Beijing.

This disillusionment with both China and the Soviet Union was spelled out in a long August 12, 1966, *Rodong Sinmun* article entitled "Let Us Defend Independency" (sometimes translated as "Let's Protect Self-Reliance"). In this article, Pyongyang pledged neutrality during the Sino-Soviet split and implicitly criticized Soviet revisionism and China's Cultural Revolution. The article states, "We should fight against all the erroneous deviations from Marxism-Leninism and defend its purity." The article continues, "It is not big Parties or Parties with a long history of revolution alone that garner fine experience. A small Party or a young one too can create experience beneficial to the international communist movement if it holds fast to independency on the values of Marxism-Leninism." The article said that the Vietnam War "is an aggression against the entire socialist camp, a challenge to the national liberation movement and a grave danger to peace in Asia and the rest of the world."[112] This article was a foundational piece of Juche-based discourse in North Korea's early political culture.

The ideological importance of this article can be substantiated by the fact that Kim Il Sung brought it up in a conversation with a visiting East German delegation, which included the GDR's chief ideologue Dr. Kurt Hager, in 1968. Kim told Hager, "Our self-reliance is not directed against the Cultural Revolution. The latter is an internal matter of our neighbor. We will not promote that." Kim continued, "Self-reliance is an action of self-defense for the education of the party and the people. Therefore we have published the article 'Let's Protect Self-Reliance' and talked about it during our party conference in October 1966." Kim added, "We are for self-reliance. It is not directed against the unity of the socialist camp and doesn't mean any interference in the internal matters of other countries. . . . We opt for self-reliance because we want to strengthen solidarity with the socialist camp and the national liberation movement."[113] Kim Il Sung identified self-reliance as an essential element of socialist internationalism. He spoke the language of Juche as a way to reassert his neutralism in the Sino-Soviet split and carve out his own ideological space within Third World socialism.

In September 1966, the North Korean request to send an air force regiment to Vietnam was finally approved by Hanoi. According to an official Vietnamese People's Army historical publication, "The request stated that their [North Korea's] personnel would be organized into individual companies that would be integrated into our air force regiments, that they would wear our uniforms, and that they would operate from the same airfields as our air force."[114] A protocol agreement between the two Communist governments stipulated that North Korea would send enough specialists to man a Vietnamese MiG-17 company in Fall 1966, and then later in the same year, it would send another group of pilots to command a MiG-17 company. If Vietnam was able to gather enough aircraft, the North Koreans would send another group of specialists in 1967 to man a MiG-21 company.[115] According to a retired North Vietnamese major general who had worked with the North Koreans, a total of eighty-seven air force personnel from the DPRK served in North Vietnam between 1967 and early 1969.[116]

The deployment of North Korean pilots to aid the North Vietnamese was kept secret from the general public until 2000.[117] A high-ranking North Korean defector, who previously served as vice president for North Korea's state-run news agency, told the United Nations armistice commission in 1967 that Kim Il Sung had secretly sent around one hundred pilots to Vietnam. The French Foreign Ministry, which kept close tabs on its former colony in Southeast Asia, said this information suggests, "Pyongyang is not content to just verbally support the opponents of the U.S. in Vietnam." The ministry also noted, "Marshal Kim Il Sung himself repeatedly recommended the sending of volunteers to Vietnam by all socialist countries" and that he had declared in December 1966 that North Korea was going to bring "even more diverse forms of active aid to the Vietnamese people." The ministry concluded, "It seems difficult, from these too few pieces of info, to speak of a true North Korean commitment to the National Liberation Front or North Vietnamese sides."[118] During the war, DPRK's large amounts of assistance to the Vietnamese Communists were kept relatively secret.

Nonetheless, North Korea did not escape the death and destruction of the Vietnam War. Fourteen North Korean Air Force personnel died in the conflict and were subsequently buried in Bắc Giang Province in Vietnam.[119] U.S. bombs also reportedly damaged the North Korean embassy in Hanoi on May 19, 1967. The North Korean ambassador showcased rocket shrapnel and photos of this "U.S. criminal act" during a May 20, 1967, press conference as evidence of further U.S. barbarity in Vietnam.[120] In that same month, a Soviet report described the degree of cooperation between Hanoi and Pyongyang during the war: "The DPRK is developing active political, economic, and cultural ties with the DRV [Democratic Republic of Vietnam] and vigorously supporting and helping fighting Vietnam."[121] The memo explained that the DPRK had sent around one hundred pilots to North Vietnam along with large amounts of free aid in 1966.

In 1966, around four hundred North Vietnamese students were attending universities in the DPRK on North Korean government scholarships, with two hundred more North Vietnamese students expected to arrive in 1967.[122] On March 12, 1966, teachers and students at Kim Il Sung University in Pyongyang held a meeting in support of the Vietnamese struggle. A North Vietnamese student studying at Kim Il Sung University gave a speech at the meeting in which he said, "The Vietnamese people will fight resolutely until they drive the U.S. aggressors out of South Vietnam and win a final victory."[123] North Korean support for the Vietnamese struggle extended into the educational realm as well.

The Soviet Union saw the DPRK's active assistance to Hanoi as being primarily motivated by self-interest, not internationalist sensibilities. As the May 1967 Soviet memo states, "It should be taken into account that the Korean comrades view the Vietnamese events primarily from the point of view of their possible consequences for Korea." The memo continues, "In their opinion, the security of the DPRK, an expansion of the aggression of the American imperialists in Asia, and the prospects for the revolutionary movement in South Korea depend to a large degree on the outcome of developments of the war in Vietnam."[124] Moscow viewed North Korea's support of the Vietnamese liberation struggle as self-centered.

This observation by the Soviets was not necessarily wrong; Kim Il Sung had previously told the Chinese that he saw the failure of U.S. actions in Vietnam as the beginning of the end to U.S. imperialism in Asia. In August 1965, Kim had bluntly told a visiting Chinese friendship delegation, "If the American imperialists fail in Vietnam, then they will collapse in Asia." Kim then went on to say, "We are supporting Vietnam as if it were our own war. When Vietnam has a request, we will disrupt our own plans in order to try to meet their demands."[125] Eastern European officials and diplomats could not interpret Kim's ability to blend national and international goals. Thus, they cynically viewed the North Korean leader's actions as solely self-serving. Kim strategically used the Vietnam War as a way to weaken the U.S. military presence in Asia and envisioned that if the U.S. lost the war in Vietnam, it would withdraw its armed forces from South Korea. Kim also believed North Korea could serve as a potential developmental model for postwar Vietnam. "Kim Il Sung offers his country's rapid reconstruction as an example to the Vietnamese whom he urges to perform a similar feat after the United States is defeated," reported the U.S. embassy in Paris in August 1967.[126] In 1967, the North Korean leader was already predicting U.S. defeat in Southeast Asia and planning the postwar development of a reunified Vietnam. As part of his attempts to build up his own international prestige, Kim wanted the DPRK to serve as a Third World model of socialist construction and postcolonial development.

In addition, there is evidence that Kim Il Sung advocated for a greater North Korean military presence in Vietnam as a way to assess South Korea's military capabilities and conduct intelligence operations. A delegate of the Vietnamese National Liberation Front, Nguyen Long, told a Romanian diplomat in Pyongyang, "The North Koreans had plenty of people active in South Vietnam." Nguyen continued, "They are active in those areas where South Korean troops are operating, so as to study their fighting tactics, techniques, combat readiness and the morale of the South Korean Army, and to use propaganda against the South Koreans." According to Nguyen, the North Koreans wanted to send more personnel to South Vietnam but language barriers impeded communications between North Koreans and the Vietnamese guerilla fighters.[127]

The Vietnamese Ministry of Defense's official history of the Vietnam War noted that a "cell" of North Korean cadres planned to "launch an ideological offensive aimed at South Korean troops" in 1968 and "proselytize" in South Vietnam.[128] According to an April 1971 Vietnamese Ministry of Public Security publication, a three-man North Korean intelligence cell was suddenly caught in the middle of a military battle between Vietnamese Communist forces and South Korea's "Tiger" division in the Bình Định Province of central Vietnam.[129] While the team of North Korean pilots left in 1969, intelligence specialists from the DPRK seemed to have stayed in Vietnam until at least April 1971 in an attempt to undermine South Korean troops' morale and potentially lure them to the Communist side. As historian Sin Jae Lee explains, the North Korean intelligence cell in Vietnam produced and disseminated over one million propaganda leaflets directed at South Korean troops, provided Korean language lessons to Vietcong soldiers, helped the Vietnamese Communists kidnap South Korean soldiers, broadcast Korean-language propaganda on the radio, and conducted data research and radio monitoring of South Korean armed forces.[130]

In an effort to portray Seoul as an inherently aggressive force in the Third World, North Korean officials would tell African governments that South Korea sent troops to Vietnam in order to start World War III.[131] In actuality, the Vietnam War presented a unique opportunity for Kim Il Sung to evaluate South Korea's military without directly engaging them in an all-out war on the Korean peninsula. The Vietnam War served as a useful litmus test for the North Korean military and intelligence. The North

Korean government continued to press the Vietnamese Communists to officially allow North Koreans to fight alongside their armed forces. On February 12, 1968, the DPRK's Ministry of Foreign Affairs released a declaration that stated, "The Korean people are effectively prepared and always ready to fight alongside the Vietnamese people, whenever the Vietnamese people need it." The declaration added, "The US aggression against the Vietnamese people is also an act of aggression against the Korean people and therefore, upon the request of the Vietnamese people, the DPRK is always ready to offer it all the help it needs."[132] The Vietnamese Communists, who were revolutionary nationalists at their core, never officially permitted North Korean armed forces to fight in their war for national reunification.

While the North Koreans contributed relatively large amounts of aid to the Vietnamese struggle, the relatively harmonious relationship between Hanoi and Pyongyang lasted only until the end of that conflict. Hanoi would soon grow tired of North Korea's rigid stances in international forums and collusion with the Chinese in ousting the North Vietnamese from positions of power within the Non-Aligned Movement. As this section described, Kim Il Sung actively assisted the Vietnamese struggle as a way to further his own interests and contribute to his growing prestige in the Third World. Kim felt that he had a special role to play in the international revolutionary movement and promoted a radical vision of the Third World movement that would emanate from Pyongyang.

Kim Il Sung viewed the Third World as fertile ground to spread his brand of autonomous anti-colonialism and bolster his global fame. In the late 1960s, Kim Il Sung viewed the DPRK, Cuba, and North Vietnam as the vanguard of world revolution and sought to lead a formal political organization of small countries unified under the rubric of national autonomy and anti-colonialism. In March 1969, the Soviet Union's Foreign Affairs Ministry noted, referring to North Korea's leadership, "According to their reasoning, the American imperialists prefer 'not to aggravate relations with big countries' (meaning the USSR and China) and are striving to defeat 'the little ones,' especially divided countries (the DPRK, North Vietnam, Cuba, and East Germany)." The Soviet report continued, "Based on this, Kim Il Sung is promoting a 'strategy' of fighting imperialism with the forces of 'small revolutionary' countries which are to 'tear American imperialism apart' everywhere."[133]

Kim believed that small anti-colonial nations needed to band together to reject Western dominance and resist influence from all big powers, including the Soviet Union and China. According to the Soviet Foreign Ministry, "The KWP leadership has recently stepped up activity to organize a group of 'Parties of small countries,' whose goal in the conditions of the differences between the CPSU [Communist Party of the Soviet Union] and CPC [Communist Party of China], so the (North) Korean leaders believe, is to exert their influence on the CPSU and CPC and thus achieve unity." The ministry added, "In the opinion of the Korean leaders, the DPRK, Cuba, and the DRV [Democratic Republic of Vietnam, official name of North Vietnam], who stand 'at the front lines of the revolutionary anti-imperialist struggle,' should become the nucleus of such an organization."[134] Kim wanted to be the leading figure of a newly forged anti-colonial front that was based on anti–Great Powerism.

Kim Il Sung viewed the international revolutionary movement spatially and regarded those small nations that were in direct conflict and proximity to U.S. aggression as the most authentic. This approach irritated the Soviet Union, which stated that Kim's proposal for a unified front of small revolutionary states "contradicts the Marxist-Leninist position about the growing role of the world socialist system as the chief anti-imperialist revolutionary force of modern times."[135] The next chapter delves into Kim Il Sung's shift to covert support of non-state actors and the beginning of an expansive public diplomacy campaign in the Third World.

2

Kimilsungism beyond North Korean Borders 1968–1971

IN 1967, a faction of former guerillas from the 1930s anti-Japanese struggle attempted to usurp Kim Il Sung's absolute authority within the DPRK. This group, known as the Kapsan faction, failed in its efforts to confront Kim Il Sung's pervasive personality cult and implement some moderate measures of economic liberalization. The Kapsan faction, which included the fourth-ranking member of the KWP Central Committee's Political Committee Pak Geumcheol and North Korean vice premier Ko Hyeok, protested Kim Il Sung's dual development policy (known as *byungjin*), which emphasized national defense and heavy industry. These high-level dissenters sought to improve living conditions in the DPRK and rightfully take their place alongside Kim Il Sung as anti-colonial heroes. Kim Il Sung strongly rejected this political dissent, and members of the Kapsan faction were subsequently purged from their leadership positions.[1] After 1967, cultish leader worship of Kim Il Sung intensified within the DPRK and the Monolithic Ideological System was cemented.[2]

The Monolithic Ideological System, based on ten sycophantic principles, placed Kim Il Sung at the center of all sociocultural life within the DPRK and eliminated political pluralism within the KWP. During the late 1960s and early 1970s, this theocratic-like system, known as Kimilsungism, dominated North Korean political culture and deeply influenced the regime's foreign policy decisions. Aie-Rie Lee, Hyun-chool Lee, Ji-Yong Lee, and Il-Gi Kim explain, "Kimilsungism is a mixture of socialism, nationalism, and Kim Il Sung worship. North Korean propagandists have forged Kim Il Sung as the world's greatest nationalist, enabling Korea to emancipate itself from the imperial powers of Japan, the U.S., the Soviet Union, and China."[3]

Most importantly for our purposes, the implementation of the Monolithic Ideological System affected the DPRK's Third World diplomacy. During the late 1960s and early 1970s, the North Korean government invested heavily in a global propaganda campaign to promote Kim Il Sung as a world revolutionary leader and champion of anti-colonial rebellions. In their 1972 foundational study of North Korean communism, scholars Robert A. Scalapino and Chong-sik Lee wrote, "In recent years particularly, Kim's international prestige has been stressed, with the suggestion that his theories and the [North] Korean road to socialism are the most appropriate models for all peoples seeking revolution."[4] Pyongyang's Third Worldism was multifaceted: the North Korean government sought to improve both the image of the DPRK nation-state itself and its Great Leader internationally.

After the establishment of the Monolithic Ideological System, North Korean diplomacy had an even more sycophantic character as cultish leader worship of Kim Il Sung became ubiquitous and obligatory both within the DPRK's borders and beyond them. From 1967 to 1972, North Korea's ideological export gradually changed from Juche to Kimilsungism. Aie-Rie Lee, Hyun-chool Lee, Ji-Yong Lee, and Il-Gi Kim explain, "Juche ideologues began gradually to replace the importance of nationalism with the 'greatness' of Kim Il-Sung himself, and it was a turning point when the 'Juche ideology' transmuted into 'Kimilsungism.'"[5] In 1968, the Czechoslovak Foreign Ministry noticed that "the intensification of Kim Il Sung's personality cult is inseparable from two other issues—namely, the importance of the DPRK example for the struggling nations of Asia, Africa and Latin America, and the embellishment of Kim Il Sung's role in the context of the international communist and workers' movement."[6] In many respects, North Korea's foreign policy and the global promotion of Kimilsungism were intimately linked during the late 1960s and early 1970s. A book published by Pyongyang's Foreign Languages Publishing House explains, "The great significance of the revolutionary theory of Kimilsungism . . . finds expression in the fact that this theory has enabled the peoples of underdeveloped countries to win the cause of national liberation by extricating them from a flunkeyist viewpoint and enhancing their revolutionary zeal and initiative."[7]

Within the field of North Korean studies, there has been an increased effort by scholars to separate the North Korean people from the leadership. As historian Andre Schmid explains in his 2018 *American Historical Review* article, scholarship on the DPRK often unintentionally reproduces the dominant messages of North Korean propaganda, such as the preeminence of the Kim family and their dominance over all state-related affairs.[8] While Schmid makes a valid argument that the Kims are too often leaned upon as the key to unlocking all North Korean histories, his focus is on the domestic sector. As unfortunate as it was, the DPRK's foreign policy was made and shaped by Kim Il Sung, not the citizenry of North Korea. This chapter explores the North Korean government's efforts to promote Kim Il Sung in the Third World as a world revolutionary leader and why DPRK foreign policy wasted so much time and effort on this global propaganda campaign.

In addition to the worldwide dissemination of its propaganda, the North Korean government provided guerilla warfare training and military support to Third World insurgents and revolutionaries in the late 1960s and early 1970s. By aiding Third World liberation movements, Kim blended national and international goals. Kim understood that each successful liberation movement and recently decolonized nation would eventually have a vote in the United Nations as a nascent government, and these leaderships would remember which Korean government assisted them during their period of anti-colonial struggle. In other words, Kim's vision of world revolution was as much about promoting anti-colonial rebellion as it was about furthering Pyongyang's self-interests in its inter-Korean competition with Seoul for international legitimacy.

This chapter focuses first on North Korea's support of Third World guerillas as a way to spread anti-colonial fervor and undermine U.S. and South Korean influence. This chapter then shifts to a discussion of North Korean propaganda in the Third World and the various forms of public diplomacy that Pyongyang invested in. By presenting photo exhibitions and film screenings, publishing propaganda in newspapers, offering free trips to the DPRK, and setting up friendship societies, Pyongyang hoped to gain prestige and status among Third World peoples as an alternative version of socialist modernity. This idea of North Korea as a developmental model would diminish the ROK's status in the Third World and bolster Kim Il Sung's prominence in the international revolutionary movement. North Korea's top-down approach to public diplomacy and its lack of an independent civil society damaged any chance of meaningful cultural exchange with Third World peoples.

Assisting Non-State Actors

During the Cold War, Che Guevara, Fidel Castro, and Ho Chi Minh earned recognition around the world for being revolutionary leaders. Although Kim Il Sung's role was less well known in the world revolutionary movement, the DPRK's role as a supporter of Third World insurgents did not go unnoticed by foreign governments. For example, a report from the Canadian Ministry of External Affairs explained, "North Korea is a strong supporter of Third World national liberation movements and probably provides more aid to these groups, in the form of training courses in revolutionary tactics and ideology, than any other country including Cuba."[9] By sowing discord and revolution abroad, Kim Il Sung enhanced his reputation in the Third World as an anti-imperialist stalwart and defender of anti-colonial peoples. In 1968, the Czech Foreign Ministry noted, "Kim Il Sung sets aside a special, clearly exaggerated role in the anti-imperialist [struggle] to the 'revolutionary' peoples of Asia, Africa, and Latin America."[10] In a bid to increase his prestige in the Third World as a revolutionary figure, Kim prioritized global insurrection and anti-colonial struggle over international stability.

During the Cold War, North Korea hosted and trained many Third World insurgents. The CIA stated in 1971, "North Korea has, in fact, both copied and competed with China in the training of guerilla movements." The CIA report continued, "Although no comparative figures of Chinese and North Korean assistance to these groups are available, Pyongyang apparently found that the training of guerillas is a relatively cheap and easy undertaking in which a small country can compete on fairly even terms for influence among radical groups."[11] According to one estimate, China trained around 3,000 foreign revolutionaries on its soil from 1956 to 1977, while North Korean military training camps hosted 2,500 Third World guerillas by 1971.[12] Thus, based on these estimates, Chinese and North Korean training camps were comparable in size. According to a May 1971 article in the *Economist*, Pyongyang's desire to evangelize the greatness of Kim Il Sung internationally fueled this "worldwide program of support for guerilla struggles which in some areas outdoes similar operations by Moscow and Beijing." The article labeled North Koreans "the last true revolutionary mavericks" and concluded that North Korea was acting on its own accord. The article proclaimed, "It would be wrong to see the Chinese as the instigators of all [North] Korean actions."[13] K. Q. F. Manning, an official in the Far Eastern department of the British Foreign Office, read this article and said that its main conclusions are "probably correct" and that the fact that DPRK's national interests "rarely coincide with those of either China or the USSR [confirms] that North Korea is acting on its own initiative."[14] The DPRK's ability to compete with the much larger nation of China in this sector demonstrates the degree to which Pyongyang committed itself to Kim's global propaganda campaign.

The two most notorious cases of North Korean support of radical Third World insurgencies happened in Mexico and Sri Lanka. In 1970, the North Korean government secretly trained fifty-three members of the Mexican Movement for Revolutionary Action (MAR) on the outskirts of Pyongyang. The Mexican revolutionaries had initially approached the Cubans, but Havana did not want to damage relations with the Mexican government. The Cubans introduced the MAR to the North Koreans.[15] A majority of the MAR militants who traveled to North Korea came from the Mexican state of Michoacán. In a March 1971 memorandum, Mexico's director for federal security Luis de la Barreda Moreno explained, "This is due to the fact that the students in the state university there, unlike those from the rest of the state, have a long tradition of revolutionary struggle, and as a consequence, there is a high level of politicization within the student body."[16]

In early 1970, the DPRK government paid for the airfare and brought the Mexican revolutionaries to Pyongyang via East Berlin and the Soviet Union. In East Berlin, the MAR militants "exchanged their Mexican passports for North Korean ones, then traveled from there by rail to Moscow, without being harassed by immigration authorities, even though their ethnic features and language made it evident that they were not, in fact, North Korean citizens."[17] Once in the DPRK, the North Korean military trained MAR members in methods of guerilla warfare and instructed them on ideological matters. In a military camp located an hour outside of Pyongyang, the MAR members learned taekwondo and underwent rigorous physical training, such as running five hours at night with heavy sandbags over treacherous terrain.[18] Rogelio Raya Morales, a member of the MAR, later explained in a police interrogation, "This instruction and training, given by North Korean soldiers, consisted of theoretical teaching on Marxist philosophy and economics, and the theory and practice of handling and using firearms, bazookas, grenades, ambush tactics, the preparation and use of explosives." Morales continued, "The trainers consistently pointed out the best way to carry out acts of sabotage and the vital points at which to apply them, and taught general guerrilla war tactics, with the understanding that they always would use green military uniforms."[19] In North Korea, the MAR members "received extensive training in [the use of] Western weapons: M-1 rifles, L-14 and L-15 carbines, .38 and .45 pistols, bazookas, mortars, and grenade launchers."[20] After six months of intense military training on the outskirts of Pyongyang, the MAR militants returned to Mexico in late August 1970.[21]

In February 1971, Mexican police raided the houses of MAR members and found North Korean propaganda, pistols, notes on weaponry and guerilla tactics, writings on Marxism, and a clandestine organization plan.[22] Nineteen MAR members were arrested, and the North Korean connection was exposed to the Mexican public and quickly hit the front pages of Mexican newspapers.[23] On March 15, 1971, the Mexican solicitor general concluded, "The objective for which this group was trained by North Korean soldiers was to impose a Marxist-Leninist regime in Mexico, for which they also received training in theory, alternating with preparation in using all types of weapons, high-powered explosives, urban and rural guerrilla tactics, karate, and self-defense."[24] In response to the North Korean government's support of the MAR, the Mexican government denied DPRK requests to establish a diplomatic mission in Mexico City.[25] The mayor of Los Angeles Sam Yorty applauded the Mexican leadership "for its speedy action in breaking up a plot by North Korean–trained Mexican guerrillas to overthrow the government and establish a communist regime."[26] The South Korean Ministry of Foreign Affairs said that the incident revealed North Korea's "wanton disregard of international peace and order [that] deserves condemnation by all freedom and peace loving peoples throughout the world."[27]

In addition to the Mexican case, the most publicized North Korean support of rebels was in Ceylon, now known as Sri Lanka. In April 1971, a North Korean–funded and –supplied dissident organization, known as the People's Liberation Front, attempted to overthrow the Ceylonese government. The North Korean embassy in Colombo supplied the rebels with money, arms, and explosives. This group, which the local Ceylonese press described as "Che Guevaristas" and "Maoists," aimed to establish a "pure socialist government" on the island. The uprising failed and the North Korean connection was quickly uncovered. The Ceylonese government took immediate action and ordered the closure of the North Korean embassy.[28] However, the chaos of the insurrection caused an island-wide school shutdown and curfew.[29]

After the instances of North Korean subversion in Mexico and Ceylon were discovered, the South Korean Ministry of Foreign Affairs issued a statement that said, "It is now common knowledge that North Korea has become the hatchery and distributor of the so-called people's guerilla war. They have trained more than 2,000 foreigners of various nationalities for guerilla warfare and exported them to more than thirty countries in Southeast Asia, Africa, and Latin America."[30] North Korea's covert support of rebels abroad was now out in the open. Ultimately, North Korea's risky practice of assisting radical movements proved detrimental to Pyongyang's international standing. However, the DPRK government engaged in this behavior because it boosted the image of Kim Il Sung as an influential figure in the international revolutionary movement and genuine supporter of anti-colonial rebellion. According to a telegram from the U.S. embassy in Colombo, "Sri Lankan officials said that North Korea would not be permitted to re-open [their] embassy and 'that trials by the criminal justice commission of captured insurgents will reveal facts that would be highly embarrassing to North Korea.' "[31] During the late 1960s and early 1970s, North Korea's Third World diplomacy fomented global insurrection as Kim Il Sung's regime undermined stability in many parts of the developing world.

Kim Il Sung's increasingly recognized role as a supporter of subversive groups in the Third World worried foreign governments and hampered the DPRK's official diplomatic outreach. The U.S. government also used it as leverage to warn Third World governments of the dangers of establishing diplomatic relations with the DPRK. In March 1971, the Mauritanian foreign minister Gaetan Duval met with the U.S. ambassador and discussed North Korea's recent support of Mexican revolutionaries because a North Korean delegation had recently visited Port Louis. According to a 1971 telegram from the U.S. embassy in Mauritania, "After the U.S. ambassador explained to Duval the recent press reports of the [Mexican] incident, Duval joked that his government had 'lost' the North Korean delegation for one hour while they were visiting the country."[32] Some countries took the North Korean threat more seriously. For example, a 1971 editorial in the Bolivian newspaper *El Diario* about a visit by a North Korean delegation accused the DPRK of "international subversion and espionage in India, Mexico, and Ceylon." The editorial also noted, "North Korea is one of the principal centers for the training of insurgents for Latin America," and it ended with a warning, "North Koreans do not engage in tourism for itself. Their trips are for other objectives: subversion."[33] This warning was well warranted as North Korea reportedly provided $280,000 to anti-government leftist forces in Bolivia from 1965 to 1975.[34]

Perhaps the most notable foreign revolutionaries hosted by North Korea are the members of the Japanese Red Army Faction (JRAF) who still call the DPRK their home. On March 30, 1970, nine members of the JRAF, a group of radical communists from Japan, hijacked a plane and landed it in Pyongyang. These Japanese revolutionaries initially wanted to fly the plane to Cuba and learn the Che Guevara–inspired brand of guerilla warfare. However, the plane was too small for long-distance travel, so the JRAF settled on Pyongyang. Kim Il Sung welcomed the hijackers and viewed it as a way to publicly embarrass the Japanese government. The North Koreans soon indoctrinated the hijackers with the ideas of Kimilsungism and later used them to help kidnap Japanese citizens.[35] In addition, there is strong evidence that the North Korean government planned and provided military support for the Lod Airport massacre, in which three JRAF members killed twenty-six people at the Israeli airport on May 30, 1972.[36] The North Korean government used the JRAF as proxies for their revolutionary activities abroad.

Despite the geographic remoteness of North Korea, Third World revolutionaries were allured by Kim Il Sung's radical brand of anti-colonial politics and came from all over the world to covertly learn his style of armed struggle that was symbolized in the Manchurian tradition. North Korea's insistence on national autonomy and anti-colonialism appealed to Third World rebels who sought an anti-Western ideology for their national liberation movements. On the surface, Kimilsungism appeared applicable to a wide range of anti-colonial struggles and radical movements. In fact, North Korean propaganda stated that Kimilsungism promoted "a sacred liberation struggle for hundreds of millions of oppressed and humiliated people in Asia, Africa, and Latin America."[37]

Newspapers

Beginning in the late 1960s, newspapers were one of the primary spaces where North Korea waged its ideological battle in the Third World as Kim Il Sung's regime regularly published full-page ads in local newspapers. By publishing these ads, the North Korean government attempted to raise the international stature of Kim Il Sung as a leading revolutionary theorist and promote pro-DPRK sympathies among leaderships in the Third World. The Czechoslovak Foreign Ministry explained in a February 1968 report, "Countries of the Third World are considered especially important for their pivotal role in increasing the authority and prestige of the DPRK in international affairs." The report added, "At the same time, the DPRK strives to promote its own example for these countries and to exert influence there by doctrines of 'building with own resources,' of 'independence from big countries,' and by radicalism of the [North] Korean positions."[38] On one hand, this public diplomacy campaign cost the North Korean government considerable sums of money. On the other hand, this diplomatic offensive expanded Kim Il Sung's global reputation as a military strategist and revolutionary theorist.

The translation, publication, and dissemination of Communist propaganda for foreign audiences were tactics used by many socialist governments during the Cold War era. China invested heavily in disseminating its propaganda abroad, as Chi-Kwan Mark's book and Çağdaş Üngör's dissertation have shown.[39] From English-language magazines such as *Peking Review* to foreign-oriented radio shows such as *Radio Peking*, China's foreign propaganda was intended to foster a pro-PRC climate abroad and promote Beijing's international positions. The Soviet Union also had an extensive international propaganda apparatus. Patryk Babiracki's book on Soviet soft power in Poland relates how Moscow sent cultural officers to Poland in the mid to late 1940s and attempted to convince Poles of the benefits of adopting the Soviet system via the press, literature, and the arts.[40] The Cuban government also invested heavily in foreign propaganda work by broadcasting Radio Havana in eight different languages and for more than four hundred hours per week.[41] In other words, North Korea was not unique in its attempt to spread its propaganda abroad. However, North Korea diverged from the foreign propaganda policies of other Communist states by devoting such a large percentage of its limited financial resources to disseminating propaganda abroad. According to foreign diplomats based in Pyongyang, North Korea had spent over $100 million by 1982 on its various lobbying efforts in the Third World.[42] Although exact figures are not available, some of this money was likely spent on propaganda advertisements in Asian, African, and Latin American newspapers.

Pictures and writings of Kim Il Sung became common sights in Third World newspapers during the late 1960s. According to U.S. embassy officials in Aden, pictures of Kim Il Sung appeared daily in South Yemeni newspapers in 1969, and "at times, as much as a quarter of these newspapers [were] taken up with the writings of Kim Il Sung or other news items relating to North Korea."[43] In Tanzania, the North Koreans published over fifty articles in two of the most popular newspapers between April 1967 and October 1969.[44] A U.S. diplomat in Tanzania commented in 1970, "North Korea was more active than any other country except perhaps Russia in mailing propaganda upcountry."[45] British officials in East Africa observed the DPRK's propaganda offensive in Somalia and noted that it followed a "similar pattern" to

North Korean actions in Tanzania as Kim Il Sung's speeches monopolized the pages of the Somali newspaper *Horseid* (Vanguard).[46] Jim Bourn, a British diplomat in Mogadishu, commented, "There has been page after page in English of turgid stuff quoting the speeches of Kim Il Sung to the North Korean Party Congress and now I see that it is all being repeated in the Arabic section of the paper." Bourn added, "The general belief here is that the North Koreans finance 'Vanguard' and this is how they get their material published—though I can hardly believe that anyone reads it. The paper is becoming known locally as the 'North Korean Times.'"[47]

When a North Korean delegation visited a capital city in the Third World, the DPRK government would step up its propaganda offensive and purchase more full-page ads in the local press. When a visiting North Korean delegation visited Freetown, Sierra Leone, in early May 1971, for example, eight of sixteen total pages in the May 2, 1971, and May 3, 1971, issues of the Sierra Leone government-owned *Daily Mail* were devoted to lauding the exploits of Kim Il Sung. In addition, five of ten pages of the May 1, 1971, issue of *We Yone*, the weekly newspaper of Sierra Leone's ruling All People's Congress (APC) Party, and twelve of fourteen pages in the May 3, 1971, issue of the pro-government paper *Unity* were also purchased by North Koreans.[48]

The DPRK spared little expense in placing ads in local newspapers. In Nigeria, North Korea published lengthy speeches by Kim Il Sung in both of Ibadan's daily newspapers, the *Nigerian Tribune* and the *Daily Sketch*. A total of sixteen pages in eight issues of the two newspapers in May 1973 were devoted to Kim's speeches, which included his "Theses on the Socialist Rural Question," a speech to visiting journalists entitled "On Some Problems of Our Party's Juche Idea and the Government of the Republic's Internal and External Policies," and an address to the Fifth Supreme People's Assembly entitled "Let Us Further Strengthen the Socialist System of Our Country."[49] During the previous year, the North Koreans published twenty-six pages' worth of Kim Il Sung's writings in two other newspapers. U.S. officials in Lagos calculated that these ads cost the North Koreans nearly US$10,000 in 1972.[50]

Nigerian newspaper publishers soon learned that the government in Pyongyang was willing to pay for column space, so they drove up the prices to earn extra income from the North Koreans. The U.S. embassy in Lagos commented, "It is beginning to appear that the DPRK is willing to pay for this strange, unremunerative exercise as an annual event. They will find Nigerians who are only too happy to take their money."[51] The North Koreans were not always so willing to pay high prices for ads in local newspapers. For example, a North Korean delegation tried to persuade C. C. Dennis, Sr., publisher of the Liberian newspaper *Daily Listener*, to print an anti-American and anti-Israeli ad. Dennis quoted an unreasonably high price that turned off the persistent North Koreans.[52]

In some anti-Communist Third World nations, local publishers that were desperate for quick cash took risks and published the North Korean ads despite government censorship. For example, a full page of Cameroon's sole daily newspaper, *La Presse du Cameroun*, was devoted to Kim Il Sung's sixtieth birthday, which surprised the local French correspondent of the *Agence France-Presse* since the conservative Cameroonian government was known for censoring leftist propaganda in the national press. The correspondent said, "The fee paid must have been enough to make the risk acceptable."[53] In Jakarta, the anti-Communist Indonesian government warned the DPRK embassy numerous times to stop disseminating propaganda. In 1969, an editor for a daily vernacular paper in Jakarta was arrested for publishing one of Kim Il Sung's speeches, which the North Koreans had paid the editor a hefty sum for the privilege to do so. The North Korean embassy also disseminated Kim Il Sung's speeches to South Korean nationals living in Jakarta.[54]

The content of these North Korean ads varied from anti-American tirades to ones celebrating the birthday of the Great Leader Kim Il Sung. For example in Pakistan, North Korean officials published a variety of propaganda in the local newspapers *Leader*, *Indus Times*, and *Azad* that ranged from anti–South Korean capitalist harangues to editorials on the progress of DPRK socialism and even a biography of Kim Il Sung's mother, Kang Pan-sŏk, on the fifty-sixth birthday of Kim Il Sung.[55] On January 9, 1971, *Azad*, a leftist Urdu-language newspaper based in Lahore, Pakistan, published a front-page reprint of Kim Il Sung's speech entitled "Expel Imperialism From Your Country." The article praised Kim "as the greatest Marxist and Leninist of the present time."[56] In Nepal, North Korean ads focused on celebrating the achievements of Kim Il Sung while anti-American pieces were also published, such as one entitled "On U.S. Imperialists' Aggressive Crimes in Korea," which irked the local U.S. embassy.[57] From January 12 to 29, 1971, the Kuwaiti English-language newspaper *Daily News* published sixteen installments that reproduced Kim Il Sung's "Report on the Work of the Central Committee of the 5th Congress of the Workers' Party of the Democratic Republic of Korea."[58] Public reception of these North Korean ads in the Third World was highly dependent on local politics and the degree to which Kim Il Sung's anti-imperialist messaging resonated with readers.

North Korean propaganda in Third World newspapers was not always harmless. In early 1970s Ceylon, the North Koreans published ads that included instructions on guerilla warfare and ways to construct grenades, bombs, and other weapons. Local anti-government insurgents used these ads as manuals on how to conduct an effective guerilla struggle in Ceylon. The Ceylonese government estimated that North Korean ads in local newspapers cost Pyongyang around US$14,000. This exportation of North Korea's revolutionary theory undermined Ceylonese government authority and

FIGURE 3. Artist unnamed. "Machine Tools Exhibition of the Democratic People's Republic of Korea." Source: Leiden University Libraries, digital collection.

helped to later provoke a 1971 armed anti-government insurrection by the People's Liberation Front on the island.[59]

The North Korean government often published its Third World newspaper ads in the local language. This had utility for the DPRK's domestic propaganda as Pyongyang oftentimes claimed these ads were articles written by foreigners adoring the Great Leader Kim Il Sung.[60] For example, the front page of the October 19, 1973, *Rodong Sinmun* proclaimed that books describing Kim Il Sung's revolutionary history were being advertised in Pakistani newspapers.[61] Some of these newspaper ads were also displayed in North Korea's International Friendship Exhibition, located near Mount Myohyang, as evidence that their country's "Supreme Leader" was widely respected around the world.[62] These ads reinforced the message conveyed by the DPRK's domestic propaganda that Kim Il Sung was not only the leader of the Korean Revolution but also a driving force behind the world revolutionary movement. In Burundi, the North Koreans published ads in the national Kirundi language.[63] North Korean ads were also published in French, Urdu, English, Russian, Nepali, and Swahili. However, North Korean translators lacked sophisticated knowledge of other cultures and would commit religious faux pas on occasion. For example, they translated the title of one of Kim Il Sung's works, *Kim Il Sung: A Divine Man* in English, into Arabic as *Kim Il Sung Is God*, which enraged devout Muslims and surely curbed the North Korean leader's popularity in the Middle East as an appropriate revolutionary figure.[64] In 1970, Egyptian president and de facto leader of Pan-Arabism Gamal Abdel Nasser condemned the cultish leader-worship systems of Communist Asia and was quoted in an Egyptian newspaper as saying, "I really cannot understand the philosophy on which the personality cult rests and the attribution of miracles to him."[65]

There was often an incompatibility between North Korea's strategic messaging and local conditions. A U.S. embassy official in Rangoon noted that the DPRK consul general in Burma "periodically purchased large newspaper advertisements consisting of deathless quotes from Kim Il Sung's more turgid speeches."[66] A U.S. embassy official in Freetown said that these ads "certainly do not represent or inspire any conceivable interest on part of readers, if any, in crushingly dull prose offered."[67] The U.S. embassy in Kathmandu noted that the DPRK consulate general in Nepal "suddenly burst forth as a major financial contributor to local newspapers" in 1970 but wondered why it was "wasting its time and money" on these ads due to the low readership of these papers.[68] Despite the mostly negative reception in the Third World to these DPRK-funded ads, North Korean diplomats continued to disseminate Kim Il Sung's works around the world.

Due to the sheer volume of North Korean ads in Third World newspapers, the South Korean government could not protest every single North Korean ad abroad. However, ROK embassies regularly protested North Korean ads that misrepresented the nature of the Seoul government or the political situation in Korea. For example, on July 12, 1971, the South Korean consulate general in Islamabad sent a letter to the director of Pakistan's Information and National Affairs Division protesting the publication of two anti-ROK ads in the Pakistani press that were paid for by the North Korean mission in Pakistan. The ROK consulate general objected to the "disparaging remarks" about South Korean president Park Chung Hee and "the very harsh and degrading language" in the two articles. The letter ended with the warning, "This sort of hostile propaganda against the Republic of Korea, if allowed to go on freely in Pakistan by a third country, I am afraid, may badly affect the already existing friendly relations between our two countries."[69]

Pyongyang's use of newspaper ads to project North Korean influence in the Third World ultimately cost the regime millions of dollars. Despite this waste of financial resources, the North Korean government continued to export Kim Il Sung's theories abroad as a way to promote Pyongyang as the legitimate Korean government and undermine South Korean influence. The North Koreans used the Third World press as a way to promote their push for reunification of Korea and shape international opinion in favor of the DPRK's political positions. While North Korean ads ultimately failed to impress Third World readers, the ads may have bolstered Kim Il Sung's popularity at home as North Korean readers may have genuinely believed these ads were articles written by devout followers of Kim Il Sung in the Third World. This image of Kim Il Sung as a global leader reinforced the propaganda that North Koreans received domestically. Chang Ki-Hong, a North Korean laborer who worked at a timber camp in Russia and later defected to South Korea stated, "We are taught that the whole world worships Kim Il Sung. I met Russians who made fun of this Kim worship, and then I realized that he was not in fact worshipped by the whole world."[70]

Photo Exhibits and Film Screenings

In addition to trying to win the war of ideas on the front pages of Third World newspapers, North Korea also began setting up photo exhibits and holding film screenings in Third World countries during the late 1960s and early 1970s. Kim Il Sung was a godlike figure within the DPRK but his personality cult struggled to extend beyond the North Korean borders. While Mao Zedong's international prestige was greatly enhanced by the convenience and popularity of the "Little Red Book," Kim Il Sung did not have his own pocket-sized book. According to the North Korean worldview, the utterances of the Great Leader were far too important to be contained within such a small book. Thus, massive volumes of Kim Il Sung's speeches and writings were sent to Third World libraries and governments, which often had trouble figuring out a way to store them.[71] In one case, the North Korean government even established the Kim Il Sung Works' Library on the small Indian Ocean island nation of

Mauritius.[72] In Zambia, the DPRK donated Kim Il Sung's books to the Mineworkers' Union's library.[73] Given the large amount of space required for these volumes and the impracticality of establishing numerous North Korean–funded libraries around the Third World, it is no surprise that many of the volumes ended up in the trash or were "promptly sent to the incinerator," as Shaikh Isa of Kuwait did in 1973.[74]

Because the North Korean government wanted Kim Il Sung to be as recognizable in the Third World as China's "Great Helmsman," it funded photo exhibits and film screenings in southern Asia, Latin America, and, most of all, Africa. Much like Maoism, Kimilsungism was to be a global ideology based on Kim's guerilla tradition and revolutionary literature. North Korean photo exhibits in the Third World promoted the revolutionary feats and leadership skills of Kim Il Sung. For example, in April 1968, a large board placed outside the Malian government-owned Librairie Populaire featured several dozen photographs of Kim Il Sung from his early days fighting the Japanese colonialists in Manchuria, organizing his band of anti-Japanese guerilla partisans, and forming the nascent Korean Workers' Party during the postliberation period. According to U.S. officials stationed in Bamako, "Many of the photographs were of stylized paintings of Kim Il Sung in assorted benevolent poses with soldiers, workers, and party leaders admiringly gathered around him. The accent in this display was on his achievements in building the party and socialism rather than his military achievements."[75] U.S. officials noted that the exhibit in Bamako was devoid of any references to U.S. imperialism or the Korean War.

North Korea photo exhibits in the Third World often contained anti-American motifs, which irked U.S. diplomatic personnel. For example, in 1968, North Korean diplomats set up a photo exhibit at a school assembly hall in Dar es Salaam, Tanzania. The exhibit mostly focused on praising the leadership of Kim Il Sung but it also contained some anti-American sentiments. U.S. officials in Dar es Salaam raised this issue with the Tanzanian Foreign Ministry "as yet another example of the North Korean embassy's refusal to abide by the Ministry's rule against propaganda activity by foreign missions defaming third countries with which Tanzania has friendly relations."[76]

DPRK film screenings were held in Burundi, Somalia, Uganda, Niger, Guinea, Liberia, Mali, and Botswana from the late 1960s to the mid-1970s. Due to the anti-Western and propaganda-filled nature of these films, these screenings often left viewers bored and foreign governments disgruntled. For example, on May 1, 1968, around seventy Malians, mostly children, watched a film that detailed the life of Kim Il Sung in a very large public theater. U.S. officials in Bamako attributed the poor attendance to the tedious style of North Korean films. An airgram from the U.S. embassy in Mali to the U.S. State Department noted, "It is possible that previous exposure to dull North Korean films has left its mark on Malian audiences. Previous North Korean film shows with their verbose repetition of the party line and paucity of action bored the unboreable at that time and the word may be out."[77] In addition to the lack of positive reception to their films, North Koreans also had to deal with the politics of host countries.

North Korean diplomats regularly showed movies at their embassies. For example, in late July 1971, the DPRK embassy in Somalia opened a film festival that focused on U.S. imperialism in Korea.[78] However, some governments of the host countries were generally unsupportive of these events. For example, on July 22, 1968, the North Korean embassy in Burundi planned a film screening in conjunction with a ceremony where the new North Korean ambassador presented his credentials to the president of Burundi Michel Micombero, whose country had close economic ties to the United States.[79] Burundian officials pretended that they were unable to supply a projector in order to prevent embarrassment over the showing of what would likely be an anti-American film.[80]

A similar situation arose in Burma when the new DPRK consul general Park Jong Oh tried to show a film about the USS *Pueblo*, the U.S. navy intelligence vessel that was captured off the coast of North Korea on January 23, 1968, to a group of Burmese citizens and journalists in August 1968.[81] Park sent out invitations, but the film showing was never held. U.S. officials in Rangoon speculated that the Burmese government warned Park to not hold the showing, or the invited Burmese citizens were warned not to go.[82] As demonstrated by many Third World governments' discomfort with North Korean film screenings in public venues, leaders often prioritized their own strategic interests on this issue in order to not alienate the United States.

Due to host governments' uneasiness with the showing of these DPRK-made films in public spaces, North Korean official would sometimes show the film in the residence of a foreign leader who was more sympathetic towards Pyongyang's positions in private. For example, in 1969, the government of Niger denied a visiting North Korean delegation's request to show a propaganda film in a public theater due to the fear that the film would be anti-Western.[83] A few days later, the North Koreans brought the film to the presidential palace where the president of Niger Hamani Diori and various Nigerian government officials watched the film in private.[84]

The discontinuation of North Korean film screenings also indicated tensions within diplomatic relationships. For example, the Hungarian embassy in Conakry noted in 1978 that a "cooling of relations" between the Guinean and DPRK governments was indicated by the stopping of North Korea film screenings in the country. The Hungarian ambassador to Guinea József Kertész reported that these screenings "used to be held on every possible anniversary, and at which the Guineans always attended at a high level and made extremely positive speeches that unequivocally supported the DPRK."[85] A Third World government's attitude towards North Korean film screenings often revealed their general relations with the DPRK government.

While North Korean films appeared overly propagandistic to most Third World viewers, some viewers enjoyed the perceived strangeness and anti-American sentiment of these films. In Burundi, North Korean diplomats showed anti-American propaganda films at the public functions of the ruling party's youth organ, the Jeunesse Revolutionnaire Rwagasore (JRR). The U.S. embassy in Bujumbura noted that the JRR's reaction to these films was "sympathetic with an element of faddish interest in these strange little people . . . who make bold, thrilling attacks on the United States."[86]

North Korean films became so well known in Africa that North Korean filmmakers were called in to shoot a Tanzanian documentary film, entitled *Tanzania Yasonga Mbele* (Tanzania Forges Ahead), in 1970. However, the lack of Swahili speakers in the DPRK delayed the completion of the film. Nonetheless, the British High Commission in Dar es Salaam commented, "If the film is any good, it promises to be an effective piece of propaganda because it will not only show Tanzanians parading in the North Korean way but will add to the meager total of films in the national language which at present average one a year in the cinemas here." The High Commission added that Tanzanian demand for films was huge and the North Koreans "may be astute enough to capture" this potentially large audience.[87] Sudanese president Gaafar Nimeiry paid filmmakers from the DPRK to make revolutionary films for his nation. In May 1971, a North Korean film crew went to Khartoum to make a documentary on the Sudanese revolution for the Sudanese government.[88] While most Third World governments disliked the public showing of anti-American North Korean films due to the possibility of offending local U.S. embassies, Third World viewers did not universally abhor North Korean films.

North Korean film screenings in foreign nations continued into the late 1970s. For example, in July 1979, East German security services complained that the DPRK embassy's film screenings were deliberately used to indoctrinate foreign students from the Third World, chiefly those from African countries. A file from the Stasi archive reports, "The emotional arrangement of the film was exclusively aimed at people from developing countries and resulted in active interest among the students who were present."[89] The propagandistic content of the North Korean film in East Germany focused on the greatness of DPRK's social system and its applicability to other Third World nations.

Screenings of North Korean films in Third World nations were used to popularize the revolutionary exploits of Kim Il Sung and the DPRK's unique brand of socialism. North Korean diplomats dedicated large portions of their time to disseminating the image of Kim Il Sung in their host countries. Kimilsungism had no boundaries or borders but rather sought to join the pantheon of great communist theories, such as Marxism, Leninism, and Maoism. However, North Korean diplomats' detachment from local conditions undercut the DPRK's attempts to popularize the image of Kim Il Sung abroad.

Trips to the "Socialist Paradise"

In an attempt to showcase its socialist development and postwar reconstruction, the DPRK government started to regularly offer free trips to Third World officials, politicians, businessmen, academics, and cultural figures in the late 1960s. During these official trips, visitors would tour North Korean factories, historic sites, schools, and scenic tourist spots. Pyongyang hoped that these Third World visitors would return to their homelands and tell others about the greatness of Kim Il Sung. The North Korean government used the visits of distinguished Third World guests as an opportunity to export and promote the greatness of Kimilsungism. Pyongyang hoped this would then naturally promote a pro-DPRK climate abroad. However, visitors were not always as impressed with the DPRK's socialist system as their North Korean hosts had intended.

The primary reason why the North Korean government invited foreigners to visit was for propagandistic purposes. These visits were routinely reported in the North Korean state-run media. For example, the *Pyongyang Times* had a special section entitled, "DPRK through the Eyes of Foreigners." On January 6, 1969, Gaston Soumialot, the head of a Congolese delegation, told the *Pyongyang Times* that his trip to the DPRK provided an opportunity to witness "the brilliant fruits of the idea of Juche set forth by Comrade Kim Il Sung, the respected and beloved leader of the forty million Korean people."[90] In an issue of *Korea Today*, a Colombian professor was reported as saying, "I have visited the five continents except the Antarctic zone. But, I have never seen such miracles as in the DPRK with a small area and population."[91] The image of foreigners of all different races and nations praising the DPRK's socialist construction was useful for North Korea's propaganda apparatus.

The emphasis on propaganda often made short trips in the DPRK feel like long ones for Third World visitors. A government delegation from Botswana, headed by the minister of information and broadcasting E. M. K. Kgabo, visited North Korea in the summer of 1973. According to Minister Kgabo, the delegation was "treated to 'non-stop propaganda' " during their seven-day stay in Pyongyang. He added that the Botswanan government officials quickly tired of hearing of the virtues of Kim Il Sung and rantings against 'Yankee imperialists and their running dogs.' " Kgabo also visited "a museum of some sixty rooms dedicated to North Korean history, but after twenty-or-so rooms containing much the same propaganda, the Batswana asked to proceed to the next item on their itinerary." As Kgabo described it, the delegation also visited a "not very impressive agricultural commune" and a steel mill. The delegation's journey to Pyongyang and their return home were delayed because the North Koreans refused to book them on "unfriendly" airlines through the United Kingdom. The U.S. embassy in Botswana reported, "During the extra week the delegation was away from Gaborone, the joke in the Office of the [Botswana] President was that the party had been kidnapped and Botswana would shortly be receiving a ransom note from the North Koreans."[92]

Bacary Coulibaly, a member of the Mauritanian National Assembly, said after his November 1971 trip to the DPRK that he "had been impressed by North Korea's industrial development, but disillusioned by the repetition of standard responses to his questions and by the omnipresent shadow of Kim Il Sung."[93] Coulibaly's remark regarding the overbearing presence of Kim Il Sung's personality cult was customary for many Third World visitors to the DPRK. Honduran academic Jorge Arturo Reina visited North Korea for a week in 1978. During his visit, he met Kim Il Sung, but before meeting him, he had to be examined by a North Korean doctor because, Reina was told, "Many people faint or are rendered speechless upon seeing the Great Leader." The U.S. embassy in Tegucigalpa expected Reina, a Marxist, to come back from the trip with glowing remarks about the DPRK. Instead, Reina thought the "cult of personality was extreme" and that the DPRK, due to large cultural differences, did not offer an appropriate model for Honduran development. The U.S. embassy noted that Reina was "distinctly unimpressed" by the DPRK.[94]

Sometimes, these trips to the DPRK acted as free vacations for governmental personnel from Third World nations. For example, in September 1970, a junior government official from Sierra Leone visited North Korea. This worried U.S. diplomats in Freetown, who feared the Sierra Leonean government would change its political orientation to the radical left. The Sierra Leonean Ministry of External Affairs reassured U.S. diplomats that no significance should be attached to the Sierra Leonean junior official's recent trip to North Korea as Kim Il Sung's regime was "very generous in providing free trips, especially to non-aligned diplomats." The Sierra Leonean government essentially viewed these North Korean trips as free vacations and saw "no reason why junior officials should not accept as they obviously cannot commit the government of Sierra Leone."[95]

The praises from foreign visitors were often quoted in the North Korean state-run media, but this may have been the price of admission to the DPRK. The U.S. embassy in Conakry reported on the various Guinean delegations to visit the DPRK in 1967. According to the U.S. embassy in Guinea, "Trips for business and pleasure to North Korea are arranged regularly during which the guests are generally expected to give at least lip service publicly to the North Korean position on international issues as well as to praise its domestic achievements." The embassy added, "While in the case of many Guineans, such sentiments may be genuinely felt, some have made it clear that they have made such statements only because of North Korean pressure that failure to do so would be a mark of ingratitude for the warm welcome they have received."[96]

However, the praises of foreigners should not always be seen as mere propaganda. For some coming from developing countries, North Korea's industrialization and socialist system was impressive and admirable. Alfred Vaz, the Indian consul general in Pyongyang, told U.S. officials in 1969 "that food was plentiful [in North Korea] and that his ration was 22 kilos of grain per month. People appeared well-fed and fish, rice, and other staples were available in shops."[97] Third World visitors to the DPRK reported on the wide availability of food in the DPRK in the late 1960s, which was in sharp contrast to the famine-like conditions of postwar North Korea in the mid- to late 1950s. The Sierra Leonean ambassador to the USSR Harrison E. Tucker went on a two week "private trip" to the DPRK in October 1967. After coming back from his trip, "Tucker told a [U.S.] embassy officer about [the] 'royal treatment' he and his wife received [that] naturally made a very favorable impression. They were especially impressed by the apparent abundance of foodstuffs and the 'contentment' of the North Korean population."[98]

Some Third World officials even went to North Korea in order to learn about DPRK-style development and hoped to apply these same strategies to their home countries. In fall 1968, a five-man Tanzanian delegation appointed by the minister of rural development and local government traveled to North Korea in order to observe rural development projects on a four-week trip.[99] Somalia was especially interested in North Korea's model of development and sent many government officials to the DPRK in 1971. The British embassy in Mogadishu reported, "The Somalis seem to find in [the] North Korean experience a situation similar to their own."[100] Likewise, the Soviet government noted in 1971 that the North Koreans viewed Somalia as their primary hub of influence on the African continent.[101] In April 1971, all eight Somali regional governors took a month-long study tour in North Korea, and then later in September 1971 all forty-eight Somali district development affairs officers did the same. According to the U.S. embassy in Mogadishu, "the purpose of the trips was to learn about the North Korean approach to regional and local government."[102] A group of Somali education ministry officials, led by the secretary of state for education Major Abdirazak Mohamed Abucar, also visited the DPRK in the spring of 1971 in order to learn the North Korean style of socialist-based education.[103]

The U.S. embassy in Mogadishu reported in March 1972 that "over past year and half Somalia has looked to North Korea for inspiration in revamping [its] governmental apparatus along scientific socialist lines."[104] The East Africa department of the British Foreign Office explained, "The two governments [Somalia and DPRK] have considerable similarities in their philosophies, and I doubt if the North Koreans would be interested in changing the complexion of the Somali government in the way that they might be interested in changing those in India, Pakistan, and Singapore."[105] This seemed apt as Somalia's secretary of information and national guidance, Ismail

Ali Abokor, called North Korea the "best model of socialist construction" in 1972.[106] However, the British embassy in Mogadishu concluded, "Unless it be in self-help schemes, we have come across little evidence to show that much worth to Somalia has come from these jaunts [to the DPRK]."[107] For some Somali government officials, North Korean governance appeared admirable and suitable for emulation in their developing nation.

North Korea's offer of free trips also extended to Third World–oriented organizations in the West, such as the Black Panther Party (BPP) of Oakland, California. Although the Black Panthers were from the capitalist West, they strongly identified with the Third World movement. The BPP viewed African Americans as a semi-colonized people in an imperialist country. The North Korean government supported the U.S. black freedom struggle and similarly saw Black America as an internal colony of U.S. imperialism. Kim Il Sung said in 1969, "Imperialism is attacked not only from without but also from within and is facing an acute crisis. The black people's struggle against racial discrimination and for freedom and democratic rights and an anti-war movement of the masses of the people are continuing on a wide scale in the United States."[108] A 1963 *Chollima* article proclaimed, "In the U.S., the black people's domestic struggle against barbaric assaults by U.S. imperialist authorities and racists has widened and dealt a harsh blow to the U.S. imperialist leadership."[109]

In September 1969, the BPP's minister of information Eldridge Cleaver traveled to North Korea for the International Conference on Tasks of Journalists of the Whole World in their Fight against U.S. Imperialist Aggression.[110] During his time in North Korea, Cleaver wrote a letter to the Central Committee of the Black Panther Party in which he stated, "The [North] Koreans are the most revolutionary people outside of the United States in terms of their specific opposition to the United States of America." Cleaver continued, "The [North] Koreans don't bite their tongues at all, they tell it like it is and they take a very revolutionary attitude, an anti-imperialist attitude and I can say they are serious." He noted, "North Korea is an industrialized country. It's a very beautiful country. The people have a very high socialist culture."[111] After Cleaver's return from the DPRK, the Black Panther Party's newspaper published glowing accounts of North Korean socialism and Kim Il Sung's leadership.[112]

By showing Cleaver the best aspects of their society on this free trip, the North Korean government promoted its version of socialist modernity in U.S. radical circles and presented its nation as a model of anti-capitalist development. North Korea seemed to have a degree of soft power within the U.S. Black Power movement. The Black Vanguard Party, a black revolutionary organization based in California's Bay Area, also lauded North Korea's socialist construction and routinely mentioned Juche in its newspaper. Meanwhile, on the U.S. East Coast in Cambridge, Massachusetts, white radicals and close allies to the BPP formed a socialist collective known as Juche, which published a newspaper with the same name.[113] This soft power in the U.S. enhanced Kim Il Sung's status as a supporter of all oppressed peoples, regardless of their nationality. Cleaver explained, "One thing the United States lacks is a unified national will, defined, analyzed, formulated, and articulated by a leader of genius. Such a leader is Comrade Kim Il Sung. This fact may be a threat to Americans."[114]

These free trips bolstered the image of North Korea internationally. Many Third World travelers to the DPRK shunned Kim Il Sung's omnipresent personality cult but admired the rapid postcolonial development and industrialization of North Korean society. The emphasis on national unity and communalism within North Korean society appealed to governments that sought quick solutions to their developmental issues.

Friendship Societies

In an attempt to foster local support from Third World peoples, Pyongyang formed and funded friendship societies throughout Asia, Africa, and Latin America. These friendship societies consisted of locals who disseminated North Korean propaganda and held regular meetings discussing the glorious leadership of Kim Il Sung, the wickedness of the U.S. government, and the division of the Korean peninsula. Pyongyang recruited members, especially people with high-ranking positions in local communities, for these friendship societies and used these groups to cultivate political support in Third World countries. North Korean friendship societies became one of the main tools used by Pyongyang to export Kimilsungism.

North Korea adopted the use of friendship societies from the two large Communist powers, China and the USSR, that also used similar groups of their own making to influence policies in non-Communist countries. The Soviet Union sponsored friendship societies in friendly socialist nations, in the neutral postcolonial world, and in rival Western countries.[115] China also supported friendship organizations throughout the developing world, especially in Africa.[116] In a 1949 journal article on Soviet Friendship Societies, scholar Louis Nemzer said, "They are primarily instruments for reaching an audience which is normally unreceptive to the propaganda of the Communist movement, and through which appeals may be made for support of Soviet policy in the language of peace, humanism, and cultural understanding."[117] North Korean friendship societies were used to circulate information about the Korean situation worldwide, persuade individuals to support the DPRK's political positions, and promote the image of Kim Il Sung as a global revolutionary figure.

One of the earliest and most powerful North Korea friendship societies developed in Pakistan. The Pakistan–North Korea Friendship Society, founded in 1968, promoted the image of Kim Il Sung in Pakistan and routinely hosted lectures for North Korean diplomats and dignitaries. In an attempt to gain popularity with the locals, North Korean lecturers often voiced their support for Pakistan's position on the Kashmir dispute with India. For example, on April 8, 1968, the North Korean consul general in Pakistan gave a lecture at a reception held by the Pakistan-Korean Friendship Association where "he spoke along expected lines. He fully supported Pakistan in its struggle for the liberation of Kashmir from the yoke of the Indian imperialists."[118] More than a year later, on March 3, 1970, a visiting North Korean dignitary spoke at a Pakistan–North Korea Friendship Society event, where he stated, "The Kashmir dispute should be solved in a free and just manner on the basis of self-determination."[119] In order to fit into local political climates and advance its own interests, the North Korean government used friendship societies as an informal form of diplomacy.

In the early 1970s, the Pakistan–North Korea Friendship Society was so influential that it penetrated high political offices in the Pakistani government. In 1972, the new Pakistani leader Zulfikar Ali Bhutto's pro-DPRK position worried U.S. and South Korea officials. The U.S. political counselor in Islamabad reported that Yong Hoon Lee, South Korean consul-in-charge in Pakistan, said that "certain local leaders in Bhutto's own party, the Pakistan People's Party, were members of Pakistan–North Korea Friendship Association and suspects they might seize opportunity to press for recognition [of North Korea] at this time."[120] In Islamabad, the Pakistan–North Korea Friendship Society was both influential and powerful.

Most members of North Korean friendship societies did not advance Pyongyang's positions because they believed in Kimilsungism. Rather, Pyongyang often paid locals in the Third World to become members of their friendship societies. In Sierra Leone, there was a DPRK friendship society that held a "one-day solidarity meeting" at the Freetown Town Hall, where members gave away free DPRK souvenirs and refreshments. U.S. embassy officials described the local members of this group as "paid sponsors" of the DPRK who were "otherwise unemployed youthful hangers-on of [the ruling] All People's Congress (APC) Party, like Monty Cole who tore down [the] U.S. flag at [the] embassy in [a] demonstration [in] October 1970."[121] Members of North Korean friendship societies in the Third World were usually far more interested in the free goods and paychecks from Pyongyang than in discussing the works of Kim Il Sung.

Members of the Tanzania-Korea Friendship Society likewise used Pyongyang's enthusiasm in disseminating its propaganda as a way to skim money off the North Koreans. The secretary of the Tanzania-Korea Friendship Society, Peter Msungu, received money in 1970 from the North Korean government because the group wanted to translate articles from the *Pyongyang Times* into Swahili. According to a British diplomat in Tanzania, Msungu "pretended to do the work himself but instead gave the work to a friend and took a commission." The DPRK government wanted to directly supervise the translation efforts but Msungu said that the present lucrative arrangement should continue as "friendship with North Korea has not been quite cemented yet."[122] Some ostensibly pro-DPRK individuals in the Third World used North Korean government funds to line their own pockets. The North Koreans remained profoundly ignorant of this local corruption.

From publicly referring to Kim Il Sung as the "beloved and respected leader of the 40 million Koreans" to printing North Korean propaganda in local newspapers, North Korean friendship societies in the Third World often acted as extensions of Kim Il Sung's regime and promoted Pyongyang's line on international issues in the local press. For example, in September 1970, the U.S. embassy in Kathmandu noted that the North Korean consulate and indirectly the Nepal-Korean Friendship Society "were publishing great hordes of material" in two English-language, three Nepali-language, and one Newari-language newspapers in Kathmandu.[123] In May 1972, the Nigeria–North Korea Friendship Society's publication of DPRK propaganda in the local press gained the attention of South Korean diplomats in Africa. The ROK ambassador-designate to Cameroon, as there was no ROK diplomatic accreditation to Nigeria at the time, wanted to form South Korean–Nigerian Friendship Societies similar to the North Korean–Nigerian Friendship Societies that were already active in Nigeria. The U.S. ambassador to Nigeria told Ambassador Moon that "North Koreans got less than their money's worth because of [the] sheer lack [of] interest by [the] Nigerian reading public." The U.S. ambassador added that the U.S. embassy considered "friendship societies of little use, since they [are] most frequently organized and participated in by Nigerians looking for personal gain and prestige, and [the] U.S. government does not support such organizations."[124] Despite this warning from its U.S. ally, the South Korean government would later form its own friendship societies in the Third World in an attempt to curb the DPRK's influence.

North Korean friendship societies continuously irked U.S. and South Korean officials in the Third World. A 1971 CIA report explained, "Friendship societies or cultural associations (or institutes as they are sometimes called) are a favorite North Korean device for gaining access to foreign areas, and have been established in some thirty to forty countries, many of which have no official relations with North Korea." The report continued, "They may be used as a wedge for establishment of trade, commercial, or diplomatic relations at some later date. They also serve as covers for propaganda activity and, in certain instances, for guerilla training."[125] The Tanzania–North Korea Friendship Society, which hosted its monthly meetings in the DPRK's embassy in Dar es Salaam, held a 1970 public photo exhibition entitled "U.S. Imperialism Is a Permanent Enemy of the People of Korea." This offended the U.S. ambassador to Tanzania, Claude Ross, who personally discussed the issue with Tanzanian president Julius Nyerere. Ross told Nyerere, "Since senior Tanzanian government officials were officers of [the] friendship society it created erroneous impressions that very hostile anti-American slogans, photo captions, and films at exhibit were subscribed to by Tanzania." Nyerere admitted that "this sort of thing should not happen but observed that [the] North Koreans had lots of money and did [a] great deal of 'advertising.'" Nyerere said that his government was looking into the issue and "was presently working out rules to cover this kind of situation" as he did not want foreign governments to bring their conflicts to his country.[126] Friendship societies often functioned as propaganda wings of Pyongyang that parroted the party line.

Friendship societies also arranged trips to the DPRK for influential locals and political elites as a way to foster the image of North Korea as a socialist paradise and Third World model. In 1967, the Nepalese foreign minister said that "the limited number of Nepalese visitors to North Korea were loud in their praises of that area, granted most of them went under the auspices of the Nepal–North Korea Friendship Society, while those who had visited South Korea hadn't even bothered to share their impressions with the government."[127] Some of the friendship society–sponsored tours even met the Great Leader. For example, in August 1969, the Lebanon–North Korea Friendship Society organized a two-week tour of the DPRK. Five Lebanese parliamentarians joined the tour group, which met with Kim Il Sung.[128]

In Pakistan, the North Korea Friendship Society helped to invite notable British-Pakistani journalist Tariq Ali to the DPRK in 1970. In his diary, Ali explains, "The letter came via a local Communist known as Rahim 'Koreawallah,' secretary of the Pak-Korea Friendship Society. Short, paunchy, loquacious and full of beer, he was out of breath as he handed me the letter from Pyongyang." Ali added, "I had to leave straightaway, he said. Why? Because the North Koreans were convinced that the US was preparing to invade and needed global solidarity."[129] These friendship society–sponsored trips to the DPRK burdened North Korea's increasingly stagnant economy. However, the trips provided useful propagandistic output for the regime in Pyongyang as the image of foreigners visiting its nation reinforced the image of Kim Il Sung as a world revolutionary leader.

North Korea's use of friendship societies to cultivate support in the Third World grows out of a Communist tradition of using a fifth column to evoke sympathy and spread disinformation in hostile countries. However, the DPRK's use of such groups is unique because they often focused their efforts on non-aligned Third World countries, rather than overtly hostile countries such as the U.S. or Japan. This suggests that the DPRK government saw the Third World as a new frontier in its struggle to gain recognition as the legitimate Korean government and genuinely believed Kimilsungism could function as a useful anti-colonial ideology for the decolonizing world.

During the late 1960s and early 1970s, North Korea prioritized international revolution and the global promotion of Kimilsungism over peaceful coexistence with capitalist countries, which caught the attention of Western governments. This strategy involved assisting anti-colonial rebels in the Third World and disseminating pro-DPRK propaganda around the globe. Beginning in the late 1960s, North Korea undertook a diplomatic offensive aimed at promoting Kim Il Sung's status abroad and gaining Third World allies in its fight for greater international recognition as the legitimate, sole Korean government.

North Korea's strict government-run form of public diplomacy and cultish leader worship appeared out of touch, outlandish, and at times threatening to many Third World governments and peoples. From publishing propaganda in newspapers to establishing friendship societies, North Korean diplomats were committed to disseminating Kimilsungism. Rather than focus on people-to-people exchange as a form of soft power, the North Korean government forcibly spread its unattractive propaganda. This ultimately doomed the DPRK's soft power in the Third World.[130] North Korea spent large amounts of money on cultivating a sociopolitical presence in the Third World, which failed to win the hearts and minds of most local peoples. To most people in the Third World, North Korea appeared as a strange country with a tyrannical dictator that spoke wildly about world revolution. Despite the obvious futility of their public diplomacy, the DPRK government would continue to export various forms of propaganda to the Third World from the mid-1970s to the late 1980s.

3

Kim Il Sung's "Korea First" Policy 1972–1979

IN THE MID- TO LATE 1970S, South Korea's economy surpassed the DPRK and effectively became the economic leader on the peninsula. Soon, the South Korean economy would take off and become known as an "Asian tiger" economy.[1] Meanwhile, the DPRK's industrial productivity stalled and Pyongyang became the first Communist government to default on its foreign debts in 1974.[2] In that same year, Venezuelan Communist poet Ali Lameda was released from a North Korean political prison camp after more than six years of imprisonment. Arrested for allegedly spying in the DPRK while working as a propaganda translator at the invitation of the North Korean government, Lameda suffered solitary confinement and faced starvation. After his release, Lameda wrote a report for Amnesty International about conditions in North Korean political prisons. He noted, "The food provided in the prison was fit only for animals. For months, a prisoner is deprived of adequate food. In my opinion, it is preferable to be beaten, as it is possible to grit one's teeth and withstand physical beating. To be continually starving is worse."[3] Lameda's personal account was "the first published report about the life of political prisoners" in the DPRK, and Western news outlets, such as the *New York Times*, picked up his story.[4] A Communist poet from Venezuela had shed light for the first time on the horrendous conditions of North Korean political prison camps. During the mid-1970s, the two Koreas were on two vastly different developmental paths. South Korea prioritized economic development, while state security and military power dictated North Korea's developmental agenda.

In addition to the DPRK's economic troubles and international image issues, the increasingly militant state of North Korea caused further tensions on the peninsula.

During the so-called Second Korean War of the late 1960s, border skirmishes in the DMZ and North Korean guerilla raids into South Korean territory frequently occurred.[5] In addition, after the 1968 *Pueblo* incident, heightened tensions between Pyongyang and Washington further militarized the DPRK's socioeconomic life.[6] In addition to the buildup of offensive weaponry such as tanks, the number of North Korean troops swelled from about 400,000 in 1970 to 700,000 in 1975 and to approximately 1 million by the late 1970s.[7] This domestic militarization also shaped North Korea's foreign policy in the mid-1970s as Kim Il Sung secretly sent advisors and pilots to conflict zones in the Third World. This covert deployment of North Korean military specialists served as a way for Kim Il Sung to test his armed forces' strength and aptitude on the battlefield in preparation for a possible Second Korean War. Pyongyang often gained political support or economic concessions from Third World governments with which it had military ties.

In addition to using the Third World for military aims, the government in Pyongyang continued to actively export its brand of autonomous anti-colonialism in the mid-1970s as a way to strengthen Kim Il Sung's personality cult and represent the DPRK as a symbol of national self-reliance vis-à-vis the "U.S. puppet regime" in Seoul. North Korea also joined the Non-Aligned Movement and used this international body as a way to politically undermine South Korea and gain international support for its cause of Korean reunification under the DPRK's terms. Moreover, North Korean workers and builders functioned as extensions of Kim Il Sung's regime as they built palaces, museums, and other structures for Third World governments and left a profoundly DPRK-style aesthetic in the decolonizing world. While chapter 1 focused on the DPRK's solidarity with like-minded Third World states and chapter 2 examined the global dissemination of Kimilsungism, chapter 3 investigates the movement of North Korean people and materials beyond the country's borders in order to advance Kim Il Sung's "Korea First" policy. This new direction in Kim's Third World diplomacy asserted inter-Korean competition and agitation of the ROK government as the leading policy initiative.

From the mid- to late 1970s, political mission and self-interest stood at the heart of North Korea's Third Word diplomacy. Despite offering many forms of assistance to Third World governments free of charge, Kim Il Sung often expected something in return, such as political support in international forums, trade concessions, or the ability to establish a North Korean embassy or mission in the aid-receiving country. Whether that actually happened depended on the Third World government's internal politics, but Kim Il Sung remained focused on his main goal of Korean reunification under the DPRK's terms. In a 1975 conversation with Romanian leader Nicolae Ceauşescu, Kim said, "We are making efforts for strengthening and developing the relations and strengthening the unity and solidarity with all socialist countries, as well as for earning new friends and supporters of our positions across the Third World, precisely with the purpose of bringing to fruition our wish—the unification of the homeland."[8] Kim's admission to Ceaușescu that he intended to use allies in the Third World to further his reunification goals should not be surprising. The North Korean leader said in an April 19, 1975, speech in Beijing, "The current struggle of our people for the reunification of their divided fatherland is an important link in the chain of the global anti-imperialist national liberation struggle."[9] Kim Il Sung's regime had wished to unify the peninsula under the DPRK's flag since the initial division of Korea in 1945. With the U.S. military still bogged down in Vietnam and war fatigue settling in among the U.S. population, Kim increasingly felt the time was right to achieve the "final victory" of reunification during the mid- to late 1970s. In addition, Kim's band of guerillas from the anti-Japanese struggle in the 1930s were aging, and their final wish of reunification under Communist rule was fading. The aging guerillas' wish was expressed in North Korean propaganda with the revolutionary slogan "It is necessary to unify Korea still within the lifetime of the current generation."[10]

In the mid- to late 1970s, inter-Korean competition stood at the forefront of Kim Il Sung's Third World policy. Adrian Buzo aptly explains, "The evidence for DPRK preparedness to pursue a military option for reunification during the 1970s is substantial."[11] As South Korea's economy roared and emerged as a global industrial power, North Korea retreated into paranoid militarism and assumed a victim-like siege mentality. Beginning in the mid-1970s, the North Korean leadership determined the Third World was less of a space for revolutionary collaboration and more of an opportunity for advancing its nationalist agenda. An April 1976 report from the Soviet embassy in Poland explained, "DPRK diplomatic relations rose in 1975 from 78 to 90 countries. At that time South Korea kept diplomatic relations with 94 countries." The report continued, "The DPRK chose rapprochement with the developing countries and cooperation with parties in those countries, especially those that support so-called revolutionary views of the [North] Korean leadership, also with respect to Korean reunification." The report concluded, "DPRK policy vis-à-vis the developing countries is characterized by narrow pragmatism."[12] To borrow Donald Trump's phraseology, "Korea First" became Kim Il Sung's de facto Third World policy in the mid- to late 1970s.

North Korean Builders and Workers Abroad

Since the early 1960s, North Korea sent technical experts and agricultural specialists abroad. Third World nations were often more than willing to accept cheap or free North Korean developmental assistance in building massive palaces, irrigation projects, and factories. During the 1960s and 1970s, North Korean workers and engineers were all over Africa building factories, palaces, and stadiums. Since there were so many North Koreans in Africa during the mid-1970s, the CIA even tried recruiting some of them.[13] According to a 1983 British Foreign Office report on DPRK activities in Africa, Kim Il Sung's regime had undertaken aid programs in twenty African countries, which mostly consisted of "small-scale unsophisticated industrial projects, irrigation and other agricultural projects, and some educational assistance." The report added that the DPRK "offered development assistance that was perceived as relatively cheap and effective, and as carrying no implications of implanting great-power influence."[14] North Korean assistance appealed to African nations because it ostensibly did not come with strings attached, unlike Western development aid. In reality, North Korea often expected some sort of diplomatic favor in return for its developmental assistance. For example, Pyongyang expected support in international forums on Korea-related issues and for these newly independent countries to recognize the DPRK as the sole legitimate Korean government. Ko Young-hwan, the former head of the Africa section in the DPRK's Ministry of Foreign Affairs from 1985 to 1987, who defected to South Korea in 1991, said in an interview, "Kim Il Sung took Africa seriously because he wanted to use votes in the United Nations for the withdrawal of US troops from South Korea. He believed that if he could get the socialist Eastern bloc and African countries on board, then he could make the withdrawal happen."[15]

In Somalia alone, North Koreans were involved in building a cement factory, a polytechnic institute, and an irrigation system during the late 1970s.[16] North Korean agricultural specialists assisted Tanzanian farmers in 1975 and made an irrigation survey of a large Dakawa rice farm, which produced 6,000–7,000 tons of rice annually.[17] Technicians from the DPRK also helped to build a munitions factory in Madagascar for the Malagasy military.[18] According to a 1980 speech from Rwandan president Juvénal Habyarimana, North Korea assisted his countrymen in the construction of a hospital and a technical school. North Korean technical workers also assisted the Rwandans in maize farming, urban sewage system planning, and fish farming.[19] North Korea left a deep developmental mark on the African continent.

North Korea's specialty in building palaces was particularly sought after by some African governments. For example, in the Central African Empire, North Korea agreed in 1978 to build Emperor Bokassa a presidential palace in the style of Pyongyang's Kumsusan Palace of the Sun.[20] In 1979, North Korea agreed to assist the Burundian government in constructing a new 8,000-square-meter presidential palace, and the Malagasy government in building a new presidential palace "made of marble" that would include "an underground bunker and barracks for a presidential guard of 750 to 1,000 men."[21] In addition to presidential palaces, the DPRK sent workers to Rwanda to build a youth palace.[22] The palaces of North Korea appealed to African governments that seemingly admired the extravagance of the DPRK's architectural style.

The DPRK's construction projects often resulted in severe delays or sheer disaster. The completion of the youth palace in Rwanda was delayed for over two years and was described by the U.S. embassy in Kigali as an "albatross" around North Korea's neck in high-level DPRK-Rwanda relations.[23] In Mali, a North Korean–built ceramics factory was described as "unprofitable" by the U.S. embassy.[24] The U.S. embassy's information officer in Mali recalls that the North Korean ceramics factory produced dinner plates that "your knife went through as you sawed on a piece of tough meat."[25] In Burundi, North Korean engineers built a farm implements factory during the late 1970s. The U.S. embassy noted, "The quality of the output is widely considered to be very poor. It is unlikely that the factory has achieved its planned production rates of 100,000 hoes and 150,000 machetes annually."[26] Meanwhile, in Guinea, a North Korean–built factory had an even worse fate. The Hungarian embassy in Guinea reported in May 1978, "The factory that the DPRK had built in the vicinity of Conakry for the production of porcelain household and sanitary wares ceased to operate due to technological problems and the deficiencies of the mechanical equipment."[27] This failure in Guinea even pushed the government in Conakry to reach out to the Czechoslovakian government to help repair the North Korean factory's machines and engage South Korea in economic cooperation. While North Korea was extremely enthusiastic in offering technical assistance, it frequently lacked the skills, commitment, and resources required for successfully completing these construction projects in Africa.

Due to North Korea's initiative in building factories and palaces around Africa, Park Chung Hee encouraged South Korean construction companies to look at Africa as a potential site of profit making that would also further the ROK government's anti-DPRK agenda on the continent. The best example of South Korean construction in Africa is the massive fifteen-story department store, Immeuble Renovation, in Libreville, Gabon. Built in 1977 by the South Korean company SsangYong, this was the first department store in Gabon to have escalators and likely the highest building in all of Africa at the time.[28] According to the Romanian Embassy in Libreville, Immeuble Renovation was so large that it also housed Gabon's Ministry of Trade and Industry and other governmental institutions. In addition, South Korea provided doctors free of charge to the Gabonese government in the late 1970s.[29]

North Korea tried to counter South Korea's offensive by agreeing to build, free of charge, a party cadre training school in Gabon. The DPRK government also sent, free of charge, ten specialists to Libreville in order to build a large statue of the Gabonese leader Omar Bongo. Furthermore, the North Koreans held discussions with the Gabonese government about sending Mass Games instructors and doctors to the African country.[30] Gabon, a relatively small non-aligned West African country, became an unlikely site for inter-Korean competition in the Third World. This competition began with the building of a massive department store and soon spread to other sectors. The Bongo government was more than willing to take aid from both sides. The competition was so fierce between the two Koreas in Gabon that the DPRK's chargé d'affaires in Libreville tried to get Gabonese governmental approval to set up an exhibit that displayed North Korean products in an attempt to outdo an existing Gabonese–South Korean shop.[31]

Despite the internationalism of North Korean technical assistance, the DPRK's state-run media rarely published articles in the Korean language on the exploits of North Korean development experts and specialists abroad. The North Korean government may have purposely kept its Third World development assistance secret in order to prevent domestic protest at home. Most North Korean citizens would have seemingly preferred governmental development efforts to focus on the homeland rather than nation-building projects of distant Third World countries.

While the DPRK's domestic propaganda rarely highlighted the activities of its citizens abroad, North Korea's foreign-oriented propaganda, such as the *Pyongyang Times*, frequently discussed DPRK development projects abroad. For example, on March 6, 1971, the *Pyongyang Times* proudly announced the groundbreaking for the construction of a North Korean–built porcelain factory in Matoto, Guinea. Karim Banggoura, Guinea's secretary of state for industry and mining, said the building of a porcelain factory by the North Koreans "is a great encouragement to the Guinean people who are fighting against imperialism and colonialism."[32]

In addition, the North Korean magazine *Foreign Trade* promoted North Korean construction services abroad. A June 1978 advertisement for the Korea Equipment Export Corporation noted, "The great leader Kim Il Sung taught, 'In creating our architecture, we should pay attention to develop it into modern and beautiful one [*sic*] while keeping the national peculiarity.' With the teaching of the great leader as our guiding principle, we do our best to reflect the national character of the given country and the modern sense of the buildings in which we undertake abroad."[33] After North Korea hosted a symposium of the nonaligned countries on increasing food and agricultural production in August 1981, Kim Il Sung's regime established agricultural institutes in Guinea and Tanzania and sent agricultural specialists to visit these institutes, which was detailed in the *Pyongyang Times*.[34] The North Korean state-run media delivered different messages to domestic and foreign populations. The domestic message focused on the world-renowned greatness of Kim Il Sung, while the foreign message, more capitalistic in tone, advertised North Korean construction services.

Global Juche

Prior to 1972, Juche was a developmental guideline and utopian thought for Kim Il Sung's regime. However, the North Korean government revised its constitution in 1972 and made Juche the official ideology of the DPRK. Article 4 in the 1972 constitution asserted, "The Democratic People's Republic of Korea is guided in its activity by the Juche idea of the Workers' Party of Korea, a creative application of Marxism-Leninism to the conditions of our country."[35] The constitution also stressed absolute independence and declared that it would deal only with foreign governments that adhered to principles of national sovereignty. Legal scholar Christopher Hale said, "All in all, it would be accurate to call the [1972] constitution a Juche constitution in light of its saturation with Juche ideology."[36] While Juche was part of the DPRK's ideological mission since the mid-1950s, the revision of the constitution in 1972 signaled that the philosophy became the vanguard ideology of the DPRK. The North Korean propaganda apparatus spread "the assumption that Korea is the center of the world . . . radiating outward the rays of *chuch'e* (Juche), especially to Third World nations that are thought by the North Koreans to be ready for *chuch'e*."[37]

In a 1972 interview with Japanese journalists from *Mainichi Shimbun*, Kim Il Sung elaborated on the newfound centrality of Juche in North Korea's political culture. He told the journalists, "In a nutshell, the idea of Juche means that the masters of the revolution and the work of construction are the masses of the people and that they are also the motive force of the revolution and the work of construction." He continued, "Independence is what keeps man alive. If he loses independence in society, he cannot be called a man; he differs little from an animal." Kim also explained the role of Juche in the world revolutionary movement. He said, "Today progressive people in the world want to live in accordance with the Juche idea and many countries demand independence. No one wants to be subjugated by others." He added," No nation will tolerate interference in its internal affairs and infringement upon its dignity; not only the socialist countries but also the newly independent countries oppose foreign interference and restrictions, and are taking the road to independence and self-reliance."[38] Since Kim Il Sung's personal promotion under the guise of Kimilsungism failed to gain popularity in the Third World, Pyongyang promoted Juche as a more accessible and applicable ideology for newly independent countries in the 1970s.

The most fertile space to export Juche was the Third World, which identified with the main principles of the philosophy such as autarky, self-strengthening, and self-sufficiency. One of the most attractive aspects of Juche was its emphasis on self-reliance. Yokoko Yamba, a Congolese journalist, wrote, "The Korean nation had long groaned under the yoke of Japanese colonialism. But, though in a state of underdevelopment, it rejected servitude and was united under the banner of the Juche Idea of Comrade Kim Il Sung, the great brilliant commander, who laid bare the barbarities of the Japanese imperialists."[39] Thomas Menyassan, a journalist from the African country of Dahomey (Benin) said after a 1975 trip to the DPRK, "[North] Korea, once subjected to aggression, exploitation, oppression, and maltreatment, has become a dignified, prosperous country where the banner of independence, self-sustenance, and self-defense is flying high in the rays of the Juche Idea."[40] Regina Kessy, a Tanzanian student who studied at Wonsan Agricultural University during the 1980s, said, "Juche was the way we were supposed to think. It underpinned everything. It was quite attractive for an African to learn that Man is master of everything and self-reliance is attainable."[41] Despite the fact that Kim Il Sung borrowed large amounts of money from Moscow and Beijing, the party-state portrayed itself as economically independent.[42] This idea of self-reliance was embodied in the Juche idea.

Juche also served an important purpose within the DPRK's propaganda apparatus. North Korean propaganda claimed Juche was Kim Il Sung's own creation and personal contribution to Marxist-Leninist theory. North Korean propagandists intended Juche would compete with Maoism abroad and bolster Kim Il Sung's global status vis-à-vis Mao Zedong as the leading revolutionary figure. A Bulgarian diplomat in Pyongyang noted in 1973, "Kim Il Sung himself wanted to be recognized as the leader of world revolution."[43] In fact, North Korea had deep theoretical disagreements with China, as the East German embassy in Pyongyang noted in 1977, because it claimed Juche, not Maoism, was the most advanced form of Marxism-Leninism in the world and Kim Il Sung, not Mao Zedong, was the leader of the international proletarian movement.[44] Kimilsungism was too openly sycophantic to succeed abroad, but Juche, with its messages of self-reliance and self-strengthening, appealed to many in the decolonizing world.

Third World governments started to take notice of Juche in the mid-1970s. When an Ethiopian delegation visited the DPRK in March 1976, the head diplomat, Moges Wolde-Michael, "praised the Juche idea that had enabled the DPRK to perform miracles, 'which is attributable to the genial guidance of President Kim Il Sung, the great and excellent leader, and to the diligent work of the Korean people.'" Wolde-Michael also "declared that the example of Korea was worth following and stated that 'the political independence and economic self-reliance, which is resolutely defended by the Korean people, is an excellent model for the socialist Ethiopian people.'"[45] Two months later, the Malian head of state visited North Korea and also praised the Juche idea. He "called the achievements and experiences of the DPRK a model for the developing countries."[46] In 1978, a Mozambican government delegation traveled to the DPRK to learn from the North Korean experience of building Juche-style socialism, especially its training of cadres.[47] Juche initially appealed to some Third World governments that were disillusioned with domineering world superpowers.

The DPRK's foreign minister Pak Seong-cheol told Polish foreign ministry officials in 1969, "Small countries cannot do without independent development; independence should concern all aspects of the life and activity of a state, including the strengthening of the defense capacity of the country." Pak then suggested to his Polish counterparts that a Juche-based attitude could also be beneficial for their situation. Pak said, "But what would you do if West Germans attacked Poland? Who would help you? You need to count on your own resources in this matter first and foremost." Pak continued, "When each country has the capability to rebuff an aggressor then it will be able to help one another. For example, if the Germans attack you, then we Koreans could help you, and if the Americans attack us, you could help us."[48] In his articulation of Juche, Pak paradoxically merged the principles of self-reliance with socialist internationalism. Nonetheless, Juche eventually won out. As the Soviet embassy in Poland commented in 1976, "The Korean comrades do not recognize the socialist countries' system and do not accept the principle of socialist internationalism."[49] Juche meant putting Korea first, and this nationalistic mentality influenced North Korea's Third World policy, beginning in the mid-1970s.

In addition to inviting visitors to the DPRK and educating them about the Juche idea, North Korea actively exported the concept to the Third World via conferences. International seminars on the Juche idea were routinely held in Pyongyang and in Third World cities. In 1977, an international seminar on the Juche idea brought eighty-nine delegations from seventy-three countries to Pyongyang. A Cameroonian representative said that conference "accords with the good African saying that he who is thirsty should go to the spring," and a representative of the South West Africa People's Organization (SWAPO) noted the "Namibian struggle for national and social liberation draws profound inspirations from the gallant struggle of the Korean people against both Japanese and U.S. imperialism."[50]

Sometimes, Third World peoples would try to connect Juche to their own indigenous concepts that stressed self-reliance. Juche joined a Third World modernization discourse that emphasized independence, autonomy, and anti-colonialism. For example, the U.S. Black Panther Party, which championed self-determination for African American communities, explained in its newspaper in 1970, "Broken wine bottles and hypodermic needles are very effective. Pork chop and chicken bones can even be utilized as weapons. This is 'Juche' relying on what you have, to sustain your resistance." The Panthers explained that Juche "basically means relying on yourself, and supporting and supplying yourself."[51] Black Panther Party leader Eldridge Cleaver said, "Juche is carrying out the Korean Revolution. Juche for us means . . . to carry out our revolution."[52] The Panthers Americanized Juche for their armed struggle.

Meanwhile, the African interpretation of Juche had a less militant tone. For example, during the DPRK vice president's March 1973 visit to Dar es Salaam, a Tanzanian newspaper published an editorial that noted the "close political and ideological affinities" between Tanzanians and North Koreans. The editorial continued, "Foremost among those is their common commitment to building a socialist society on the basis of self-reliance. In Tanzania, we call it the spirit of *ujamaa* and *kujitegemea*. In [North] Korea, they call it the spirit of Juche. But the objective is similar, to establish a society free of exploitation comprising materially well-off people who are proud and independent."[53] During his 1974 speech in Pyongyang, Zaire's president Mobutu Sese Seko compared North Korea's Juche ideology to the Zairian concept of "Authenticité." Mobutu explained, "Authenticité means that as Koreans are proud of being Koreans, so the Zairese [are] proud of being Zairese. We do not have an inferiority complex in the fact that we are Negroes with frizzled hair. You too do not have any inferiority complex because you are as you are now."[54] In the Caribbean region, the Guyanese chairman responsible for diplomatic talks with North Korea recalls, "Self-reliance was the golden thread that held co-operative socialism (Guyana's version of Marxism-Leninism) and Juche together."[55] Third World notions of self-reliance often combined indigenous ideas and traditions with a Marxian framework.

The North Korean government exaggerated the degree to which Juche could be realistically applied in the decolonizing world as a nation-building theory. For example, in India, it was overeager in its exportation of Juche, and some locals took advantage of this North Korean overenthusiasm. In 1979, the fifth international seminar on the Juche idea was held in New Delhi since India had supposedly "achieved many successes in the work of studying and pervading the Juche idea."[56] More than eighty countries were represented at the conference. The Indian press questioned who paid for this elaborate conference, which took place in New Delhi's most expensive hotels. In addition, they reported that representatives staged fake political squabbles and that participants pocketed funds from the conference organizers. The Bombay edition of the Indian magazine *CURRENT* stated that "money flowed like water; wine and women were available in abundance" at the Juche seminar.[57]

Despite criticism from many Indians in 1979, New Delhi hosted another international seminar on the Juche idea three years later. A group of Indian students protested the seminar and interrupted the event for fifteen minutes by yelling and throwing pamphlets. Two of the student protesters ended up going to the hospital after physical altercations with guards. Along with the usual pocketing of North Korean funds, participants apparently could not even pronounce *Juche* correctly, calling it "juicy" and "juchi." The chairman of the seminar's preparatory committee, S. S. Mahaptra, admitted to Indian reporters in a press conference that Juche "was nothing new" and the concept could be found in Greek philosophy and in the writings of Marx, Engels, Lenin, and Mao. According to Mahaptra, Gandhi himself even believed and propagated the same principles.[58] Juche conferences in India were thus a waste of North Korea's increasingly limited financial resources. False Juche believers in India had essentially swindled Kim Il Sung's regime.

North Korea continued to spend large amounts of money on spreading Juche via conferences, study groups, and literature. Domestically, North Korean propaganda portrayed Juche as a world-renowned theory and the country's leader as a global intellectual genius. This outweighed the financial costs of globalizing Juche. The Swedish embassy in Pyongyang compared Juche to an "angling worm" that was used as "bait" in developing countries. It said, "One can not form a study group to read Kim Il Sung's writings anywhere in Africa without it being extensively reported in the [North] Korean press."[59] The export of Juche served important domestic purposes because the establishment of Juche study groups abroad made North Koreans think their national leader was world-famous and respected. Adrian Buzo explains, "An unsophisticated, isolated population may well have come to believe that Kim Il Sung had become a major international statesman—as perhaps did an unsophisticated, isolated leader who allowed such practices to continue."[60]

In the 1980s, Juche continued to appeal to some Third World peoples. There was genuine intellectual curiosity regarding this anti-colonial ideology from a radical Asian nation. For example, a South African political activist, Karrim Essack, published *Juche-Korea,* a two-volume series on the North Korean revolution, in 1982 and 1983. In the introduction, Essack explains, "The thread that runs through all the chapters and links them up is the Juche idea, that the Korean people are the masters of Korea and they alone can make their own revolution basing themselves on Korean realities." Essack said that since the end of the Korean War, the DPRK "has become an ideal society for mankind to live in" and that the Third World saw the DPRK as a model "because it shows them, despite backwardness in all spheres, it is possible for the once colonized people to raise themselves up." Essack naturally attributed North Korea's postwar success to Juche.[61]

In addition to Essack's book was the small booklet comparing Juche with Irish Republicanism's idea of national dignity by Gerry MacLochlainn, a prominent Irish Republican, published in 1985. MacLochlainn stated that the Juche Idea "propounded by Korea's great leader Comrade Kim Il Sung expresses so clearly the aspirations and the needs of colonial and semi-colonial peoples struggling for freedom."[62] One of the leading Western proponents of the Juche ideology was prominent West German writer and Green Party politician Luise Rinser. After visiting the DPRK on several occasions in the early 1980s and meeting with Kim Il Sung, Rinser said that North Korea was a "model not just for the Third World" and its Juche ideology was a "third possibility" distinct from Soviet-style socialism and U.S.-style liberal capitalism. Rinser viewed the DPRK as a "farm-loving country owned by a farmer father" and Kim Il Sung as a man of the people because he "does not govern from his desk, he goes out to the people, giving and receiving advice at the grassroots."[63] Despite being a Western intellectual and politician, Rinser was deeply invested in Third World politics. She wrote a book on the Iranian Revolution in the late 1970s, visited a leper colony in Indonesia, and later wrote a book based on her conversations with the Dalai Lama in northern India.[64]

The Juche ideology, even during North Korea's economic downturn in the 1980s, continued to make positive impressions on Third World–oriented intellectuals and politicians such as Rinser. According to scholar Joanne Miyang Cho, the characteristics of the Juche ideology that most appealed to Rinser were its radical departure from traditional Marxism and its emphasis on political and economic independence.[65] Rinser and the rest of these foreign Juche evangelists neglected to realize that the ideology offered little concrete instruction for economic development. As historian Jon Halliday describes in a 1981 article on Third World development, "Volumes on Juche and the texts of Kim are not priority items in planning ministries or bibliographies on world development."[66]

While national self-reliance was a rallying cry for many governments in the decolonizing world, some found the expression troubling. For example, a Kenyan government official said at a Pan-African conference in the 1970s, "I accept the slogan of self-reliance. The man in the bush has always been self-reliant and that is the reason why he is still in the bush."[67] Despite these outliers, national self-reliance was a common goal for many Third World political movements. Juche was a theoretical concept that put an intellectual gloss over Kim Il Sung's political aspirations. For many in the Third World, national self-reliance advanced postcolonial development and opened a path to a revolutionary future devoid of Western exploitation.

Fighting Imperialism in Egypt and Assisting Zaire

Along with the militarization of North Korean society, Kim Il Sung prepared his military specialists for the "final victory" by deploying them covertly to the Third World, primarily the Middle East and Africa. These secretive deployments functioned as a way for Kim Il Sung to gain hard currency and give his military specialists battleground experience. While anti-colonial solidarity was in the backdrop of these Third World military partnerships, Korea-First nationalism and potential Korean reunification stood at the forefront.

In a 1971 interview with an Iraqi journalist, Kim Il Sung said, "The Arab people are vigorously fighting in arms against U.S. imperialism and the Israeli aggressors. It is quite natural that the gallant Arab people resist the armed aggressors with arms."[68] Kim's dislike of Israel stemmed from the fact that he saw Israel as a puppet of the United States government. Similar to the way he saw South Korea as a U.S. puppet state, Kim saw Israel as a tool of Washington in a divided region. Kim's rhetorical support for Arab states transferred into direct action two years later, when a North Korean military aircraft squadron assisted Egyptian forces during the Yom Kippur War with Israel.[69] Kim saw supporting Egypt, the leader of the Arab world, as one of the most important anti-imperialist struggles in the Third World. Kim told a Sudanese journalist in 1974, "As in the past, the Korean people will continue to resolutely support the valiant struggle of all Arab peoples against Zionist and imperialist aggression and always remain a close comrade-in-arms of Arab peoples in fighting the common enemy."[70] In a May 1978 conversation with Romanian leader Nicolae Ceauşescu, Kim said, "The Democratic People's Republic of Korea supports the realization of Arab unity. In reality, the main country that is in conflict with Israel is Egypt."[71]

According to the deputy director of the Soviet state-media news agency TASS Leo Yedrashnikov, a suspected intelligence officer for Moscow, the North Koreans sent ninety-two pilots to Egypt in 1973. Yedrashnikov "believed [the] DPRK was involving itself more deeply in [the Egyptian] crisis because 'they are probably preparing their own surprise attack against South Korea.'"[72] Similar to the use of Korean People's Army pilots in the Vietnam War, Kim's deployment of North Korean pilots to Egypt suggests that wars in the Third World served as useful testing grounds for potential air battles on the Korean peninsula. According to a British Foreign Office report on DPRK arms deals with developing countries, North Korean pilots "conducted many operational flights" from early 1973 to 1975 in Egypt. The DPRK government also sent military supplies, such as artillery, rocket launchers, and spares for ground-force equipment, to Egypt from the early to the mid-1970s.[73]

In addition to Egypt, the North Korean government also established close military ties with Syria during the Cold War era. Beginning in the late 1960s, Kim Il Sung's regime sold "rifles, artillery, mortars, machine guns, ammunition, bombs, armored vehicles, anti-tank weapons, and multiple rocket launchers" to Hafez al-Assad's dictatorship.[74] The North Koreans also sent around two hundred tank drivers to Syria in the mid-1970s, and technicians from the DPRK updated several hundred Soviet T-54/55 tanks in the 1980s, which were still in use by Bashar al-Assad's regime during the recent Syrian civil war.[75] The DPRK state-run media regularly congratulated the Assad regime on state occasions, such as the thirty-eighth anniversary of Syrian independence in April 1984. The *Rodong Sinmun* said, "Since independence the Syrian people have endlessly struggled to defend the national dignity and sovereignty of the nation." The editorial continued, "Under the leadership of the Arab Socialist Ba'ath Party led by President Hafez al-Assad, today the Syrian people are firmly defending their national sovereignty and territorial integrity, bravely countering the intensified aggressive and interventionist moves of the U.S. imperialists and Israeli Zionists."[76]

After the 1979 overthrow of the pro-U.S. leader Mohamed Reza Shah Pahlavi, Iran and North Korea bonded over mutual feelings of anti-Americanism, anti-Zionism, and revolutionary fervor. The two governments had close military ties as Pyongyang supplied nearly 40 percent of Iran's military needs during its war with neighboring Iraq in the 1980s.[77] Pyongyang also assisted Tehran in the production of chemical weapons, such as mustard gas.[78] According to the Polish ambassador in the DPRK,

Iran gave North Korea oil in exchange for arms and military equipment deliveries. Chinese "silkworm" missiles were sent to Iran via North Korea. The Iranians also assisted the North Korean government in exploring domestic uranium deposits.[79] Tehran and Pyongyang formed a close military-based partnership.

Due to the secrecy of its military deals, North Korea never publicly discussed its Third World military assistance in its state-run media. The *Rodong Sinmun* frequently published articles in the mid-1970s condemning U.S. support of Israel and Zionist aggression. On October 23, 1976, the *Rodong Sinmun* published an article that stated, "It is an invariable design of the U.S. imperialists to stamp out the just cause of the Arab people, bring the Middle East under their control, and freely rob this region of its rich natural resources." The article continued, "In order to put their monstrous design into effect, the U.S. imperialists are manipulating the Israeli Zionists as a 'shock brigade' of aggression and fostering their 'strength' in all haste, while cunningly trying to set the Arab countries against each other by sowing the seed of discord and enmity among them."[80] A month later, an article entitled "The Israeli Invaders Are the Worst Enemy of the Arab People" asserted, "Today, the Israeli invaders, under the active support and encouragement of the U.S. imperialists, illegally occupy Arab land and for the sake of endlessly expanding into new territories are recklessly using military provocation and aggression against opposing Arab nations and Palestinian people."[81]

Despite *Rodong Sinmun*'s condemnation of Israeli aggression in the Middle East, Kim Il Sung secretly supported peace talks between Israel and Egypt in 1978. Kim told an Egyptian government delegation in September 1978 that he supported "any peace initiative launched by Egypt, including the tripartite high-level meeting in Camp David," which he regarded "as 'a new step' in the direction of finding a peaceful resolution for the [Middle East] conflict." However, Kim said that he could not "publicly express this for the moment, given the complex situation in the Middle East, as well as the fact that the Korean government wishes to be in good relations with the other Arab countries, including those that are against the direct dialogue between Egypt and Israel."[82] Kim's yearning for Middle East peace talks suggests that North Korea's state-run media's harsh rhetoric did not always accurately reflect the pragmatic stance of its leadership. Moreover, once wars in the Third World fulfilled Kim's self-interests, he was more open to peace talks between the major warring parties. Kim strategically used wars in the Third World as periodic tests for his armed forces and as a way to gain hard currency for his regime. As demonstrated by his secretive approval of the Camp David accords, Kim Il Sung's anti-imperialist rhetoric regarding Israel extended only so far. Kim's Middle East policy revolved around his policy of Korea First.

During the mid-1970s, national liberation wars and independence struggles raged in Africa. One of the most important anti-colonial wars took place in Angola, which became a microcosm of the Cold War with various world superpowers supporting warring parties and using them as proxies to advance their strategic interests in Africa. Despite global involvement in the Angolan civil war, Kim Il Sung wanted the DPRK to be on the periphery of the conflict. He even criticized Cuba for its direct military support of the Popular Movement for the Liberation of Angola (MPLA) in the Angolan conflict. Kim told Ceauşescu, "If the Cubans really wanted to contribute to the fight against imperialism, then they should have supported Egypt and the other Arab countries in their fights against Israel." Kim also said that the Cubans were fighting in Angola at the behest of the Soviet Union. Kim explained, "The Cubans were actually waging war in Africa for someone else and with the support of someone else. The participation of the (colored) Cuban military in the battles in Africa was not helping the nations on this continent at all." Stressing an autonomous worldview, Kim told Ceauşescu that the Africans should be left to solve their own problems and that the DPRK "received lots of support requests from African countries involved in conflicts, but it did not reply to any of them."[83]

Despite Kim's denial that his country ever became involved in African conflicts, North Korea indirectly participated in the Angolan civil war. In late November 1975, the British *Daily Telegraph* initially reported that hundreds of DPRK troops were fighting with the Zairian-assisted National Liberation Front (FNLA) of Angola against the MPLA and that the North Koreans replaced Chinese military instructors in northern Angola who were training FNLA troops. However, the South Korean embassy in neighboring Zaire clarified, "British reporting was not true as far as we have found. There is some information regarding Chinese instructors going back to China but North Korean instructors taking over their role is not fact." The South Korean report continued, "It seems that as for now, four hundred and fifty North Korean instructors are training one Zairian infantry division and that same division is organizing to go to Angola." The South Korean embassy in Zaire accurately concluded that the North Koreans found it "hard to deal with Angolan affairs" because they could not openly defy the Soviet Union and Cuba on the battlefield, but they also needed Zaire's support in international forums. Thus, the North Koreans covertly supported Zairian-financed armed forces in a complicated Third World proxy war that indirectly pitted Cuba against North Korea.[84]

The deployment of North Korean military advisors to Zaire was most likely linked to Kim Il Sung's initially close relationship with Zairian leader Mobutu Sese Seko, who closely backed the FNLA. Mobutu visited the DPRK in December 1974 and said to North Koreans during a speech at a Pyongyang mass rally that Kim Il Sung "has revived your country from scratch and brought it up to [the] level of great powers."[85] After visiting North Korea, Mobutu was reported to have adopted a more anti-American mentality. He also obtained the assistance of North Korean military instructors in training an elite brigade of Zairian tribesmen.[86] In 1975, *Daily Telegraph* journalist Bruce Loudon, who was based in Lusaka, Zambia, wrote, "President Mobutu, it seems, sees in the spartan and doctrinaire North Koreans a more than adequate replacement for the departing Chinese. He has long been fascinated by Kim Il Sung's regime, and has indicated to friends that he admires its discipline and purpose."[87]

DPRK-Zairian relations started to sour in October 1975 as Mobutu sought payment for his nation's cobalt exports to North Korea.[88] "Since then," a January 1976 Swedish foreign ministry telegram explains, "the relationship between the two countries deteriorated rapidly due to developments in Angola, where the North Koreans announced their support for the MPLA."[89] North Korea subsequently recalled its military instructors from Zaire and sent patrol boats and handguns to the MPLA via Congo-Brazzaville.

As Zaire was the first sub-Saharan African nation to establish an embassy in North Korea, Zairian diplomats in Pyongyang were disgusted at the change in Kim Il Sung's policies towards Kinshasa. They said that the Organization of African Unity (OAU) would support Zaire and that North Korea would regret its involvement in African affairs, as it would cost the DPRK many African votes at the next United Nations consideration of the "Korean question." The North Korean authorities also withdrew a number of local staff from the Zairian embassy in Pyongyang.[90] Zairian diplomats told Erik Cornell, a Swedish diplomat based in Pyongyang from 1975 to 1977, that North Korean military instructors based in Zaire suddenly changed sides during the Angolan civil war and began fighting with the MPLA against the FNLA.[91] A November 11, 1976, article in the *Rodong Sinmun* declared, "After independence, the Angolan people under the proper command of President Agostinho Neto has advanced quickly, with its banner heightened and oriented towards socialism. . . . Today, there are huge transformations in the land of the new Angola."[92]

Mobutu's demand for North Korean payment for Zairian cobalt shifted Kim Il Sung's support to the MPLA. Despite calling MPLA leader Agostinho Neto "not so smart" in his 1978 conversation with Ceauşescu, Kim's Korea First policy led him to view the MPLA as the more stable, less imposing, and ultimately victorious side in the Angolan conflict.[93] Kim Il Sung had few long-lasting alliances in sub-Saharan Africa. Beginning in the mid-1970s, pragmatism and a need for African allies on Korea-related issues at international forums overrode any sense of Third World solidarity or anti-colonial comradeship. With South Korea's economic resurgence in the mid-1970s, anxiety regarding the DPRK's economic downfall made Kim Il Sung retreat into Korea First nationalism.

Entrance into the Non-Aligned Movement

In 1955, leaders from Afro-Asian countries sent representatives and officials to Bandung, Indonesia, for a meeting in which to discuss the mission of the decolonizing world. These new independent governments met in order to devise an anti-colonial agenda that sought a greater voice in global affairs and announce that an alternative international system was possible outside of Soviet-style socialism and American-style liberal capitalism.[94] Due to postwar reconstruction efforts in the DPRK, Kim Il Sung's regime did not participate in the 1955 Bandung Conference. However, this meeting established the framework for the Non-Aligned Movement (NAM), which later appealed to Kim Il Sung, who saw the organization as a powerful, independent, and revolutionary force in the Cold War world that could further his global standing and promote pro-DPRK positions vis-à-vis South Korea. Adrian Buzo aptly explains, "Kim thought he detected a valuable forum [referring to the NAM] in which to promote an anti-imperialist and anti-revisionist agenda, to promote the DPRK's approach to economic development as a model for less developed NAM member states, and of course, to promote his own image as a significant international Communist leader."[95]

Beginning as early as 1960, North Korea expressed interest in the NAM and honored the five-year anniversary of the Bandung Conference. According to the Soviet ambassador to the DPRK A. M. Puzanov's diary entry on April 16, 1960, "The Korean friends are widely noting this anniversary in the press, and the historic significance of the [Bandung] conference is being stressed demonstrating the spirit of solidarity and cooperation of the peoples of Asia and Africa for peace and independence."[96] It was not until the mid-1970s that North Korea applied for membership into the NAM and pushed for the inclusion of the Korean question (that is, the division of Korea and the diplomatic competition between the ROK and DPRK for sole legitimacy as the rightful Korean government) into the organization's main talking points. Kim Il Sung used the NAM to push his Korea First agenda, which called for the withdrawal of U.S. forces from South Korean soil.

The 1973 summit of the NAM took place in Algiers, Algeria. As the North Koreans were not yet members of the NAM, they could not directly participate in the meeting. Nevertheless, Pyongyang sent "delegations and leading personalities primarily to those countries which exert great influence on the non-aligned countries." As a Hungarian diplomat in the DPRK observed, the North Koreans held discussions with Cambodia's Prince Sihanouk, sent a delegation to Indonesia, and received delegations from Algeria and Yugoslavia. This lobbying produced positive results as Sihanouk and Yugoslav president Josip Broz Tito, the de facto leader of the NAM, "changed the atmosphere of the conference" and passed a resolution that "referred to the withdrawal of foreign troops" from South Korea. The DPRK government was "very satisfied" with this outcome and depicted the Algiers resolution in North Korean provincial committees and meetings "as a victory of [North] Korea's independent foreign policy that enjoys support of the whole world."[97]

As Leninist outlaws who diverged from the socialist paths of Moscow or Beijing, Tito and Kim Il Sung had much in common ideologically. In a May 1974 correspondence with Tito, Kim wrote, "In particular, the peoples of the Third World, who in the past were subjected to exploitation and oppression from the imperialists, have strongly taken their fates in their own hands and are acting as the masters in a historic arena. We think that today that the countries of the Third World are the main strength of the world revolution." Kim added, "You, Comrade Josip Broz Tito, as one of the generally recognized eminent leaders of the Third World, have truly done much in the name of the unity and independence of the peoples of the Third World. We hope that in the future you will make a great contribution to this noble cause." By praising Tito in such a lavish manner, Kim hoped to curry favor with the Yugoslav leader in an attempt to join the NAM as a full-fledged member. Kim explained, "Although Yugoslavia is a socialist country, but at the same time as a country belonging to the Third World, it plays a great role in the ranks of the nonaligned countries, and we think we could join the ranks of the nonaligned countries and pursue our activity among them."[98] On one hand, the North Korean leader self-interestedly viewed the NAM as a useful forum to push his Korea First agenda and gain international support for the removal of U.S. forces from South Korean soil. On the other hand, the NAM's ideological platform and revolutionary spirit most likely appealed to Kim's internationalist sensibilities as well.

The U.S. government was becoming increasingly worried about the potential membership of the DPRK in the NAM. During a March 28, 1975, discussion on U.S.-Korea relations with South Korea's foreign minister and its ambassador to the U.S., Secretary of State Henry Kissinger said, "We have to do something about the nonaligned. If Cuba and North Korea are both in the nonaligned group, we will have to make clear to that group that we do not regard them as nonaligned." South Korea's foreign minister Kim Dong-Jo responded, "It would be disastrous to our UN policy if the [Non-Aligned Movement's] Lima conference says that North Korea is nonaligned."[99] A few months later, Kissinger reiterated his concern to the Sri Lankan ambassador to the U.S., saying, "We hope that the Non-Aligned will not adopt a pro-North Korean resolution which amounts to taking sides. We would prefer that the issue not be raised at the UN."[100]

At the 1975 conference in Lima, Peru, NAM members agreed to let the DPRK join the international body.[101] The *Rodong Sinmun* proclaimed this as a victory and stated, "Our country's entry into the nonalignment conference this time through the unanimous vote was the result of our government's efforts to adhere to anti-imperialist independent policies."[102] Kissinger could not believe North Korea was allowed into the NAM while South Korea was not. He told Afghanistan's deputy foreign minister Waheed Abdullah on September 6, 1975, "I don't understand why North Korea was admitted as nonaligned and not South Korea. I could understand not admitting either one, but not the acceptance of one without the other." Afghanistan and Ghana were the only two NAM members to oppose the DPRK's membership into the NAM. Abdullah told Kissinger, "What is the meaning of alignment and nonalignment if North Korea is considered nonaligned?"[103]

Pyongyang's decision to join the NAM also angered the Soviet Union and its allies. The deputy head of the First Far Eastern Department of the Soviet Foreign Ministry, Mikhail Basmanov, told his East German counterparts on May 10, 1976, "The DPRK is still unwilling to coordinate its foreign policy actions with the socialist countries. It is acting separately and does not take into consideration positions of the Soviet Union and the socialist community of states. Sometimes Korean positions are even directed against the latter. The DPRK also joined the Non-Aligned Movement without any previous consultation with the socialist countries."[104] Basmanov interpreted North Korea's foreign policy as being purely motivated by self-interest. He said, "The DPRK conducts its foreign policy activities based on purely pragmatic considerations. The decisive question is always the following: What will benefit our interests, and what will not. The DPRK develops its relationships with individual states according to this thinking."[105] North Korea's independent-minded foreign policy frustrated the Soviet Union. The Soviet leadership wanted the DPRK to behave more like a proper client state, such as East Germany (GDR), and willingly submit to the central Communist authority in Moscow. The DPRK was no Asian GDR, but rather behaved in an independent-minded way that adhered to a policy of anti–Great Powerism.

North Korea's official entry into the NAM began at the 1976 conference, which was held in Colombo, Sri Lanka, from August 16 to 19. During the conference, on August 18, 1976, North Korean border guards in Panmunjom unleashed a brutal attack on U.S. soldiers and South Korean woodcutters over a mere poplar tree in Korea's demilitarized zone. North Korean soldiers murdered two of the U.S. troops with axes, and numerous others sustained injuries.[106] Some Western observers claimed this attack, known as the Axe Murder Incident, was an attempt by Pyongyang to portray the U.S. military as hostile imperialist forces on the Korean peninsula during the 1976 NAM Conference. An anonymous op-ed writer in the *Chicago Tribune* said, "The happening may be connected with the conference of nonaligned nations underway at Colombo, Sri Lanka. North Korea's Foreign Minister Ho Dam told this conference that 'war may break out at any minute' on his tense border." The op-ed added, "North Korea's Premier Pak Sung Chul further told the conference that the U.S. has 400,000 troops in South Korea, a ten-fold overstatement, and demanded that they be withdrawn. The U.S. 'attack' at Panmunjom can be depicted to the Third World as justification of his demand."[107] The North Korean leadership may have wanted to use this crisis to push pro-DPRK positions to the forefront of the NAM agenda.

Despite the fact that the North Korean economy was declining in the late 1970s, Kim Il Sung's regime used some of his country's limited financial resources for the 1976 NAM conference. According to the East Germany embassy in Pyongyang, "Of the $10 million needed to fund this conference in Colombo, the DPRK alone contributed $500,000."[108] Despite this generous donation, the DPRK's past troubles with the Sri Lankan government and aggressiveness in pushing the Korean question negatively affected the image of the North Korea delegation at the conference. No pro-DPRK resolutions were passed at the conference. Tito, leader of the conference, "was reported to have been irked at Pyongyang's overemphasis on political and military issues at the expense of global economic and energy problems."[109] The DPRK's narrow focus on advancing its own Korea First agenda irritated other members of the NAM.

North Korea wanted to use the NAM as a diplomatic medium to advance Kim Il Sung's goal of having U.S. armed forces removed from South Korea. The North Korean leadership soon realized the NAM was much more divided than unified. In April 1977, North Korean premier Pak Song Chol welcomed a Yugoslav delegation to Pyongyang. During a discussion with the delegation, Pak said, "The main problem within the Non-Aligned Movement is maintaining unity amongst its member states."[110] In September 1977, Tito visited North Korea and met with Kim Il Sung. During their conversation, Tito explained that "reactionary forces" in the Third World were in the midst of trying to overthrow progressive governments. Tito acknowledged that some NAM member states, such as Morocco, Egypt, and Zaire, supported these "reactionary forces," which threatened the supposed unity of the NAM. Kim Il Sung agreed with Tito and proposed "direct and permanent contact with all the states in order to explain the current global situation and to mobilize all the Non-Aligned countries so as to defend and strengthen the solidity of the movement."[111] The North Koreans quickly realized that the NAM did not function effectively as an international body as it was simply too ideologically diverse. Nonetheless, the DPRK continued to participate in NAM as it was "highly anti-imperialist in character."[112]

In March 1979, the disunity of the NAM was again invoked when the DPRK's foreign minister Ho Dam visited Belgrade. Yugoslav officials told him, "The Non-Aligned Movement should be independent of [a] 'bloc' and should not become [a] 'bloc' itself." Yugoslav officials said that there were a few countries, "such as Cuba," that wanted the NAM to function as a bloc. Ho agreed with Yugoslavia on this issue and stated that "the Non-Aligned diplomacy is the primary policy of the North Korea's diplomacy and North Korea would like to contribute as most as possible to the development of the Non-Aligned Movement." North Korea's participation in the NAM primarily focused on gaining international support for Korean reunification. Naturally, Ho Dam "asked for Yugoslavia's support for North Korea's 'initiative' in inter-Korean reunification."[113] As long as Tito remained leader of the NAM, Kim

Il Sung went along with Belgrade's NAM policies as a way to curry favor with the Yugoslavia government and gain its vital support for DPRK-led reunification of the Korean peninsula.

Despite the obvious discord among many NAM member states, North Korean propaganda represented the movement as a unified and cooperative force in international affairs. For example, an April 30, 1977, article in the *Pyongyang Times* announced, "In the countries of new emerging forces, there is a growing tendency toward unity and cooperation today," and "the peoples of new emerging forces making up the absolute majority of the world's population were all subjected to imperialist oppression and exploitation in the past and are now struggling for national independence and the building of a new society."[114] An earlier *Pyongyang Times* piece praised NAM member states' nationalization of foreign companies. The article said, "A vigorous struggle for wiping out the aggressive and predatory footholds of imperialism and building a national economy is being unfolded in the countries of new-emerging forces which are advancing under the banner of anti-imperialism and independence."[115] By depicting the NAM as a "new emerging force" in world affairs that stressed militant solidarity and cooperativeness, Pyongyang glossed over the ideological differences and division within the movement.

North Korea's use of NAM as a way to promote its goal of removing U.S. armed forces from the Korean peninsula and to cozy up to Yugoslavia, sometimes at the expense of Cuba, demonstrates the brutal Korea-First pragmatism of Kim Il Sung's foreign policy in the mid- to late 1970s. Kim Il Sung rarely hesitated to side with larger NAM powers, such as Yugoslavia or China, on international issues that advanced the DPRK's reunification initiative. In the summer of 1979, Kim attempted to expel Hanoi from the NAM as a way to gain favor with China, which had recently fought a border war with Vietnam, and advocated changing the site of the 1980 NAM conference from Havana to Pyongyang. The Vietnamese ambassador to Canada angrily told his Hungarian counterparts that the DPRK "does its best to isolate Vietnam" and that North Korea "cannot be regarded as a socialist country."[116] Kim's uncanny ability to destroy long-standing Third World friendships reflected his brutal pragmatism in trying to reach his goal of removing U.S. troops from the ROK. The fact that "U.S. imperialist bastards" remained on Korean soil deeply angered Kim Il Sung as it was a direct affront to the DPRK's national identity.

During the mid-1970s, an emerging force was gaining power within the DPRK's opaque central government. As Kim Il Sung grew older, questions started to be asked by Eastern European diplomats in Pyongyang as to who would succeed North Korea's founder as leader. Initially, Korean Workers' Party propaganda vaguely mentioned a "party center," and rumors circulated among Pyongyang's Eastern

European diplomats that this referred to Kim Il Sung's eldest son, Kim Jong Il. In April 1975, the East German ambassador to the DPRK observed at a Pyongyang exhibit that

> for the first time, the chronology of Kim Il Sung's family strongly highlights his first wife and his oldest son. Some large paintings show Kim Il Sung with his son. Other widely enlarged photos show his son instructing propagandists and film producers. He already displays the pose usually reserved for Kim Il Sung in his talks with DPRK citizens. This visual observation confirms in fact our assumption we have made earlier: Kim Il Sung's eldest son is systematically groomed to become his successor.[117]

In 1980, it became clear that Kim Jong Il was going to be Kim Il Sung's successor. Based on a September 8, 1980, conversation with the DPRK foreign ministry's Hungarian referent Bang Jong-gap, the Hungarian embassy in Pyongyang reported, "Regarding Kim Il Sung's son, Kim Jong Il, he said that he is the real leader of executive party politics. In other words, guidance is from 'The Great Leader' and Kim Jong Il is the executive leader."[118] Hereditary succession, heresy within Communist orthodoxy, seemed to be the path ahead for the DPRK leadership. The editor in chief of *Rodong Sinmun* told the editor of the Soviet state newspaper *Pravda* in October 1980 that "the classical figures of Marxism made a mistake when they did not address the issue of a proper succession of their cause" but that Kim Il Sung "learned from the mistakes of others" and appointed his son as his successor.[119] By 1980, Kim Il Sung's regime had essentially become the Kim family regime ruled by both father, "the Great Leader," and son, "the Dear Leader." This father-son leadership duo, known hereafter as the Kim family regime, would rule the DPRK until Kim Il Sung's death in 1994, when Kim Jong Il assumed full control of the North Korean government.

Unlike his father, who grew up fighting Japanese colonialists in the rugged Manchurian landscape of the 1930s, Kim Jong Il was born in the Soviet Union and grew up in an isolated and luxurious palace. Despite his lack of guerilla fighting experience, Kim Jong Il was surrounded by Kim Il Sung's closest allies from their Manchurian partisan days. As an East German diplomatic report accurately stated, "The core of the present and past leadership of the Korean Workers' Party was formed mainly from among active fighters against the Japanese fascists, organizers of and participants in the anti-Japanese resistance."[120] Thus, Kim Jong Il had to gain the trust of these aging guerillas in order to secure his place as his father's successor. As a creative individual, Kim Jong Il curried the favor of these former guerilla fighters by creating revolutionary operas based on their 1930s anti-Japanese struggle in Manchuria. Kim Jong Il's work as a nostalgia-focused propagandist earned him a foothold in the Central Committee of the Korean Workers' Party.[121]

Despite his lack of a military background, Kim Jong Il took the DPRK's foreign policy in a more militant and aggressive direction. In addition, Kim Jong Il unofficially disagreed with Kim Il Sung's policy of anti-colonial assistance, often free of charge, to Third World rebels and revolutionary governments. Under Kim Jong Il, Third World peoples would need to pay the North Koreans for their assistance. The need for hard currency to preserve the loyalty of high-level party officials and the stagnant North Korean economy made Kim Jong Il increasingly focus on illicit activities in the Third World, such as smuggling and arms proliferation. While Kim Il Sung had seen the Third World as a new revolutionary force in world politics and as a valuable ally on the Korea question, Kim Jong Il saw this global space as one where illicit activities, corruption, and violent aggression could occur more easily.

4

Kim Jong Il's World and Revolutionary Violence 1980–1983

BY THE EARLY 1980S, South Korea had surpassed the North in most indicators of state power. From its population size to its economic resurgence to its military power, the ROK easily eclipsed the DPRK.[1] During a 1980 interview with American congressman Stephen Solarz, Kim Il Sung even admitted, "We are in a state of inferiority to South Korea in all areas."[2] As a divided nation dependent on legitimacy, the DPRK leadership for the first time since its inception felt massively inferior vis-à-vis its southern brethren. However, South Korea was dealing with its own internal issues. In May 1980, the South Korean military's brutal suppression of protesters in Gwangju drew the world's attention to the poor human rights situation in the Republic of Korea.[3] With the political chaos in the South and Pyongyang's increasing desperation, the Korean peninsula was in political turmoil during the early 1980s.

Kim Jong Il saw the unrest in South Korea during the early 1980s as an opportunity to undermine Seoul's legitimacy and boost his father's legacy as the preeminent Korean statesman. Kim Il Sung had told his Communist allies in 1975 that "if a revolution flared up in South Korea, the DPRK could not remain indifferent; it would give active assistance to the South Korean people."[4] Not wanting to provoke another conventional war on the peninsula that it was bound to lose, the North Korean government carried out a brazen guerilla-style attack on the South Korean leadership in Burma in 1983. Although this bombing, which took place in Burma's capital city of Rangoon, failed to complete its objective of killing the ROK president Chun Doo Hwan, this audacious attack indicated a shift in the North Korean leadership's foreign policy. Rather than restricting the military facet of inter-Korean competition to the geographical confines of the peninsula, the DPRK leadership exported its conflict with the ROK to the Third World.

Both Kim Il Sung and Kim Jong Il shared an affinity for national autonomy and anti-colonialism. Nonetheless, the two leaders had different interpretations of diplomacy. Kim Il Sung's foreign policy was primarily based on his ego and advancing his global prestige. He also had sympathy for national liberation movements and thus promoted radical anti-colonialism. Kim Jong Il's version of diplomacy prioritized revolutionary violence as the key to undermining the ROK's legitimacy and paving the way to his succession as the next leader of the DPRK. Thus, he put North Korea's foreign policy on a more terroristic path.

Although Kim Jong Il himself was never a guerilla fighter, the North Korean Politburo primarily consisted of former anti-Japanese guerilla fighters that fought alongside Kim Il Sung in 1930s Manchuria. Besides Kim Jong Il and Oh Kuk-yol, whose father had also fought in the 1930s anti-Japanese struggle, the seventeen other members of the Politburo in 1980 had fought alongside Kim Il Sung in Manchuria as part of his guerilla band.[5] While Kim Jong Il was not a fighter himself, he was a masterful propagandist who used revolutionary operas that traced the lineage of the North Korean revolution to the 1930s anti-Japanese struggle. Kim Jong Il's artistic flare for guerilla nostalgia gained the respect of his father's former fighting comrades.[6] In order to consolidate his position as his father's eventual successor, Kim Jong Il also had to prove his military skills to the guerilla band that was now the aging DPRK leadership. He saw the Third World as fertile territory to capitalize on South Korea's security lapses and help achieve his father's long-sought goal of removing U.S. troops from Korean soil. Most importantly, diplomatic and military victories in the Third World would solidify his internal position as the next leader of the DPRK.

As a lover of the arts, Kim Jong Il viewed mass culture as an important diplomatic medium in fostering his father's global status and the idea of the DPRK as a Third World developmental model. Kim Jong Il said in a 1965 speech to Korean Workers' Party (KWP) leadership, "The leader's greatness is in reality the greatness of our nation. Upholding the leader, national hero and peerlessly great man, as the leader of our nation is the great honor and pride of the entire Korean nation."[7] In that same year, Kim Jong Il also said in a speech to DPRK foreign ministry officials that North Korea's experience in building socialism "can help the peoples of newly emergent countries a great deal in their struggle to consolidate their national independence and build new societies."[8] Kim Jong Il saw the Great Leader, the party, and the Korean nation as inseparable entities. To promote his father's greatness in the Third World was akin to promoting the DPRK nation-state itself.

The hereditary succession of Kim Jong Il was officially announced to the socialist and decolonizing worlds at the Sixth Congress of the KWP in 1980, which was held in Pyongyang October 10–14, 1983. This nepotistic transfer of power angered many Communists and leftist-leaning fellow travelers who attended the Sixth Party Congress. The delegates of the Socialist People's Party of Denmark, the Social Democratic Labor Party of Norway, the People's National Congress of Guyana, and the Socialist Party of Lebanon criticized the "dynasty-founding efforts seen in the KWP," while the representative of the National Liberation Party of Costa Rica "condemned the non-existent democratism in the KWP, and the fathomless cult of personality as its result." In addition, leftist Australian journalist Wilfred Burchett, a long-standing admirer of Kim Il Sung's regime, said after the Sixth Party Congress that the DPRK was "moving further away from Marxist-Leninist ideologies."[9] The Mongolian People's Revolutionary Party's delegation "concluded that the cult of personality around Kim Il Sung and his son is intensifying, and this [is] detrimental to the DPRK. The Korean nationalist line is growing stronger. They are attempting to replace Marxism-Leninism by the 'Juche' ideology. The latter one is a revisionist tendency."[10] The event of the Sixth Party Congress made it clear that the KWP's continuing ideological ties to Marxist orthodoxy would be extremely loose and shallow.

Before 1980, Juche was officially depicted in the DPRK as a creative interpretation of Marxism-Leninism according to national conditions. At the Sixth Party Congress, North Korea's homegrown ideology of Juche replaced all references to European-imported Marxism-Leninism. Juche was then understood as a concept that stressed radical chauvinism and extreme nativism. Thus, the Sixth Party Congress was also important because it marked a significant shift in the ideological structure of the KWP. During the Sixth Party Congress, Kim Il Sung described the DPRK and the Juche ideology as a model for developing countries. He said at the congress, "In the public eye of the world, our nation is widely regarded as the country of Juche, and the model country for socialism." The Hungarian delegates at the congress noted, "Emphasizing the uniqueness of the Korean road, the independent model for building socialism was presented to set an example mainly for the developing countries."[11]

After this congress, Juche formally supplanted Marxism-Leninism as the ruling philosophy of the DPRK and was an openly Korean nationalistic concept. Hungarian delegates at the Sixth Party Congress later stated, "This [Juche] idea is mainly the product of the particular Korean circumstances, but its Korean advocates mention ambitious plans: they formulate their messages in this spirit to the so-called Third World, and to the countries of the Non-Aligned Movement above all, and on the long term, they are aspiring to lead the movement itself."[12] Hereditary succession and a more radical interpretation of Juche worked hand in hand. This shift from a Marxist-framed understanding of Juche to a more ethnocentric Juche was intended to legitimate the hereditary succession of Kim Jong Il and promote the continuation of the Kim family's revolutionary "Paektu" bloodline.[13] This ideological heterodoxy had ramifications for North Korea's foreign policy as Kim Jong Il's regime increasingly saw ultranationalism and revolutionary violence as the answer to issues of national sovereignty and domestic legitimacy.

The 1983 Rangoon bombing, which was reported to be Kim Jong Il's idea, proved useful for solidifying Kim Jong Il's succession but was a public relations disaster in the Third World. Prior to 1983, many Third World governments respected the ardent anti-imperialist stance of the North Korean government and desired peaceful reunification on the Korean peninsula.[14] The Rangoon bombing quickly changed public opinion of the DPRK in the Third World, and the increasingly terroristic nature of the Kim family regime could no longer be ignored or tolerated by nonaligned nations. This chapter begins with a discussion of the export of North Korea's Mass Games to the Third World, which was personally promoted by Kim Jong Il. The Mass Games embodied the importance of mass culture in Kim Jong Il's DPRK. Next, this chapter shifts to the Rangoon bombing as Kim Jong Il's first politically motivated use of violence. This chapter then examines North Korea's support of anti-imperialist forces in the Middle East and the use of the Palestinian conflict to mobilize citizens at home. This chapter concludes with an investigation of North Korea's efforts to gain allies in the faraway Caribbean and South Pacific regions and the degree to which inter-Korean competition motivated foreign-policy-making decisions in Pyongyang.

Mass Games in the Third World

As a former anti-Japanese guerilla fighter, Kim Il Sung's expertise was primarily in the realm of military affairs. The artistic authority within the Kim family regime was his son and successor Kim Jong Il, who took a special interest in further developing his father's Mass Games and exporting them abroad. North Korean Mass Games featured a backdrop of thousands of schoolchildren holding placards with revolutionary slogans and skilled gymnasts in the foreground performing choreographed dances and acrobatic moves.[15] This highly choreographed gymnastics and calisthenics event was used by the regime as a tool to mobilize youth and bolster national unity.[16] For example, in 1987, Kim Jong Il told a group of North Korean Mass Games experts, "To be a fully developed communist man, one must acquire a revolutionary ideology, the knowledge of many fields, rich cultural attainments and a healthy and strong physique. . . . Mass gymnastics play an important role in training schoolchildren to acquire these communist qualities."[17]

Kim Jong Il emphasized that the Mass Games equipped participants with the Korean Workers' Party's concept of Juche. As the DPRK's Vice Chairman of the Mass Gymnastics Production Company Kim Jong Ho explained, the Mass Games "represents the ideological theme of the country and nation splendidly through the combination of gymnastics formations, backdrops involving tens of thousands of

FIGURE 4. Artist name: Song Siyŏp. "Let the youth of the Third World unite firmly under the banner of anti-imperialism and independence!" Source: Leiden University Libraries, digital collection.

people, and music" and, that unlike sports where athletes compete for a prize, the Mass Games "brings pleasure and satisfaction to the performers as well as to the audience, and instills in their hearts hope for the future."[18] Juche's focus on the "masses" as a revolutionary force in world politics naturally meshed with the tenets of the Mass Games: collectivism, organization, and mobilization. In his 1987 speech, Kim Jong Il said, "Through mass gymnastic performances, the Party members and other working people are firmly equipped with our Party's Juche idea, and the validity and great vitality of our Party's lines and policies, the embodiment of the idea, are demonstrated far and wide at home and abroad." Kim Jong Il later added in the speech, "Only when you deal with the Juche idea and the Party's lines and policies properly in your works can you produce genuine mass gymnastics that can actively contribute to the revolution and construction."[19] The Mass Games in North Korea were a vehicle for disseminating the Juche idea and thus further consolidating the Kim family regime's absolute autocracy.

Thus, the Mass Games presents a unique window into North Korea's soft power. Kim Jong Il explained, "Mass gymnastics make an active contribution to the development of friendly relations with other countries. Many mass gymnastic performances are now shown to foreign visitors to our country, and our experts are sent abroad to produce and disseminate mass gymnastics." He continued, "In the course of this, trust between our country and other countries are deepened, and exchanges steadily strengthen ties of friendship, as they support and encourage each other."[20] In other words, the Mass Games were an important tool of Pyongyang's foreign policy and diplomatic efforts with Third World countries during the Cold War era. They expressed North Korean anti-colonial solidarity and articulated Pyongyang's core values in an artistic format. With their emphasis on discipline, national unity, and communalism, the Mass Games were a creative expression of North Korea's value system.

Many nascent leaders in the Third World, particularly in sub-Saharan Africa, also understood the power of the Mass Games in mobilizing youth populations and fostering patriotism during the era of decolonization. Thus, they sought North Korean assistance in forming their own local versions. According to a 2002 North Korean book, the DPRK government sent Mass Games instructors to forty-eight countries, most of which were located in the Third World, on ninety-four different occasions.[21] Beginning in the mid-1970s, North Korea exported this particular type of collectivist culture to sub-Saharan Africa as a way to spread the virtues of the Kim family regime and promote the ideals of the proper socialist citizen, such as selflessness, physical fitness, and solidarity. The Mass Games were an artistic manifestation of North Korea's authoritarian "single-minded unity" (*ilsim-dangyeol*) concept.[22]

The first foreign leader to recognize the value of North Korea's version of the Mass Games was Somali president Siad Barre, who visited the DPRK in 1971. Diplomatic ties between Somalia and North Korea had begun four years earlier when a North Korean delegation visited Somalia in early 1967 and established diplomatic relations with Aden Abdulle Osman Daar's government. At a dinner party honoring the North Korean delegation, the president of the Somali National Assembly Sheikh Mukhtar Mohamed Hussein said, "The dimensions of the historical tragedy, engineered by imperialists in our countries and our peoples have suffered from its bitterness and ferocity, is manifested in dividing great Korea into two parts and peaceful Somalia into five parts."[23] Two years later, Somali military general Siad Barre ousted the democratic government in a bloodless coup. Barre visited the DPRK for the first time in 1971 and met Kim Il Sung.[24] Shortly after returning from the DPRK and with the help of the Somali Supreme Revolutionary Council's commanding officer Abdirizak Mohamud Abubakar, the two established a pervasive personality cult based on the Kim Il Sung model. Similar to the North Korean leader, Barre assumed titles that stressed his greatness and absolute authority, such as the "father of wisdom," "father of the nation," and "teacher of the revolution."[25] In 1972, a joint communiqué was signed between North Korea and Somalia in which "both sides expressed their firm convictions that the only way to liberate Southern Africa and other colonially held territories is by waging an armed struggle."[26]

In addition to adopting Kim Il Sung-style titles and a DPRK-inspired personality cult, President Barre also borrowed North Korea's mass gymnastics event. According to Somalia scholar I. M. Lewis, "Wherever he went, the President was greeted by mass applause and adulation, feted and saluted by his loyal subjects who literally danced before him—to [North] Korean choreography." Lewis recalled that the "intriguingly oriental flavor" of this extravagant state pageantry conflicted with the traditional egalitarian ways of pastoral Somali society.[27] Islamic influences in Somalia, given Islam's belief in the Prophet Muhammad as the supreme deity, clashed with the Asian Communist aesthetics of the Mass Games that promoted the national leader as godlike and almost divine in his revolutionary genius. Pastoral traditions, Islam, and North Korean influences made for strange bedfellows in Barre's Somalia.

For a welcoming ceremony for Ugandan dictator Idi Amin on October 22, 1972, the Somali government performed a North Korean–style Mass Games event. With placards displaying revolutionary slogans such as "Long Live Comrade Siad" and "Let Us Develop Industry" and images of flourishing Somali irrigation systems, Barre's regime indigenized Kim Il Sung's Mass Games. Based on archival video footage, Amin seemed impressed by the choreographed event. The sheer visual similarity between North Korean and Somali Mass Games footage most likely indicates that North Korean specialists directly helped Barre's regime organize the event.[28] Somalia was the starting point for the diffusion of North Korean–style Mass Games around the Third World.

In 1973, Amin began seeking North Korean assistance in forming his own version of the Mass Games. According to a May 1973 report from the U.S. embassy in Rwanda, Amin reportedly "talked highly of the high standard of gymnastics in North Korea."[29] In late November 1973, a North Korean–directed Mass Games instruction course began in the Ugandan region of Eastern Buganda. The district commissioner Solomon Jubilee "said that the importance of gymnastics exercises cannot be overemphasized" and that "the idea behind such courses is to produce strong, efficient, healthy, and courageous men and women who can sustain every situation such as the economic war."[30]

Beginning in late 1972, Amin's "economic war" expelled South Asians from Uganda and confiscated businesses and property owned by South Asian and European residents. This economic policy attempted to redistribute Uganda's wealth to the indigenous population but instead created hardships and mass poverty.[31] The "Ugandization" of Uganda's national economy naturally found parallels with North Korea's Juche ideology, which stressed self-reliance and self-sufficiency. The editor of the state-run newspaper *Voice of Uganda* noted the similarities between the two approaches in an op-ed and said that "the great Juche idea is a phrase for economic war."[32] During a May 1974 visit to Uganda, the DPRK's foreign minister Ho Dam stated that North Korea "highly appreciated the progressive reforms introduced by the Second Republic of Uganda to eliminate the aftermaths of the imperialist and colonialist rule, build the national economy and culture, and Ugandanize the economy."[33] In addition to finding common ground on the merits of the Mass Games, the Ugandan and North Korean leaderships also advocated for similar economic policies despite their disastrous outcomes.

Some Ugandan officials did not view the Mass Games as a worthwhile or productive use of time. Idi Amin held a briefing for district representatives in 1973 in order "to dismiss unfounded and shallow allegations spread by some misguided elements that gymnastics was a communist oriented game." During the meeting, Amin thanked Kim Il Sung for sending the instructors free of charge but assured the district representatives that the games were not designed to promote communism. Amin said that "by doing gymnastics you keep your body physically fit." A *Voice of Uganda* article on the "advantages of gymnastics" stated "that gymnastics is a new feature in Uganda's history and some people deserve pardon when they sincerely ask themselves: 'What is gymnastics and what is the purpose of gymnastics training?'" The article concluded that the "Mass Games is one of the most powerful weapons in mobilizing and disciplining the people. It is a fine sport in educating the masses morally and physically."[34] Despite the obvious Communist North Korean connection to the Mass Games, the Ugandan government assured locals that the game merely promoted physical fitness and patriotism.

In October 1973, schoolchildren in Entebbe performed the first-ever Ugandan Mass Games on Ugandan Independence Day. According to the headmaster of the school, "Our children liked [the] gymnastics game and wanted to learn more." The headmaster added, "Almost every headmaster wanted his children to participate in the gymnastics game. Some even complained why their children were not invited for training. I have found from the schoolchildren that if one is involved in gymnastics, he always wants to learn more and more without rest."[35] North Korean–style Mass Games seemed to have a degree of genuine popularity among Ugandan teachers and students.

A few months later, in January 1974, the second North Korean–style Mass Games performance took place in Uganda, to commemorate the second anniversary of the founding of Amin's Second Republic. According to the Ugandan state-run media, Amin watched the performance and "was highly impressed by their [the North Korean instructors] high standard of cooperation, discipline, and love for the people of Uganda." Amin added that the "North Korea instructors had made many friends in Uganda and earned a good name for their country." Amin planned to invite the North Korean instructors back to Uganda for the following year's celebrations. The head of the North Korean mission in Uganda, Han Ryong Bin, told Amin "that the success of the training of Ugandans in the art of gymnastics was due to the great interest the General [Idi Amin] had taken in their work."[36] While the North Koreans struggled to export raw materials and finished products to the Third World, they succeeded in developing specific authoritarian niches, such as the Mass Games, which they exported around the world. The North Korean leadership exported these forms of soft power as a way to improve their image abroad as a modern socialist state and establish closer ties with Third World governments.

The North Korean–style Mass Games clearly made an impression on the Ugandan leadership as Amin continued to praise the work of the North Korean instructors in Uganda's state-run media. In May 1974, a North Korean delegation visited Uganda and met with Amin. During their meeting, Amin complimented the North Korean instructors who had recently left because they "helped a lot in the mass mobilization program of Uganda." Amin stated that he wanted to have the instructors back again soon.[37] Later, in October 1974, Amin again praised the work of the North Korean instructors and told the DPRK's ambassador to Uganda that "North Korea is one of the best friends of Africa because the country has experienced defeating imperialists, colonialists, and neo-colonialists."[38]

Amin spread word in Africa that North Korean–taught Mass Games were an effective political tool. In 1974, Amin "said the [North] Koreans had been such good instructors that very many leaders in East and Central Africa have been making inquiries about how they had managed to train Ugandans in such a short time."[39] This newfound interest in North Korean–orchestrated mass celebrations surely encouraged the regime in Pyongyang, which sought an increased presence in Africa. Due to the initial success in training Ugandans, the DPRK's reputation for organizing mass celebrations spread throughout sub-Saharan Africa.

North Korea sent Mass Games instructors to Burundi in early October 1974 and trained students in preparation for President Michel Micombero's Revolution Day celebrations, held in late November 1974.[40] According to the U.S. embassy in Bujumbura, the intense daily training sessions disrupted the school schedule of these students, but the hard work paid off as the students held "an impressive display for dignitaries with exercises and tableaux depicting [the] achievements of [the] Micombero era and Burundi's devotion to African causes."[41] The organization, discipline, and flashiness of North Korean–style mass celebrations appealed to African leaders and officials who admired the collectivist aesthetics and mindset of the DPRK. Four years later, the DPRK government once again sent Mass Games instructors to Burundi. According to the *Rodong Sinmun*, the president of Burundi Jean-Baptiste Bagaza met the North Korean Mass Games instructors in early October 1978 and said, "The mass gymnastic event taught by our Korean comrades is of high educational value and deeply inspires the people of Burundi in the struggle of constructing a new society free from exploitation and domination." He thanked Kim Il Sung "from the bottom of his heart" for sending a Mass Gymnastics delegation to Burundi.[42]

Although the North Korean instructors tried to modify the Mass Games to fit local traditions and customs, African Mass Games remained heavily influenced by DPRK-style aesthetics and political culture. In the summer of 1975, North Korean instructors trained Rwandan students for their National Day celebrations, which "replaced Rwandan folklore presentations with North Korean–directed mass movement tableaux and flash card spectacles featuring political themes." According to the U.S. embassy in Kigali, "Although [the] participants were Rwandan and some effort [was] made to incorporate Rwandan scenes, [the] style and content were neo-Pyongyang."[43]

North Korea later sent Mass Games instructors to Guinea and Togo in 1976 and Madagascar in 1977. In Guinea, the North Koreas organized "impressive" mass drills, music, and card displays for the sixth anniversary of the 1970 Portuguese-backed attack on Conakry.[44] In Togo, the North Koreans trained thousands of schoolchildren and a military unit in the art of the Mass Games for the tenth anniversary of Togolese leader Gnassingbé Eyadéma's rule.[45] In 1977, the North Korean instructors assisted the Malagasy government in constructing a card show for their National Day celebrations. According to the U.S. embassy in Madagascar, "The card show really turned the crowd on. North Koreans, who had been drilling all the participants for months, were very much in evidence and visibly proud of their pupils." The North Korean–inspired card show featured images of Malagasy leader Didier Ratsiraka as well as more overtly political content, such as a picture of Malagasy farmers and soldiers choking a Western capitalist. The card show also included anti-imperialist rhetoric, such as signs stating, "Death to Capitalists, Imperialists, and Racists" and "Down with Capitalism."[46] Ratsiraka met the North Korean instructors on June 28, 1977, and "spoke of the successes made by the [North] Korean mass gymnastics display experts sent by the great leader, Comrade Kim Il Sung and expressed satisfaction with the ever more excellent development of friendly and cooperative relations between [North] Korea and Madagascar."[47] North Korea used its Mass Games instructors as a cheap but effective means of spreading its anti-Western and anti-imperialist ideas in Africa.

North Korea continued to deploy Mass Games instructors as a means of spreading its influence throughout sub-Saharan Africa in the late 1970s. In 1978, the North Koreans once again assisted the Burundian government in the art of mass celebrations and organized a performance for the seventeenth anniversary of the ruling Uprona Party, which was "flawlessly executed" and included a "battalion-sized army unit which simulated tank, recoilless rifle, and bayonet fighting to the accompaniment of explosive charges set off at one end of the field."[48]

In 1978 and 1979, the North Koreans once again assisted Rwanda's ruling party, the National Republican Movement for Democracy and Development (MRND), in their National Day celebrations. According to the U.S. embassy in Kigali, the North Koreans transformed primary schoolchildren from a "rag-tag" group to a "regimented" unit that yelled cheers on cue, and the secondary schoolchildren no longer showcased their livestock at the celebrations but rather flipped and held North Korean–painted portraits of the Rwandan leader and signs with revolutionary slogans. In addition to giving the Rwandan government mobile loudspeakers for the celebrations, the North Koreans also taught the Rwandan army band, which was infamous for performing off-key renditions of Christmas music, their brand of revolutionary music.[49] In 1979, the U.S. embassy in Kigali concluded, "While we ourselves would have preferred more local folklore and less [North] Korean influence, it is clear that Rwandans take great pleasure and pride in impressive coordinated Korean-taught activities of hundreds, sometimes thousands, at a time."[50]

Journalist Philip Gourevitch, who visited Rwanda after the genocide in the mid-1990s, interviewed individuals who had a less positive recollection of the Mass Games. According to Gourevitch, "Of course, everyone turned out, as the ubiquitous MRND-party enforcers required, to chant and dance in adulation of the President at mass pageants of political 'animation,' but such mandatory civic cheer could not mask the growing political discontent in much of Rwandan society."[51] North Korean–imported Mass Games may have mobilized the youth in Rwanda but their mandatory nature and over-the-top political antics often disillusioned local peoples.

In 1979, the North Korean government expanded their Mass Games instruction beyond Africa as they sent instructors to the South American–Caribbean nation of

Guyana.[52] Janis Prince, a former student participant in the Guyanese Mass Games during the 1980s, recalls the training as primarily consisting of "baking in the sun for hours on end, with very little to do" and remembers her North Korean instructors as "stoic and highly disciplined." Prince said she never personally got to know her North Korean instructors and saw them as "robotic" rather than harsh or kind.[53]

Predictably, the official Guyanese government opinion on the Mass Games was more positive. In 1980, Guyana's state-run newspaper said that the North Korean–imported Mass Games "are here to stay" and the first official event held in Georgetown's National Park was apparently "a resounding success." After the event, the leader of the North Korean Mass Games instructor squad, Kim Il Nam, told the local press that "Guyanese children are really quick to grasp" the complex choreography of the event. After the first year, the Guyanese people increasingly took control of the content of their Mass Games. For example, in 1981, Guyana's Mass Games featured indigenous folk songs and historical spiritual hymns from African slaves. The presentation told the story of Guyana's national development, and one viewer recalled, "It was easy to feel proud."[54] In fact, a 2017 letter to the editor in the *Guyana Chronicle* fondly remembers the Mass Games of the writer's youth: "All the schoolchildren would get ready for Mass Games and enjoy being proud Guyanese, but still complain about the hot sun. Yet they loved being outside in the fresh air, avoiding class and enjoyed the positive energy of people smiling all the time."[55] North Korea's Mass Games tended to gain traction in the Third World when locals infused their own indigenous traditions and local customs into the imported event.

North Korea's reputation in the Third World for organizing mass celebrations reached its peak in the 1980s when Pyongyang exported the Mass Games to several other African countries. During his October 1980 visit to the DPRK, Zimbabwean leader Robert Mugabe brought along his minister of education and minister of youth and sport in order "to see the excellent work which the North Koreans had done in organizing youth and education and to consider what lessons Zimbabwe could draw from this." Mugabe said that he had been "most impressed with the discipline and efficiency of the various gymnastic and other demonstrations laid on for his benefit by youth groups."[56] According to one of his former supporters, Mugabe "came back almost a different man" after visiting North Korea in 1980. Mugabe "was tremendously impressed by the stadiums full of people doing mass calisthenics. He came back wanting to become president, like Kim."[57]

In the mid-1980s, the North Korean government sent Mass Games experts to Zimbabwe's capital city of Harare, which delighted Mugabe. In January 1987, Mugabe met the DPRK's ambassador to Zimbabwe, Hi Chun-Ok, and "expressed thanks to the Korean mass gymnastic display experts for their active help to Zimbabwe in gymnastic display."[58] The socialist aesthetics and collectivism fostered by North Korea's

Mass Games appealed to Mugabe. The event's illiberal emphasis on regimentation and social control allured Mugabe, who sought the same degree of dictatorial control and power that Kim Il Sung wielded inside the DPRK. Demonstrating the continuing importance of this event in Harare, the Mass Games recently became a part of Zimbabwe's primary school curriculum.[59]

In May 1984, Pyongyang sent seven Mass Games instructors, four men and three women, to Burkina Faso and trained students for the first anniversary of the Burkinabe Revolution. According to a government-run Burkinabe newspaper, the North Korean–inspired collective movements were "the most beautiful spectacle of the celebration."[60] Pyongyang also sent seven Mass Games instructors to Ghana in December 1984 and trained nearly 5,500 Ghanaian students for a Ghanaian Revolution ceremony. A Ghanaian newspaper labeled the Mass Games "spectacular gymnastics."[61] North Korean Mass Games instructors also trained Zambian youth in 1984 for the country's independence celebrations and met with Zambia's president Kenneth Kaunda.[62]

In addition, the North Koreans dispatched instructors to Angola in 1989 for its first national cultural festival, which featured a large Mass Games event of eight thousand people, and to Namibia in 1990 for its independence day.[63] In 1996, North Korean instructors helped the Nigerian government coordinate Mass Games performances for its independence day celebrations. In honor of Nigeria's gold medal in soccer at the 1996 Olympics, one of the scenes featured a soccer player kicking a ball into the goal. This scene excited spectators so much that some even ran onto the field and danced with the gymnasts during the performance. Wahab Rawal, a spectator at the event, said, "Our football team was very successful at the Olympic Games in Atlanta, creating a global sensation, but today's performance has given our people as much delight as our football team did." Rawal enthusiastically added, "I would like to extend my utmost thanks to Comrade Kim Jong Il, who has sent excellent mass gymnastics specialists to bring about a second ecstasy in Nigeria."[64]

The Mass Games were one of the few areas in which Pyongyang eclipsed Seoul in international status. The DPRK's style of Mass Games, with its emphasis on grandiosity, communalism, and precision, acquired such an international reputation that North Korean instructors even taught their Chinese neighbors how to perform mass gymnastic pieces. Chen Weiya, a Chinese director famous internationally for his choreography of large events such as the opening ceremonies of the 2008 Summer Olympics in Beijing, said of a May 2001 North Korean–instructed performance in Beijing, "This is a piece of very high quality which cannot be produced by either the United States or Australia. Such a great piece can be created only by the [North] Korean specialists."[65]

The Kim family regime's niche as an effective organizer of mass celebrations popularized the DPRK's image in the Third World. Due to its small size and relatively weak economy, North Korea could never coerce a foreign country into accepting its political positions or viewing Kim Il Sung as an international statesman of great significance. Thus, Pyongyang deployed Mass Games instructors, mostly free of charge, as a form of soft power with which to attract Third World governments to its version of socialist construction. The Mass Games were more popular than other forms of North Korean soft power in the Third World as they were not overt propaganda. Many peoples in the Third World seemingly appreciated the physical benefits, flashy aesthetics, militaristic style, and collectivist approach of the Mass Games. The Mass Games were political education hidden under a veneer of creativity and revolutionary spirit.

The Rangoon Bombing

On October 9, 1983, South Korean president Chun Doo Hwan planned to visit the Aung San Martyrs' Mausoleum in Rangoon, Burma, and lay a wreath. Moments before the presidential delegation's car reached the front of the mausoleum, the roof exploded. The blast ended up killing four Burmese and seventeen South Koreans, which were security forces, presidential advisors, cabinet members, and journalists accompanying Chun's delegation during his tour of Southeast Asia. After the smoke cleared, suspicions naturally turned towards North Korea as the culprit of this attack that aimed to kill the South Korean president. The CIA explained that the Rangoon bombing had much in common with previous North Korean agents' incursions into South Korea. An October 19, 1983, CIA Directorate of Intelligence note stated, "The radio-detonated explosives used in Rangoon are similar to those used in a North Korean attempt to assassinate Park Chung Hee in Seoul in 1970," and "nearly all North Korean agent operations into South Korea in recent years have been conducted by three-man teams."[66] The Rangoon bombing was an important step in Kim Jong Il's succession process as it bolstered his credentials as a military leader.

Two North Korean agents in Burma—a Korean People's Army major and captain—were later arrested in connection with the blast. A third North Korean agent died when gunfire was exchanged during the attempted capture.[67] The Rangoon bombing illustrates the terroristic foreign policy undertaken by the North Korean leadership in the 1980s. The use of a friendly nonaligned country as a space to execute an attack against the South Korean president demonstrated a shift in North Korea's Third World policy. Rather than focus on assisting anti-colonial fighters in their own anti-imperialist struggles and disseminating its propaganda, North Korea itself engaged in guerilla-style attacks on South Korean targets in the Third World. This brazen use of political violence was very much in line with Kim Jong Il's more aggressive and provocative foreign policy.

The attack was reportedly planned a month in advance with the help of the North Korean embassy in Burma. The three North Korean agents arrived in Burma on September 22 via a North Korean trading vessel. According to one of the captured North Korean agents, General Kang Chung Su, who trained commandos in the DPRK, planned the attack.[68] However, South Korean officials tied Kim Jong Il to the attack. The *Washington Post* reported, "'General Kang could not have done it alone,' one high South Korean official said this week. 'We believe it was Kim Jong Il. He probably thought that if the assassination were successful and killed the president Chun, South Korea would be in chaos.'"[69] According to actress Ch'oe Un-hui and director Shin Sang-ok, the famous South Korean couple that was kidnapped by North Korean agents in 1978 and later escaped the DPRK in 1986, Kim Jong Il told them about the Rangoon bombing in Pyongyang and was the main architect of the incident.[70] Chinese leader Deng Xiaoping refused to meet with Kim Jong Il as he believed the junior Kim was personally responsible for the Rangoon bombing.[71] Hwang Jang Yop, a top-level North Korean official who later defected to South Korea, said, "Kim Jong Il boasted that the Aung San terrorist incident was a success for his secret agents, but once the terrorists were caught and North Korea's involvement revealed, world opinion turned against North Korea."[72] Although no smoking gun document directly links Kim Jong Il to the Rangoon bombing, the available evidence suggests that junior Kim personally orchestrated the Rangoon bombing.

The attempt by North Korean agents to assassinate the South Korean president in Burma surprised many around the world as North Korea previously had close ties with the nonaligned Burmese government. Kim Il Sung visited Burma in April 1965 and numerous high level Burmese officials, including the president in 1977, visited the DPRK in the late 1970s. North Korean workers also assisted the Burmese in the construction of a factory in the early 1980s. After tying the DPRK to the October 9, 1983, blast, Burma quickly severed ties with Pyongyang. The Burmese government ordered North Korean diplomats to leave the country and even withdrew recognition of the DPRK. Burma sentenced to death the two North Korean agents arrested in Burma.[73] One of these agents, Kang Min-cheol, told Burmese officials about the planning and coordination of the bombing. In return, the Burmese government spared his life and put him in Rangoon's Insein Prison. As detailed in a book written by the former deputy director of South Korea's National Intelligence Service, Kang was subsequently forgotten by Pyongyang and ignored by Seoul. He never received a single visitor from the Korean peninsula and died of liver cancer in 2008 while still in Insein Prison.[74]

Despite overwhelming evidence that the North Korean government directly planned the attack in Rangoon, Pyongyang denied any links to the bombing. The [North] Korean Central News Agency said the South Korean government carried out the incident as a way to "incite north-south confrontation and further increase tensions." The KCNA's official statement said, "What on earth have we to do with the explosions which took place in far-off Burma?"[75] The DPRK's foreign ministry also released a statement in the state-run media that alleged Chun Doo Hwan's regime planned the mausoleum bombing as a pretense for inciting anti-DPRK sentiment in South Korea and around the world. The statement explained, "We had already made it clear that we had nothing to do with the incident. We, by nature, have never resorted to individual terrorism and assassination and such a thing is alien to us." The statement added, "This is an act fanning the new war provocation moves of the South Korean puppets, a dangerous act seriously endangering peace in Asia and the world."[76] The *Rodong Sinmun* released a series of articles denying the DPRK's involvement in the Rangoon bombing and proclaimed, "The truth of the conspiracy that surrounds the Rangoon explosion will surely be revealed."[77] Another *Rodong Sinmun* headline reads, "Denouncing the International Conspiracy of the South Korean Puppet Regime to Shift Responsibility for the Rangoon Explosion."[78] The *Pyongyang Times* claimed that Chun Doo Hwan was "hell-bent on kicking up a frantic anti-communist, anti-DPRK racket almost everyday."[79] Denial, a fixture of North Korea's guerilla-style tactics, played an important role in distancing Pyongyang from its agents' terrorist attacks abroad and gave the regime a veneer of acceptability in the Third World.

In addition to vehemently denying any links to the Rangoon bombing, the North Korean state-run media cited sympathetic foreign media outlets, organizations, or figures that denied the DPRK's involvement in the attack in order to further corroborate its position. For example, the *Rodong Sinmun* cited Soviet newspapers, such as *Pravda* and *Izvestia*, and a pro-DPRK newspaper in Japan, *Choson Sinbo*, which repeated Pyongyang's line on the North Korean government's noninvolvement in the Rangoon bombing.[80] The *Pyongyang Times* cited Nuran Nabie, the general of the Bangladesh–(North) Korea Friendship Association, who compared South Korea's use of the Rangoon bombing to Adolf Hitler's "false flag" Reichstag fire, which helped the Nazis gain power in 1933 Germany. In that same article, the pro-Pyongyang Benin Committee for Friendship and Solidarity with the DPRK stated the incident "was a drama staged by the traitor Chun Doo Hwan, a faithful stooge of the U.S. and Japan."[81]

In late November 1983, a pro-DPRK "Support for Korean Reunification" event in Japan similarly denied any connection between Pyongyang and the Rangoon bombing and claimed Chun's regime was behind the attack. At the event, Seya Hideyuki, a Socialist Party member in Japan's House of Councilors, said,

> It is beyond common knowledge that South Korean 'ministers' had been waiting inside the mausoleum building before Chun Doo Hwan arrived there. Suppose they had come earlier, ignoring the practice of accompanying Chun Doo Hwan, then why were

> they already within the mausoleum building, not waiting at its entrance? It is a thing unthinkable that members of a delegation enter the mausoleum ahead of its head.[82]

The North Korean state-run media also lambasted the Japanese government for offering aid, such as rice and money, to the Burmese government after the bombing. The *Pyongyang Times* said the aid was a reward for the Burmese government blaming the attack on the DPRK and that this aid was a "sinister plot" by the "Japanese reactionaries" to "bind [Burma] hand and foot so as to prevent her from escaping from their snare."[83] While the North Korean state-run media offered an alternative "fake news" version of events surrounding the Rangoon bombing, most American and South Korean newspapers almost unanimously linked Pyongyang to the attack.[84]

The South Korean press used the Rangoon bombing to showcase North Korea's duplicitousness in the Third World. A November 5, 1983, *Tong-A Ilbo* newspaper article, entitled "A Terrorist Group Condemned," explains,

> It is almost a cliché that where there is an international dispute there are bound to be North Koreans. They have been accused of selling watches on the black market, liquor and cigarettes in other countries, and have been expelled for trafficking in drugs. Money made was often used to finance terrorist operations. North Korean agents and arms were recently spotted in the Caribbean in Grenada, in Africa, in Iraq, in Cairo, and in Asia in Sri Lanka.

The *Tong-A Ilbo* article added that the Rangoon bombing "inflicted serious injuries on the Third World which can hardly be healed. It thus behooves members of the Third World to condemn North Korea."[85] The November 5, 1983, *Kyŏnghyang Sinmun* said, "Although North Korea is notorious for its terrorist adventures in many parts of the world, it is still shocking to learn that officers of its regular army were the special agents who perpetrated the Rangoon bombing attack." The article continued, "Such an act of provocation by officers in active service is tantamount to a declaration of war against the Republic of Korea."[86] The press was not the only ROK media entity that portrayed the Rangoon bombing as yet another confirmation of the DPRK's aggressive and unpredictable foreign policy.

The Korea Overseas Information Service, a South Korean government-run agency formed to promote (South) Korean culture abroad, published an information booklet in December 1983 entitled *International Renegades: North Korean Diplomacy through Terror.* With a cover photo featuring the destroyed Aung San Martyrs' Mausoleum, the book describes the events of the Rangoon bombing and the subsequent investigation linking Pyongyang to the attack. Similar to the way the North Korean state-run media cited sympathetic foreign voices supporting their view of the Rangoon bombing, the Korea Overseas Information Service included foreign news articles that highlighted Pyongyang's role in the attack. For example, the booklet republished a *Saudi Gazette* article that stated, "The Chun regime does not consider it coincidental that the deadly attack took place in Burma, a neutralist nation. South Korea has been assiduously courting nonaligned and left-leaning Third World countries in an effort to win support they've traditionally given to Kim's hermit dictatorship in Pyongyang." The booklet also included a Thai newspaper editorial from *The Nation* that called the Rangoon bombing "a mindless act" by North Korea as "we cannot understand what that country hoped to achieve."[87] As evidenced by the inclusion of foreign news articles in their media, international opinion surrounding the Rangoon bombing mattered greatly to both Korean governments and constituted a sort of information war between Pyongyang and Seoul.

The Rangoon bombing ultimately hurt North Korea's international image and its diplomatic presence in the Third World. In addition to Burma, the governments in Comoros, Costa Rica, and Western Samoa also cut diplomatic ties with North Korea after the Rangoon bombing. On December 3, 1983, the Islamic Federal Republic of the Comoros, a small archipelago island nation in the Indian Ocean, announced that in being "faithful to its principles of peace and justice," it was "obliged to break diplomatic relations with the DPRK." South Korean President Chun Doo Hwan "warmly welcomed the courageous decision" by the Comorian government to condemn North Korea's "wild act of terrorism" and cut ties with the Kim family regime.[88] Three days later, the Costa Rican government announced at the United Nations that it terminated all ties with the DPRK. In response, South Korea's vice foreign minister Roh Jae-won said, "The ROK government hopes all peace-loving nations of the world will take strong sanctions against North Korea, as did the Costa Rican government, to prevent a recurrence of North Korea's terrorism."[89] The Rangoon bombing undeniably harmed North Korea's once-rising status in the Third World.

The nonaligned Western Samoan government, which established diplomatic relations with the ROK in 1972 and with the DPRK in 1978, released an official statement on December 22, 1983, that said, "Western Samoa does not wish to continue diplomatic relations with a country which clearly does not intend to conform to internationally accepted norms of behavior between nations." The statement noted, "Western Samoa can condone neither terrorism nor callous disregard for human life and for civilized behaviors between states as displayed by North Korea in the tragic Rangoon incident." On December 23, 1983, South Korean president Chun Doo Hwan sent a letter to Western Samoa's prime minister Tofilau Eti that expressed the ROK government's appreciation of the country's "resolute decision to sever diplomatic relations with North Korea as a measure of punitive sanction against the latter's terrorist act in Rangoon."[90] Although Thailand did not formally end diplomatic ties with the DPRK, the government in Bangkok rejected Pyongyang's request to establish an embassy in the capital city. The Thai government expressed "outrage" at North Korea's actions in Burma and would not allow the DPRK to open an embassy "now or in the foreseeable future."[91]

North Korea's terroristic actions in the Third World doomed its foreign policy as governments began to view the DPRK as a rebellious state that operated outside of international norms. Although the governments in Comoros, Costa Rica, Western Samoa, and Thailand were not world superpowers, their disillusionment with Pyongyang signaled to the wider international community that the DPRK's aggressive actions in the Third World should not be taken lightly and ostracizing North Korea might be the best policy in the future.

North Korea and the Palestinian Conflict

On October 10, 1981, Yasser Arafat, chairman of the Executive Committee of the Palestine Liberation Organization (PLO), arrived in North Korea. He was greeted at the Pyongyang airport by Korean Workers' Party cadres and after leaving the airport was welcomed by 100,000 North Koreans who lined the streets of the capital city to enthusiastically welcome the PLO leader. Shortly after arriving in the DPRK, Arafat met Kim Il Sung at the Kumsusan Assembly Hall, where he was warmly embraced by the North Korean leader. A banquet was held in Arafat's honor, where Kim proclaimed, "The Korean people have always expressed firm support to the just struggle of the Palestinian people to retake Palestine, their sacred homeland, and restore their inalienable, legitimate national rights, including the right to return home, the right to self-determination, and the right to found a sovereign state."[92] Arafat's visit to North Korea was the culmination of years of close ties between the DPRK and the PLO. As a testament to the enduring nature of this close comradeship, Arafat would return to Pyongyang eight years later and meet with the North Korean leadership. The Kim family regime saw the Palestinian conflict as one of the most important anti-colonial struggles in the Third World and routinely voiced support for the Palestinian cause. In the 1980s, North Korea's Middle East policy increasingly concentrated on supporting Palestinian allies in the region, rhetorically and militarily, while also undermining South Korean influence in the region.

In many respects, North Korea's Palestine policy mirrored that of another divided Communist nation, East Germany. Historian Jeffrey Herf explains that to East German Communists, "Zionism was an anachronism, a form of reactionary nationalism. Anti-imperialist nationalism was fine but not Zionist nationalism."[93] The Soviet Union, and in turn its allies, turned the language of anti-fascism used during World War II into a rhetorical weapon against Israel.[94] North Korea adopted a similar approach and viewed Zionism as an outdated imperialistic ideology. For example, the North Korean magazine *Kulloja* published an article in 1985 entitled "Israel Is the Cancer of Peace in the Middle East" and said, "Israel's invasion strategy, which Arab people oppose, has been executed for a long time, and the source of the bastards' invasion strategy is the reactionary Zionist ideologues." The article continued, "The Zionists' ideology is reactionary, which was distributed by Jewish bourgeois nationalists who had been living in a series of European cities during the end of the nineteenth century." [95]

In addition, South Korea adopted West Germany's Hallstein Doctrine, which deemed the government in Pyongyang illegitimate and made it officially illegal to establish diplomatic relations with countries that also recognized the DPRK. As a way to counteract the doctrine in South Korea, North Korea, much like East Germany, supported Palestine as a way to appeal to Arab governments in the Middle East and gain diplomatic recognition in the region. This pro-Palestine policy vastly improved the DPRK's status and prestige in the Middle East.

The earliest contact between the DPRK and the PLO took place in 1963 when Khalil al-Wazir, a founding member of the PLO's largest faction, Fatah, traveled to North Korea for military training. In addition to al-Wazir, notable PLO members Sabri al-Banna, leader of the notoriously violent PLO splinter group Abu Nidal Organization, and Muhammad Da'ud Awda, one of the planners of the attack on Israeli athletes at the 1972 Munich Olympics, traveled to the DPRK for military training during the early 1970s. Besides providing military training to high-level PLO members, Pyongyang also provided the Palestinian militants with BM-11 rocket launchers.[96] In 1969, a Lebanese journalist asked Kim Il Sung to give advice to Palestinian guerillas based on his previous experiences fighting the Japanese colonialists as a guerilla fighter. Kim gave the journalist a brief history of his anti-Japanese guerilla army during the 1930s and said, "Victory will be hastened if the Palestinian people further strengthen their armed guerilla force organizationally, ideologically, and militarily, lay the solid mass base of the struggle, rally all the revolutionary and mass organizations firmly so as to cement the unity of the revolutionary forces."[97]

As illustrated by Kim Il Sung's advice to the Lebanese journalist, the DPRK's public support for the Palestinian struggle came primarily through its rhetoric of anticolonial solidarity. From celebrating the "day of world solidarity with the Palestinian people" to announcing a "week of Palestinian solidarity" in its propaganda, the North Korean state media rarely missed an opportunity to show unity with their Palestinian comrades. In 1971, Kim Il Sung told an Iraqi journalist, "The Korean people will continue to resolutely support the valiant struggle of the Palestinian people for liberating their fatherland and the struggle of the entire Arab people against Zionism and imperialist aggression and will always remain a close comrade-in-arms of the Arab people in the struggle against the common enemy."[98]

The DPRK government saw Israel as a lackey of Washington and the "common enemy" of the Palestinian and North Korean peoples. A February 1983 article in the North Korean magazine *Chollima*, entitled "The Identity of Israel and the People Who Control It," explains Pyongyang's view of the Israeli state. The article notes, "The existence of Israel and their invasion strategy is totally the result of the U.S. and UK imperialists' anti-Arab policy, which is to use Israeli Zionists as 'shock troops' for controlling the Middle East." An image in this article features a large, cloaked American capitalist wearing a top hat and with a large nose slyly handing money to a small Israeli air pilot who will use the funds to bomb Arab countries. Meanwhile, the two-faced American capitalist holds an olive branch as a fake gesture for peace.[99] This anti-Israeli image encapsulated North Korea's view of the U.S.-Israel relationship. The DPRK's depiction of Israeli soldiers often echoed anti-Semitic themes from the World War II era. In one North Korean image, a cowering Israeli soldier, with a hooked nose and fang-like teeth, is holding a flag of surrender while being pelted by rocks.[100]

The North Korean government galvanized domestic support for the Palestinian cause by hosting mass rallies. For example, during a "week of support for the struggle of the Palestinian people" in May 1977, hundreds of North Koreans attended a meeting at Pyongyang's Chollima House of Culture, where the chief of the PLO mission in the DPRK Marwan Hassan Abdullah spoke and "expressed thanks to the Korean people for arranging a mass meeting every year to express [an] unshaken stand toward the cause of Palestine."[101] In 1980, the North Korean state-run media hosted another series of mass rallies during the "week of support for the struggle of the Palestinian people." The *Pyongyang Times* declared the start of this week and stated, "At the active instigation of U.S. imperialism, Zionists, challenging the unanimous demand of the world's people, deport themselves more haughtily and insolently and intensify their aggressive and expansionist maneuvers."[102]

North Koreans also celebrated November 29 as "the day of world solidarity with the Palestinian people." According to the *Pyongyang Times*, "On this occasion, the Korean people send militant greetings to the Palestinian people and the resistance fighters who are waging a hard-fought struggle to restore their country and found an independent Palestinian state." The piece asserted that North Korea in the future "will stand four-square behind the Palestinian people until final victory is won."[103] By establishing events such as the "week of support for the struggle of the Palestinian people" and celebrating "the day of world solidarity with the Palestinian people," the DPRK government brought the Palestinian conflict into the forefront of North Korea's national consciousness.

North Korea advocated guerilla warfare as one way to promote Palestinian self-rule and combat Israeli oppression. From 1963 to the early 1990s, the DPRK covertly trained fighters from the Palestinian liberation movement and supplied them with weapons. As Joseph Bermudez explains, North Korean military advisors traveled to Lebanon in the mid-1970s to train various Palestinian guerilla organizations. In 1979, twenty-one members of the PLO traveled to Pyongyang for military training. The Kim family regime also provided Palestinian guerillas with weapons, such as hand grenades and BM-11 rocket launchers.[104] This military support continued in the 1980s. According to the Polish ambassador in Pyongyang, the purpose of Arafat's 1989 visit to the DPRK "was to deepen the traditional cooperation in the new circumstances (following the proclamation of the Palestinian state), particularly in the political and military sphere (mainly the training of several hundred Palestinian airborne troops by the local special forces, supplies of North Korean arms, handguns mostly)."[105] Similar views of revolutionary violence and anti-Zionism bonded the North Korean government and the Palestinian liberation movement.

North Korea formed close ties with the Palestinian liberation movement for two primary reasons. First, the North Koreans saw the Israeli government as a puppet of the U.S. government and represented Israeli Zionists in their propaganda as cunning puppets determined to carry out their American masters' imperialistic orders in the Middle East. Second, the Israeli-Palestinian conflict had some of the same David-versus-Goliath elements of the Korean conflict. As an oppressed people using armed guerilla struggle to resist the imperialist Israeli occupiers, the Palestinian cause naturally resonated with the North Korean leadership, who once used guerilla warfare to oppose Japanese colonialism and saw U.S. troops in South Korea as imperialist occupiers. The DPRK government used this historical parallel as a way to politically mobilize its citizens and generate the image of another besieged freedom-fighting people in the Third World fiercely battling U.S. imperialism. As part of its imagination of a unified global anti-imperialist front, the DPRK's propaganda apparatus played a major role in bringing the Palestinian struggle into North Korea's revolutionary consciousness.

Island Hopping

As part of its effort to increase its diplomatic presence around the world and undermine South Korean influence, North Korea expanded its diplomatic contacts to small island nations in the early 1980s. Although the U.S. had historically dominated the Caribbean and South Pacific regions, North Korea felt it could make inroads in newly independent island nations that preferred nonalignment to U.S. interventionism. Soon, North Korean diplomats were hopping from island to island in the South Pacific and Caribbean. One of the first stops for North Korean diplomats was Jamaica.

Under Michael Manley's socialist government, Jamaica increased its contacts with the Communist bloc in the late 1970s. North Korea jumped at this opportunity and opened an embassy in Kingston in July 1979. In August 1980, the DPRK's vice premier

Kim Kyong Ryon visited Jamaica for three days. Similar to their patterns in other Third World countries, North Korean diplomats in Jamaica pressured local newspapers to print their propaganda materials. Initially, the North Koreans met resistance from the Jamaican government-controlled *Daily News*.[106] The North Koreans later spread their propaganda via other outlets on the island. For example, the North Koreans published a piece in Jamaica's *Star* magazine on April 13, 1983, marking Kim Il Sung's seventy-first birthday. The North Koreans also put on a photography and handiworks exhibition at a Kingston hotel from May 11 to 17, 1983. Jamaica's minister of culture, Ed Bartlett, said at the opening of the exhibition, "Even though Jamaicans are thousands of miles away from Korea, through a movement of ideas and contact they could learn about the culture of another people."[107] In 1984, North Korea published propaganda glorifying Kim Il Sung in Jamaica's *Daily Gleaner* newspaper. Despite most Jamaicans never experiencing snow, one *Daily Gleaner* article, entitled "The Most Benevolent Leader of the People," told the story of Kim Il Sung helping farmers on a cold, snowy day and proclaimed, "The respected President Kim Il Sung is the great leader of the working people, who is possessed of the noblest personality."[108]

Kingston became a microcosm of inter-Korean competition as North and South Korean embassies in Jamaica rhetorically sparred with each other. For example, on January 17, 1983, the DPRK's chargé d'affaires in Jamaica, Han Bong Rim, gave a press conference in Kingston where he objected to the formation of a "triangular military alliance" between South Korea, Japan, and the U.S. He added that the U.S. aimed to use this alliance to "divide Asia and the world." The South Korean embassy in Jamaica swiftly responded to Han's press conference by disseminating a news release on the island, which described the accusation as "unjustifiable" and "purely speculative." The release explained that South Korea "has no military pact with Japan as does North Korea with China and the Soviet Union." Jamaica's *Daily News* declared, "The historical conflict between North and South Korea has extended here to Jamaica."[109]

North Korea's embassy in Kingston increasingly became a hotbed of subversion and illicit activity. In late July 1983, the North Korean embassy gave about 20,000 Jamaican dollars to the National Workers' Union in support of its strike against the Jamaican International Telecommunications, Ltd. The North Koreans also provided funds to striking Jamaican dockworkers and Manley's People's National Party, which had been voted out of office in 1980. There were also rumors that the North Korean embassy provided arms, funds, ammunition, and paramilitary training to leftist insurgents on the island, known as the Brigadistas, which had initially been trained by the Cuban embassy.[110] In addition to fomenting leftist subversion on the island, North Korean diplomats were suspected of smuggling jewelry into Jamaica via diplomatic pouches in 1984. The Jamaican police observed a North Korean diplomatic vehicle being driven by the owner of a Jamaican jewelry shop, who was suspected of purchasing North Korean jewelry.[111] North Korean diplomats in Jamaica also allegedly imported expensive electronics under diplomatic privileges and resold them on the island's black market.[112] In most Third World countries, North Korean embassies rarely engaged in actual diplomacy and quickly overstayed their welcome. They disseminated unattractive propaganda and subverted host governments by supporting local anti-governmental forces and smuggling illegal goods.

The North Koreans also took great interest in establishing a presence on small newly independent Caribbean islands, such as Barbados, Grenada, St. Lucia, and St. Vincent and the Grenadines. In 1977, North Korea established diplomatic ties with Barbados and soon disseminated its propaganda in the local newspaper, the *Barbados Advocate*. On July 29, 1983, North Korea published Kim Il Sung's principles for national reunification in the *Barbados Advocate*. The North Koreans also invited a Barbadian journalist, Norman Pryor, to a 1983 conference in Pyongyang. The impressionable journalist described the DPRK's command economy as being "way out in front compared with a number of Asian countries under a free enterprise system" and said that Pyongyang "has none of the slums that exist in other Asian countries."[113] However, the most active North Korean presence in the Caribbean was on the small spice island of Grenada, where North Koreans assisted the nascent socialist government in infrastructure development, agricultural projects, and enhancement of its military power.[114]

In 1979, North Korea established diplomatic ties with St. Lucia, and in late October 1980, St. Lucia's minister for external affairs visited the DPRK. Seoul received news of his visit as St. Lucia's UN delegation mistakenly asked the South Korean delegates for information about travel to North Korea.[115] The North Koreans also made inroads into St. Vincent and the Grenadines and established diplomatic relations in 1981. The British embassy in Seoul aptly chalked this up to inter-Korean competition and said that "both countries regularly publish lists detailing their diplomatic triumphs, and unsurprisingly, these come to different conclusions as to which country is in the lead with the most ambassadors or diplomatic recognitions. This is probably the main reason for North Korea's interest in St. Vincent." The North Koreans inquired about setting up a resident mission on the island, but the British embassy in Seoul reminded the St. Vincent government of recent North Korean diplomats' troublemaking activities abroad. The British embassy in Seoul concluded, "While the opportunities for such mischief-making as this may be few in St. Vincent, the [North Koreans] would probably quickly outstay their welcome if St. Vincent allowed them a resident mission."[116] North Korea invested resources in the Caribbean region due to the participation of these island nations in international forums, such as the UN. Despite being relatively insignificant players in Cold War politics, these small islands mattered in the inter-Korean competition between Pyongyang and Seoul as both sides vied for diplomatic recognition.

Nicaragua, the site of an intense civil war between leftist Sandinista insurgents and U.S.-supported Contras in the 1970s and 1980s, also attracted Pyongyang's attention. The *Rodong Sinmun* criticized Washington's involvement in the conflict and said on August 10, 1983, that the encirclement of Nicaragua by U.S. naval forces "suggests that the U.S. imperialists, far from drawing a correct lesson of the bankruptcy of their Central America policy, are trying to hide their failure with 'strength.' This is nothing but a dream of 'strength' fanatics who believe a big stick is everything."[117] A day later, the *Rodong Sinmun* printed another article on the Nicaraguan situation and called U.S. president Ronald Reagan's press conference, in which he said that the U.S. desires peace in Central America, "nonsense" and that " 'peace' on the lips of the U.S. imperialists is a pronoun [*sic*] of aggression and war."[118] The North Koreans were also suspected of providing assistance to the Sandinistas, via the Cuban government, in the form of military training and weapons deals.[119] According to a declassified CIA document, the North Korean government supplied the Sandinistas with four patrol boats, worth $8 million, during the early 1980s.[120]

In addition to wreaking havoc in Central America and the Caribbean during the early 1980s, the North Koreans also invested resources in expanding their diplomatic presence in the South Pacific region. North Korean diplomats from nearby Southeast Asian countries, such as Indonesia, would travel to small island nations on goodwill missions. For example, in August 1980, a three-man North Korean delegation, consisting of two journalists from Pyongyang's Foreign Languages Publishing House and the third secretary of the DPRK's embassy in Indonesia, visited the Solomon Islands on a "familiarization and fact-finding tour." The North Korean delegation said, "The DPRK like the Solomons is a newly independent and developing country and it would be important for the two countries to establish mutual friendship in trade and cooperation" and that on their return to the DPRK, they "will be printing articles about their findings here so that their own people can know about the Solomons."[121] However, this was mere rhetoric, as this distant South Pacific island nation remained largely unknown within the DPRK.

In 1981, North Korean diplomats based in Southeast Asia would frequently show up in the Solomon Islands unannounced. From March 10 to 12, 1981, three North Korean diplomats from Indonesia, posing as tourists, visited the capital city of Honiara and met with two senior Solomon Islands civil servants to discuss possible sponsorship of Solomon Islands students for study courses and athletic events in the DPRK. On March 12, 1983, three more North Korean diplomats, who were based in Papua New Guinea, showed up in Honiara and stayed ten days. As the British High Commission in Honiara commented, "By now, the interest of [the] Solomon Islands government was well and truly aroused [but] found that keeping track of the [North Korean] visitors was a difficult task." According to the British

FIGURE 5. Artist name: Ro Ŭigŏn. "Let us unite our capacity for anti-imperialism and independence and fight!" Source: Leiden University Libraries, digital collection.

High Commission, the North Koreans "popped up everywhere, including at the door of the Prime Minister's office after [Permanent Secretary of Solomon Islands' Ministry of Foreign Affairs] Bugoto had expressly ruled out such a call. The Prime Minister did not see them."[122]

Despite the prime minister's cold shoulder in 1980, the North Koreans continued to pester the government in Honiara. After the new prime minister Solomon Mamaloni took office in August 1981, the North Koreans "lost no time in contacting him" as they were "perhaps encouraged by Mamaloni's heavily publicized statement about possibly turning to communist states for aid." However, Mamaloni turned down the North Koreans' advances.[123] The North Korean government saw these small island nations as useful pieces in its global struggle against South Korea. By first establishing its presence in the South Pacific, the DPRK could claim the region as pro-Pyongyang and deny any chance of South Korea gaining a foothold in the region.

North Korea's South Pacific policy mirrored the increased focus that the Soviet Union gave to the South Pacific region during the 1980s. Moscow saw the South Pacific as a region with economic potential and geostrategic importance.[124] Due to U.S. nuclear tests in the waters of Micronesia, anti-Americanism grew in the region during the 1980s. Naturally, the Soviets exploited this vulnerability and promoted the idea of the South Pacific as America's nuclear playpen in its propaganda. A Soviet analyst wrote in 1982, "Once blossoming islands transformed into 'radioactive cemeteries'; fertile lands completely pockmarked with bomb-craters; the black silhouettes of submarines in blue lagoons; barbed wire fences with warning notices 'U.S. property.'"[125] Unlike the Soviet Union's emphasis on establishing trade ties with South Pacific nations and combatting U.S. influence in the region, North Korea's South Pacific policy primarily focused on forming diplomatic ties with island nations and establishing it as a pro-DPRK area vis-à-vis the South Koreans.

Although North Korea failed to establish diplomatic ties with the Solomon Islands in the early 1980s, it agreed to establish relations with Vanuatu in late October 1981. Australia warned Vanuatu to not allow a North Korean ambassador to be appointed and said that "if the North Koreans do establish a foothold in (Port) Vila [the capital city of Vanuatu] they will almost certainly use it as a base from which to attempt to insinuate themselves into other South Pacific islands."[126] After failing to set up a residence in Vanuatu, the North Koreans focused their efforts on establishing a presence on the South Pacific island nations of Fiji, Kiribati, and Nauru.

Although Fiji recognized the DPRK in 1975, the diplomatic relationship resulted in few, if any, real ties between the two countries. According to the British High Commission in Fiji, the Fijian government did "not allow any substance to be put into the relationship" and routinely turned down the DPRK's request for delegations to visit the island. However, a group of three influential Fijian officials, including the deputy speaker of the parliament, visited North Korea in June 1984.[127] Ironically, this group of three belonged to the Fiji Anti-Communist League. One of the members, Maan Singh, "said he found nothing wrong in visiting North Korea despite the fact that he was a member of the Fiji Anti-Communist League." Singh explained he was "open-minded" and "would like to see the best of the two worlds."[128] The Fijian public was less than thrilled about their government officials visiting the DPRK. One Fijian citizen wrote in the local newspaper, "Are they not satisfied with the way Communist countries operate? What else do they want to know about Communist countries? The facts are already before our eyes to be judged. What I want to know is whether they are going to gain anything from this trip." Another citizen wrote, "Little is known about life in this encapsulated country but it is suspected that totalitarianism there is more complete than anywhere else. So, what might these Fiji people visiting such a place be wanting to find out?"[129] The North Korean government allured prominent Fijian politicians with free trips but, as in most other Third World countries, failed to appeal to the general public.

North Korea's unattractive and overly aggressive propaganda in Fiji did little to improve its reputation as a despotic regime. For example, on March 5, 1982, the North Korean government published a Yugoslav journalist's interview with Kim Il Sung in the *Fiji Sun* newspaper that reeked of demagoguery.[130] A North Korea friendship society was also set up at Fiji's University of the South Pacific. In 1984, the friendship society attempted to set up a two-week North Korean book display at the university's library. Three days after it opened, organizers claimed the display was forced to close amid diplomatic pressure from the South Korean ambassador and the U.S. embassy on the island. The university's main librarian denied these claims.[131] The Fijian government also continued to deny North Korean delegations' requests to visit the island. Fiji's prime minister Ratu Sir Kamisese Mara said, "Fiji would not deal with governments that resort to international terrorism."[132] News of North Korea's role in the Rangoon bombing had reached even remote island nations in the South Pacific and devastated any chance of establishing a foothold in the region. The small island nation of Kiribati also declined North Korea's advances.

Not all South Pacific island nations could resist the North Koreans, however. Nauru, a state of only 13,000 people in Micronesia, established diplomatic relations with the DPRK in 1982. This announcement alarmed South Korea's embassy in Fiji, which quickly sent a letter to the government in Nauru. The letter stated, "It is most unfortunate that the decision of your Government concerning North Korea came at a time when both the ROK and Nauru were seeking to establish a base for closer economic cooperation and further develop the traditional friendly relations between our two nations." The letter urged Nauru, as a "nation respected and admired for its nonaligned policies," to reconsider its decision to establish diplomatic ties with Pyongyang.[133] It was assumed that the North Koreans gave money to the

Nauru government in exchange for diplomatic recognition. According to the British High Commission in Fiji, Nauru's president Hammer DeRoburt felt "that he [could not] reasonably refuse to enter into diplomatic relations with anyone who [wanted] to establish them." A British diplomat "pointed out the danger of this attitude and said that there was no obligation on any country to enter into diplomatic relations if they did not wish to do." DeRoburt responded that Nauru "had already got relations with some countries they didn't really like [such as Chile] and they felt it better to be even handed." However, the British diplomat concluded, "The North Koreans made a very bad impression on Nauru and are not at all popular."[134]

In the South Pacific, the South Korean government constantly played catch-up to the North Koreans. The ROK government deployed an ambassador to Fiji, Sung Woo Kim, whose sole purpose was to disrupt and counter North Korean influence in the South Pacific region. The British High Commission in Kiribati described Ambassador Kim as "an intense man, single-minded, and persistent," who was "well-informed" about North Korean actions in the South Pacific due to "a network of informers throughout the Pacific region." He told his British counterparts in private that "his Mission was set up with the single objective of countering the influence of North Korea in the Pacific region."[135] The British High Commission in Fiji said that the ROK ambassador's "main preoccupation in life is thwarting North Korean efforts to develop their relations with the island states."[136]

However, North Korea surpassed South Korea in terms of influence in the region due to its donations of developmental aid. Naturally, most South Pacific nations prioritized pragmatism and recognized the Korean government that gave them the most financial assistance. Inter-Korean competition and Cold War politics mattered little to these developing island nations. The British Foreign Office acknowledged this and urged the South Koreans to give even a small amount of money to South Pacific governments: "The South Koreans are prepared to go to considerable lengths worldwide to counter the activities of their Northern brethren. It therefore seems strange that no [South] Korean aid monies are available for the South Pacific. The investment of even a token amount would pay dividends both in terms of counteracting North Korean influence and assisting commercial penetration."[137] Thus, the South Pacific remained dominated by North Korean influence and became one of the few spaces where Pyongyang exerted greater influence than Seoul. It was North Korea's financial assistance, and not the teachings of Kim Il Sung, that South Pacific island nations most welcomed.

As divided nations with similar political systems, North Korea and East Germany naturally formed close ties. However, their views vastly differed on the use of violence to achieve their political goals. This distinction surfaced in 1984 when the North Korean and East German governments prepared a Treaty of Friendship. As Sang-Hwan

Seong explains, "In preparation for the 1984 Treaty of Friendship, North Korea was not willing to acknowledge the principle of non-violence as compulsory within international law, whereas East Germany maintained its position that foreswearing violence was a core objective in achieving mutual understanding."[138] Seong adds, "East Germany was successfully able to persuade North Korea on this point, and the revised position was duly reflected in the Treaty of Friendship in 1984." The fact that the East Germans had to coax Pyongyang to hide its inclination to use violence shows that the North Korean government began to openly embrace its renegade status in the international order. By the mid-1980s, it was clear that international norms, laws, and treaties mattered little to the regime in Pyongyang. The Rangoon bombing had already demonstrated North Korea's willingness to conduct political violence abroad and quickly deny any responsibility. The smuggling activities of its diplomats, the awkward placement of its propaganda in Third World newspapers, and its eagerness to conduct arms deals with anti-colonial militants also showcased North Korea's inability to abide by international conventions.

With its crumbling economy and growing inability to compete with South Korea on the diplomatic front, North Korea faced a legitimacy crisis in the early 1980s. As a sign of just how underdeveloped North Korea's industrialized economy had become in the early 1980s, some German environmentalists paradoxically saw the DPRK as an eco-socialist haven untainted by capitalist-fueled pollution. Rudolf Bahro, an East German dissident, visited North Korea in 1981 with Luise Rinser and came away impressed with North Korea's socialist construction "without destroying nature." Rolf Stolz, a leading politician of the West German Green Party, also visited North Korea in the early 1980s and later told a West German newspaper, "Beginning in kindergarten, the children [in North Korea] are educated to act in ways that take nature into account. Rather than killing insects with poison chemicals, they are attracted with oil lamps and then annihilated in a way that is friendly to the environment."[139] By the early 1980s, North Korea could no longer compete with South Korea economically and faced an increasingly anti-Communist U.S. foreign policy under Ronald Reagan.

Internationally, the DPRK leadership witnessed the rapid overthrow of radical Third World regimes, such as the U.S. invasion of Grenada in 1983.[140] In order to preserve its political system amid changing international conditions and gain an upper hand over its South Korean rivals, a military deterrent was necessary. With the help of Soviet nuclear scientists, the DPRK invested heavily in nuclear development during the 1980s.[141] Under Kim Jong Il's guidance, the military acquired a stronger role in the KWP's internal affairs. With a nuclear arsenal of its own, the reunification of the Korean peninsula under the DPRK's terms suddenly seemed to be within reach for the Kim family regime.

5

Survival by Any Means Necessary 1984–1989

AFTER THE 1983 RANGOON INCIDENT, South Korean president Chun Doo Hwan made a statement to his countrymen in which he explained the importance of his "summit diplomacy" with the leaders from nonaligned nations. He explained that his 1982 trip to Africa to meet with African leaders was intended to bring "the Republic closer to the vast continent which had been dominated by North Korean penetration and thus a hotbed of its vicious activities."[1] With a renewed sense of resolve to combat North Korea's influence in the Third World after the bombing in Burma, Seoul invested more resources into establishing a larger presence in Africa during the mid-1980s. Thus, the inter-Korean conflict moved to the African continent, where the two Koreas competed for status and recognition in the mid-1980s.

This chapter focuses on three major themes of North Korea's Third World policy from 1984 to 1989. First, North Korea's reputation as a modern militaristic state helped it gain friends and customers among new African despots, such as Zimbabwe's Robert Mugabe and Uganda's Milton Obote. As the DPRK's economy stalled, Pyongyang exported its people, specifically military specialists, in the mid- to late 1980s as a way of earning the Kim family regime hard currency. Second, the personality of foreign leaders mattered a great deal to Kim Il Sung and this influenced North Korea's foreign policy. As evidenced by Kim Il Sung's close friendship with Cambodia's Prince Sihanouk, personality sometimes more than political ideologies determined who the Kim family regime supported. Third, the North Korean government invested heavily in the 1989 World Festival of Youth and Students as a way to improve global awareness of the DPRK and combat Seoul's success in hosting the 1988 Olympics.

North Korea, the Fifth Brigade, and Communist Ethiopia

After more than a decade of fighting the white minority Rhodesian government as a guerilla fighter, Robert Mugabe emerged as the leader of newly independent Zimbabwe in 1980. Faced with political rivalry and rising ethnic tensions, Mugabe sought to consolidate his fragile grip on power in the early 1980s. After visiting Pyongyang for the Sixth Korean Workers' Party Congress in 1980, Mugabe came away impressed with the DPRK's sociopolitical system and asked fellow ex-guerilla fighter Kim Il Sung for military assistance. Kim obliged and sent 106 military advisors to Zimbabwe to train Mugabe's Fifth Brigade. This North Korea–trained elite guard then went to the Matabeleland region of Zimbabwe and carried out a genocidal campaign of terror that inflicted mass chaos and casualties on the Ndebele people, an ethnic minority that historically opposed Mugabe's Shona tribe and supported his main political rival Joshua Nkomo.[2] According to a report of the atrocities, the North Korean–trained Fifth Brigade tortured more than 7,000 people and killed more than 3,000 from 1983 to 1988.[3]

North Korea's training of the notoriously brutal Fifth Brigade in Zimbabwe made British officials worry that Pyongyang would carry out this type of training in other African countries. For example, amid speculation that Ethiopia's minister of defense visited Pyongyang in July 1983, the British High Commission in Addis Ababa asked, "Shall we see an Ethiopian 'Fifth Division' operating against guerillas in Eritrea and Tigre?"[4] While an Ethiopian Fifth Brigade never developed, the North Koreans did form close ties with Mengistu Haile Mariam's military dictatorship, known as the Derg, in the mid-1980s. While visiting the DPRK in October 1983, Mengistu signed a treaty of friendship and cooperation and a general agreement on economic, scientific, technical, and cultural cooperation with the Kim family regime.[5]

Ethiopia occupied a unique space in the inter-Korean conflict as Ethiopian soldiers fought alongside South Korean troops during the Korean War. Thus, there were deep historical linkages between Addis Ababa and Seoul. For example, the South Korean government sent doctors to Ethiopian hospitals as a way to repay Ethiopia for its assistance during the Korean War. South Korean doctor Min Chul Yoo, who worked at the Black Lion Hospital in Addis Ababa for thirty years, said, "There were no comfortable days" during the violent period of Mengistu's purges, infamously known as the Red Terror. However, Yoo said, "I could not leave [Ethiopia] because my purpose of going to Ethiopia was to take care of the poor patients."[6] Although the Derg adopted Marxism-Leninism, Ethiopia never cut off diplomatic relations with Seoul. As a wily Third World leader desperate for developmental aid, Mengistu played the two Koreas off each other for large amounts of financial assistance. The Hungarian embassy in Ethiopia reported, "Since both Koreas are represented in Ethiopia, and

South Korea provides remarkable assistance, the DPRK gives a quick and positive response to every Ethiopian request." Ideologically, Mengistu viewed the DPRK as "a model of socialist construction which, due to the relative similarity of the level of development, can be taken into consideration in Ethiopia."[7]

As part of its cooperation agreement, North Korea planned to help Ethiopia build ships and fishing boats. It also planned to assist the Derg in implementing a large hydroelectric project.[8] Mengistu's blend of communism and militarism appealed to the Kim family regime. On June 1, 1984, Kim Il Sung told East German leader Erich Honecker, "Ethiopia has obviously achieved the highest level of consolidation of a Marxist party" in Africa.[9] The ROK foreign ministry said in 1985 that the Derg and the Kim family regime shared "identical ideologies" and that "North Korea has recognized that the revolutionary task has been settled in Ethiopia so North Korea has strengthened the political and financial relationship with Ethiopia and Ethiopia thus thinks very highly of this relationship."[10]

The North Koreans exerted a large amount of developmental influence on Ethiopia during the mid-1980s. For example, in a rare moment of highlighting the North Korean government's foreign assistance, the *Rodong Sinmun* proudly boasted on July 5, 1985, that North Korean engineers aided Ethiopia's agricultural development. According to the *Rodong Sinmun*, Mengistu said after visiting the dry field irrigation facilities built at the Amignahoro agricultural production cooperative, "The dry field irrigation facilities built by [North] Korean agro-technicians are very wonderful. In recent years, Ethiopia has been seriously impacted in agricultural development by adverse natural conditions." He continued, "The facilities will greatly contribute to agricultural development in Ethiopia. I express sincere thanks to the Great Leader Comrade Kim Il Sung and the Dear Leader Comrade Kim Jong Il for having sent knowledgeable agro-technicians."[11]

The North Koreans also spread their political concepts in Ethiopia. The Hungarian embassy in Ethiopia said in September 1985 that "North Korea exerts a considerable influence in certain spheres of [Ethiopian] politics" and that the North Koreans had recently aided the Derg in the construction of its constitution.[12] North Korea also obtained a place in the Ethiopian media as footage of Mengistu visiting the DPRK appeared "in sequels" on Ethiopian television.[13] In addition, a pro-DPRK piece also appeared in the *Ethiopian Herald*. On June 30, 1985, Ethiopian journalist Melese Telahoun published an article entitled "For Reunification of Korea," which repeated Pyongyang's position on reunification.[14]

The DPRK's large presence in Ethiopia surprised the Hungarian embassy in Ethiopia as North Koreans even replaced Soviet agricultural advisors. The Hungarian embassy in Addis Ababa said on November 26, 1985, "The [North] Koreans provide assistance on a very wide scale: A high number of small-scale irrigation facilities, a larger hydropower station, geological surveys, military equipment, marine fishing, and so on." The Hungarians added, "From an interest-free loan of six million dollars, they are constructing a shipbuilding factory. The Soviet experts in the Ministry of Agriculture have been largely replaced by [North] Koreans." The Hungarian embassy concluded that North Korea as a developmental model, not its ideology or politics, most appealed to the Derg. A Hungarian diplomat in Addis Ababa concluded, "In my view, it is not the ideological and political identification [with North Korea] that is important for the Ethiopian side but the fact that they regard the development of this country, which is comparable to theirs, as a model applicable [to their own conditions], and that they really receive great assistance."[15]

North Korea's vice president Ri Chong'ok toured Ethiopia in November 1985 with Mengistu. Despite his country suffering a famine at the time, Mengistu spoke about ambitious industrialization plans for Ethiopia during his tour with Ri. The Hungarian embassy commented, "This speech illuminates what has been hitherto incomprehensible in [Ethiopia's] relationship with [North] Korea. They probably cannot expect the Soviet Union to support these plans, and thus the propaganda also occasionally alludes that as far as industrialization is concerned, they rank Korea ahead of the Soviet Union."[16] Similar to the Kim family regime's idea of the DPRK as a "socialist paradise," the Derg had illusions of grandeur and believed that rural Ethiopia needed North Korean–style industrialization in order to rapidly develop.

Pyongyang wanted to alter Ethiopia's long-standing relationship with Seoul. Thus, the Kim family regime invested heavily in Ethiopia's development. It did not hurt that Mengistu looked up to the DPRK as a developmental model and his particular brand of strongman politics naturally meshed with the autocratic nature of the Kim family regime. While Ethiopia was an exceptional case in terms of the extremely large amount of North Korean developmental assistance, the DPRK sent technical and agricultural specialists all over Africa during the mid-1980s. In 1984, Kim Il Sung told Honecker, "We have agricultural specialists in nearly all African countries. Our experience in Sudan indicates that just sending a small number of specialists can help them to double or triple agricultural production and thus to solve their main problem, the issue of food." Kim added, "If all of the socialist countries together initiate more dynamic activities with respect to the nations of Africa, we will be able tear all of Africa away from imperialism and set many countries on the path to socialism."[17] Kim may have genuinely wanted to lift Africa out of poverty but grew frustrated with the lack of a unified socialist commitment to African development.

As the leader of an industrialized nation that rebuilt itself after a devastating war, Kim Il Sung felt he could help African leaders learn self-sufficiency. In November 1986, he told Jambyn Batmunk, the general secretary of the Mongolian People's Revolutionary Party, "There are many instances of the political leaders of developing countries visiting us. They ask our advice about building a new society. I say that we don't have that much experience compared to others, but we have built up a state destroyed in war." Highlighting his supposed role as a "man of the people," Kim Il Sung continued, "There are some people among the African political leaders who take a [walking] stick and travel a lot. I tell them—while you travel around with a [walking] stick, time is being lost and it will harm the people. Throw away the [walking] stick and take a shovel to lead the people [by example]. I tell them directly that this is how I began." Perhaps disappointed with African leaders, Kim Il Sung concluded, "These people say they will go back home and do things. But there are few that actually do anything."[18] Kim Il Sung's frustration with the lack of African development clearly began to show in 1986. After this year, North Korea's financial commitment to Third World development lessened.

North Korea's Military Assistance in Uganda

In 1984, North Korean military experts were present in eleven African countries—Angola, Benin, Congo, Libya, Madagascar, Mozambique, Seychelles, Tanzania, Uganda, Zambia, and Zimbabwe.[19] A relatively large number of North Korean military advisors, around fifty-five total, helped Seychelles president France-Albert René reorganize his armed forces in 1983 and 1984 after a failed military coup in August 1982 against his socialist government.[20] Meanwhile, in Madagascar, around fifty members of the North Korean military trained Malagasy armed forces and loaned four MiG-17 aircraft to president Didier Ratsiraka. In Mozambique, around one hundred North Korean military instructors trained a brigade used in anti-dissident operations.[21]

On June 20, 1986, Kim Il Sung said at a KWP meeting in Pyongyang, "The South African racist regime pursues the vicious policy of apartheid, of racial discrimination, and the policy of brutal repression. It is trampling underfoot even the basic freedom and rights of the South African people and is keeping them subjugated to the white people, who are the minority." Kim continued, "The South African racists have occupied Namibia illegally and are tightening up their colonial rule, resorting to the bloody suppression of the struggle of the Namibian people for national independence and national liberation."[22] While North Korea's military primarily focused on training the armed forces of established African governments during the mid-1980s, it also trained members of anti-apartheid movements, such as Namibia's South West African People's Organization (SWAPO) and South Africa's African National Congress (ANC), in Angola-based training camps.[23]

Of these two anti-colonial movements, the DPRK most closely supported SWAPO. Since the early 1970s, the DPRK had aided SWAPO guerillas with small arms and military training. SWAPO leader Sam Nujoma visited North Korea on three separate occasions (1975, 1983, 1984) and expressed his gratitude to the Kim family regime for supporting the liberation of Namibia.[24] In 1985, the *Rodong Sinmun* criticized the actions of the "South African racists" in Namibia. On June 20, 1985, the *Rodong Sinmun* said, "The Namibian 'provisional government' is the racists' puppet regime created by traitors of the Namibian people, excluding the South West Africa People's Organization, their only legitimate representative."[25] A couple weeks later, the *Rodong Sinmun* published another article supportive of SWAPO, which explained, "If the Namibian problem is to be solved in a just manner, the legitimate interests of the Namibian people represented by the South West Africa People's Organization should be respected, the South African racists must withdraw from the territory of Namibia at once and the imperialists' aggressive and interventionist moves against this nation must be halted."[26] After obtaining independence in 1990, the SWAPO government presumably paid Pyongyang back for its past support by giving contracts to Mansudae Overseas Project, a North Korean state-owned construction company, for the building of expensive projects, such as a war memorial, museum, and statehouse in Namibia.[27]

Sometimes, North Korea's military presence in Africa created unique spaces for resistance. After Tanzanian armed forces removed Ugandan leader Idi Amin from power in 1979, Milton Obote won an election the following year that was fraught with corruption. This rigged election led to the outbreak of a five-year-long guerilla war by anti-government rebels, led by Yoweri Museveni's National Resistance Army (NRA). One of the ways in which anti-government forces organized and recruited Ugandan youth was through the Uganda-[North] Korea Friendship Society. Mahmood Mamdani, a former anti-government dissident in Uganda and a current professor of African studies at Columbia University, had helped to found the friendship society in 1981 "as one of the few legal ways to reach out to young people in an increasingly oppressive and difficult environment." In an interview, Mamdani said the society "had roughly fifty chapters of varying strength, from ten to fifty" members, but members had "very little idea of North Korea at the time" and most of the society's discussions revolved around the situation in Uganda, not Korea. Mamdani said, "There were embassy-level interactions [with the North Koreans], limited to the provision of literature. . . . The North Koreans made Juche literature available to the society." The North Koreans had no knowledge that their friendship society was being used as a space of resistance against the Obote government, which they supported with arms and military-training assistance. Mamdani explains, "North Koreans were woefully ignorant of the domestic situation in Uganda. They also had very little idea of the actual work of the society since it happened [in] individual chapters throughout the country. Mamdani stated, "North Korea did not support any kind of struggle against Obote. Their support was limited to a general expression of anti-imperialism. There was no question of training or arms. This was a group limited to study and economic activity."[28]

Unaware of their friendship society's anti-government activities in Uganda, the North Koreans closely supported the Obote government with military assistance. North Korea's presence in Uganda showcased the turbulence of African politics during the Cold War and the ability of Pyongyang to quickly adjust to changing domestic conditions. After Obote visited Pyongyang in December 1981, the DPRK quickly sent two military training teams to Uganda. One team, composed of around fourteen members and based in Gulu and Masindi, instructed Obote's Uganda National Liberation Army (UNLA) in the maintenance of military equipment, vehicles, and radios. The other North Korean team, based in Nakasongola, instructed the UNLA on matters of personnel security and bodyguarding. The DPRK government also agreed to build Obote a school in Uganda for handicapped children and continue to provide the UNLA with military supplies.[29] Despite their noninvolvement in the actual fighting, North Korea's military in Uganda could not avoid the violence of the guerilla war. In August 1982, anti-government rebels ambushed the North Korean military training team in Gulu and killed its leader and a subordinate.[30]

North Korea's increasing military presence in Uganda impeded the development of South Korea's relations with Kampala. In February 1984, North Korea blocked a gift of twenty vehicles to Obote's government from South Korea.[31] On September 22, 1984, Obote's government gave South Korea's ambassador fourteen days to leave Uganda on the basis that "reports hostile to Uganda had appeared in the South Korean news media which had in particular attacked human rights in Uganda." The South Koreans believed the North Koreans passed on these South Korean news reports to Obote's government.[32] The North Korean state-run media celebrated Uganda's decision to "expel the puppet ambassador of South Korea late in September 1984," saying that "this was clear proof of the Ugandan people's firm support and solidarity with the just cause of the Korean people."[33] The DPRK state-run media also announced on September 26, 1984, the groundbreaking construction of a North Korean–built cadre school in Roro, Uganda. A bronze plaque made for the groundbreaking ceremony said,

> The pedestals of the Roro School of Reserve Cadres to be built as a gift of his excellency Marshal Kim Il Sung, President of the DPRK, were laid on September 12, 1984, by his excellency Milton Obote, President of the Republic of Uganda and commander-in-chief of the Defense Forces of Uganda, in memory of those who laid down their lives in the struggle for the liberation of Uganda from 1971 to 1979.[34]

The expulsion of the ROK ambassador was most likely an expression of gratitude by Obote for North Korea's continued assistance to Uganda.

The ROK's chargé d'affaires in Kampala told the British High Commission on October 24, 1984, that he believed "the aim of the North Koreans was to get Uganda to break off diplomatic relations completely" with South Korea.[35] The Ugandan vice president Paulo Muwanga told the British in early October 1984 that the North Korean military training teams were "on contract" and their training and weapons were a "practical, not ideological, matter." The British High Commission aptly concluded in late October 1984 that "the North Korean 'price' includes a political element" as representatives of South Korean–based Hyundai had also recently been asked to leave Uganda.[36]

In October 1984, North Korea's state-run media emphasized the DPRK's solidarity with Obote's government. A photo exhibition celebrating the 22nd National Day of Uganda was held at Pyongyang's Chollima House of Culture on October 7. According to the *Rodong Sinmun,* the exhibition showed "the successes of the Ugandan people in their endeavors to build a new society after the country's independence."[37] The *Rodong Sinmun* celebrated Uganda's independence day on October 9 and declared, "The Ugandan people enthusiastically advanced along the road of independence and have adhered to this road more resolutely under the leadership of President Milton Obote from 1980." The editorial added, "Friendship between the Korean and Ugandan peoples is growing in strength. President Milton Obote's visit to Korea in December 1981 was a significant event in deepening Korea-Uganda friendship."[38] The British High Commission in Kampala also considered Obote's 1981 trip to the DPRK "a significant event" as the Ugandan leader signed a secret $40-million military arms deal with the North Korean government during his visit.[39] As the North Koreans intensified their military relationship with Obote's government, the North Korean state-run media followed suit and emphasized Uganda in its propaganda. North Korean state-run media never openly mentioned the close military ties between the two countries.

In November 1984, anti-government forces in Uganda and the South Korean government spread rumors that the North Korean military training teams in Uganda participated in actual fighting on behalf of Obote's government. The director of the African division in South Korea's foreign ministry told the British High Commission that around 270 North Korean military personnel, including a senior military officer, were stationed in Uganda and were "actively involved in the fighting." However, the British High Commission said the ROK official admitted he had no hard evidence and was merely repeating BBC journalism.[40] Meanwhile, Obote's government vehemently denied rumors that foreign troops fought alongside the UNLA.[41] The ROK government routinely exaggerated the number of North Korean military personnel and mischaracterized their objectives in Third World countries as a way to highlight the DPRK government's terroristic nature.

The rumors of North Korean military training in Uganda spread to the United Kingdom. The British newspaper *The Observer* reported on June 23, 1985, that the North Korean military had trained "terror squads" of the Ugandan government army that murdered hundreds of thousands of anti-government people.[42] The North Korean state-run media denounced this "fabrication" and said that it was "a malicious challenge and intolerable insult to us." The KCNA added, "This is needless to say a crafty ruse intended to impair the authority and prestige of the DPRK rising among the African countries, driving a wedge between our country and African countries and shore up the South Korean puppets who are being further isolated from the African countries." The article concluded, "The imperialist reptile press must promptly stop such false propaganda as the training of African troops by our army and the foolish attempt to impair the authority of our republic."[43] The report of a mass slaughter by North Korean–trained Ugandan government forces was inaccurate and may have been a rumor disseminated by the South Korean security services to ruin the DPRK's growing status in Africa as a cheap supplier of military assistance. Nonetheless, the training of Ugandan armed forces by North Korean military advisors did happen although the government in Pyongyang officially denied it.

As the former colonizer of Uganda, the UK government kept close tabs on developments in the recently independent country. Although the British High Commission in Kampala stated, "We have experienced no difficulties as a result of the North Korean presence," the cheaper North Koreans replaced a group of British mercenaries, known as Falconstar, as trainers of the 5,000-man "Uganda Police Special Force" at the Naguru Barracks in late 1983.[44] The British government had recently "rehabilitated" the Naguru Barracks, which irked British diplomats in Kampala as the North Korean military trainers were now using this site.[45]

Around thirty North Korean military personnel, including at least one brigadier and two colonels, trained Uganda's Special Forces. However, their instruction suffered from communication issues as none of the trainers spoke English and the group only had one translator. According to Ugandan police sources, the North Koreans were "not generally liked."[46] The North Korean police had acquired somewhat of an international reputation for their brutality. Black Panther leader Eldridge Cleaver, who visited the DPRK in 1969 and 1970, said that the exceedingly violent North Korean police made him miss the racist police of Oakland, California.[47] The British Foreign Office suggested to the ROK government in October 1984 that if it wanted to reestablish a presence in Uganda, contacting and possibly subsidizing Falconstar might help its cause.[48]

While North Korea's military presence loomed large in Uganda, the DPRK government also carried out developmental assistance programs in the East African country. For example, in 1984, the North Koreans helped to build a school for orphans in the Loro-Apach district of Uganda. In February 1985, four North Korean agricultural technicians traveled to Uganda in order to implement the construction of an agro-scientific research center in Mupugu. In 1985, the North Koreans also proposed sending a five-man team of experts to assist the Ugandan government in wood processing, furniture manufacturing, and roofing-tile production.[49]

In July 1985, UNLA Lieutenant General Bazilio Olara-Okello and General Tito Okello deposed Obote in a military coup. Amid the chaos of the newly established military government, all North Korean military personnel, around two hundred total, pulled out of Uganda in August and September 1985.[50] However, the new Okello-led government lasted only a few months as Museveni's NRA intensified its guerilla operations and seized control of the country in January 1986. As military opportunists unshackled by allegiances to former Ugandan governments, the North Koreans quickly established ties with Museveni's government.

Desperate for arms and seemingly indifferent to the DPRK's past support of the Obote government that he recently fought against, Museveni visited the DPRK for six days in April 1987 and praised North Korea's postcolonial development. At a speech in Pyongyang attended by "Comrade President" Kim Il Sung, Museveni said, "Let me assure you Comrade President that we as a Third World people identify with these heroic achievements of the Korean people. These achievements Comrade President are not only important for Korea, they are important for the entire Third World peoples because they demonstrate the feasibility of developing on the basis of self-reliance." Museveni added, "If Korea can realize developments of such a magnitude, why can't Uganda do the same? Whether or not a Third World country makes success of a self-reliant development strategy depends on the leadership and the political line taken by that leadership."[51] North Korea's version of socialist modernity continued to impress Third World leaders in the late 1980s.

In his speech, Museveni also called South Korea "an imperialist puppet state," which infuriated the ROK embassy in Uganda. The British High Commission in Kampala said that Museveni's speech signaled "his desperate need for arms and ammunition at almost any price and his continued inability to comprehend the interaction of foreign policy statements on his relations with other countries from whom he seeks aid."[52] As wily provocateurs, Pyongyang used Third World leaders that were largely ignorant of the Korean peninsula's complexities to their advantage and pressed them to criticize the South Korean government publicly.

In exchange for Museveni's rhetorical support of the DPRK, the Kim family regime sold him antiaircraft guns, SA-7 Grail Manpads, truck-mounted multiple rocket launchers, armored personnel carriers, and ammunition in 1987.[53] Museveni would use these weapons against remnants of the UNLA, the military that the North Koreans had once trained and supported. North Korea would also send military trainers to Uganda to train Museveni's first tank crew and Special Forces. Amid criticism that Ugandan police officers continued to receive military training from North Koreans despite UN sanctions, Museveni said in 2014, "I thank the government of the Democratic People's Republic of Korea. They always give us technical support. There are people who are not happy with them, but I have not seen any problem with them."[54] As a dictator of a developing country, Museveni most likely appreciated the cheap price tag of the North Korean trainers and the brutal tactics and absolute loyalty to the ruling party that they taught to his police force.

With Kim Jong Il effectively in charge of the KWP's daily operations, he took North Korean foreign policy on a more opportunistic, economically motivated path in the 1980s. If a country was willing to pay the North Korean government for arms or military training, Pyongyang would appease its clients regardless of their past loyalties or political ideologies. The hard-currency-starved Kim family regime could no longer afford to be selective when choosing its partners abroad. According to a 1985 declassified CIA report, North Korea's hard currency debt was US$1.3 billion in mid-1984, and the Japanese government was the largest holder of this debt, with around US$240 million outstanding.[55] The North Korean government naturally gravitated towards allying themselves more closely with African strongmen, such as Mugabe, Mengistu, and Museveni. In Cold War–era Africa, where ruling governments could literally change overnight, this lack of ideological attachment paid dividends for Pyongyang.

The Royal and the Revolutionary

While Kim Il Sung's closest international friendships tended to be with Third World leaders with similar revolutionary experiences, the exception was the North Korean leader's brotherly bond with Cambodia's prince Norodom Sihanouk. After being ousted as leader of Cambodia by pro-U.S. generals in 1970, Sihanouk found refuge in North Korea and found it to be surprisingly modern. In 1971, Sihanouk gave a speech at a banquet in Pyongyang in which he said the DPRK was "one of the rare countries of Asia which has succeeded in completely breaking away from 'under-development' for her attainment of the standard of development of the European countries."[56] Kim built Sihanouk his own personal mansion on the outskirts of Pyongyang in 1974 and gave the Cambodian royal a set of luxury cars and his own personal staff. Nonetheless, from 1976 to 1979, Sihanouk returned to Cambodia and was subsequently placed under house arrest by the Khmer Rouge.

In order to give the Khmer Rouge legitimacy as the rightful rulers of "Angkor," Pol Pot used Sihanouk as the public face of his regime in order to push its dystopian program of radical agrarian reform that aimed to restore Cambodia to "Year Zero." Instead of achieving an agrarian paradise, the Khmer Rouge killed nearly a quarter of Cambodia's population in less than four years.[57] North Korea did its part to aid the Khmer Rouge's genocidal terror, as it was the second largest exporter to Democratic Kampuchea (the official name of Cambodia during the Khmer Rouge's reign) behind China and helped Pol Pot's regime build dams and irrigation projects.[58] Pol

Pot visited the DPRK in October 1977 and highlighted his brotherly and revolutionary friendship with Kim Il Sung during his speech in Pyongyang. Meanwhile, Kim Il Sung "emphasized that safeguarding the revolutionary gains of Democratic Kampuchea is 'a holy international duty.'"[59] At political meetings in Cambodia, the Khmer Rouge's revolution was approvingly compared to Kim Il Sung's brand of radical social change.[60]

After Vietnam's invasion of Cambodia in late 1978, Sihanouk served as leader of Cambodia's government-in-exile. North Korea backed up its support of Sihanouk with material aid to his countrymen. During its war with Vietnam, Pyongyang supplied the Khmer Rouge with military aid. According to an August 1978 Polish intelligence report, the North Korean government gave Cambodian armed forces two to three aircraft, arms, uniforms, and food.[61] During this tumultuous period in Cambodia, Sihanouk stayed in North Korea for months at a time and formed a close friendship with Kim Il Sung. Having spent so much time in North Korea, Sihanouk wrote a book on the country in 1983. In the foreword, he wrote that Kim's "frank and generous hospitality allowed me to take my mind off the affairs of my country and see the numerous achievements of construction which made the DPRK one of the most advanced countries in the world."[62] Later, in his 2005 memoir, Sihanouk described Kim as "my surest and most sincere friend and the most steadfast in my support. Even more than a friend: a true brother and my only 'true relative' after the death of my mother."[63]

North Korean literature even mentioned this unlikely friendship between a Communist revolutionary and a feudal monarchist. In a 1998 *Choson Munhak* fictional short story, Kim Il Sung tells U.S. president Jimmy Carter the story of his friendship with the "feudal monarchist ruler" Sihanouk. Kim tells Carter, "Even though he (Sihanouk) came to me as an exile, he believed in me like a brother and that deeply moved me. To me, that displayed an everlasting friendship and faith that was more valuable than any amount of money."[64] The moral of this story was that if a feudal leader such as Sihanouk could become close friends with Kim, Carter could as well.

In the mid-1980s, Kim Il Sung gave Sihanouk around twenty-five North Korean bodyguards for his personal protection. Sihanouk brought these bodyguards back to Cambodia, where they earned a reputation for being brutal and unapproachable. A resident journalist in Cambodia said the North Korean bodyguards are "animals" and deliberately stepped on his toes. In addition, the journalist said the North Koreans could speak only two words of English: "Speak no, no speak."[65] Sihanouk told Cambodian reporters in 1994 that he preferred keeping his North Korean bodyguards rather than an all-Khmer royal guard. Sihanouk said, "I absolutely refuse to have a royal guard because according to my own past experience and what I have observed in Africa and South America, they [leaders] are deposed by their commander in chief, their presidential guards or royal guards." Sihanouk added, "I am better protected by twenty-five North Koreans from the Democratic [People's] Republic of Korea."[66] Sihanouk valued the North Koreans' discipline and loyalty, which was a defining feature of Kim Il Sung's absolute autocracy.

This unlikely friendship between a royal and a revolutionary was not based on realpolitik or similar historical experiences. The two charismatic leaders seemingly formed a genuine friendship built on mutual trust, admiration, and love for extravagance. The megalomaniac personalities of the two and their penchant for luxurious lifestyles also naturally attracted the two figures. In a February 21, 1980, conversation with the U.S. assistant secretary of state Richard Holbrooke, Sihanouk said that Kim Il Sung "does not want any war. . . . [as] he has built schools, hospitals, cultural centers, and other facilities for his people and youth. This shows he does not want war." Sihanouk continued, "For himself he has built beautiful palaces in the mountains and at sea resorts. He has many luxury houses. He likes expensive cars, Mercedes, Lincolns. I think that since he likes luxuries so much he will not wage war." Sihanouk described Kim, Tito, and Ceauşescu as "imperial Communist" heads of state as "they are very imperialistic; very luxurious; they do not want war. They would lose their imperial style of life."[67] Sihanouk described Kim Il Sung as a lover of modern luxuries, which was a far cry from other Third World leaders who saw Kim Il Sung as a rugged ex-guerilla fighter. This juxtaposition of Kim Il Sung as a luxury-loving modernist and a militant revolutionary highlights the multiple ways in which the North Korean leader was perceived in the Third World.

Sihanouk and Kim's friendship illuminates the importance of Kim Il Sung's personality in shaping North Korea's foreign policy during the Cold War era. Unlike his son Kim Jong Il, Kim Il Sung was a charismatic leader who traveled abroad frequently and naturally bonded with foreign leaders, regardless of their political ideologies. Kim Il Sung's brand of charismatic diplomacy helped North Korea form alliances with nonaligned Third World governments such as Cambodia's.

North Korea on Soviet Imperialism

Pyongyang's anti-imperialism did not extend to criticizing Soviet "non-colonial colonialism."[68] This deviated sharply from China, which labeled the Soviets "social imperialists." When Soviet military forces invaded Afghanistan in 1979, North Korea supported the Soviet occupiers and its puppet government, the Democratic Republic of Afghanistan (DRA). On August 19, 1980, acting as if the Soviets had not invaded the previous year, Kim Il Sung sent a congratulatory message in the *Rodong Sinmun* to Soviet-installed Afghan president Babrak Karmal, celebrating Afghanistan's independence day.[69] The Hungarian embassy in Pakistan reported in September 1980 that the DPRK government officially wished to "stay neutral in the Afghan question."[70]

A year later, the *Rodong Sinmun* reported that a DRA government delegation and representatives from the DRA's youth organization visited North Korea.[71] No negative words were spoken in official North Korean rhetoric regarding Soviet intervention in Afghanistan as the two sides predictably condemned U.S. imperialism, their convenient scapegoat. Despite officially promoting noninterventionism in its propaganda, North Korea's anti-imperialism in reality was highly selective and pragmatic. North Korea's anti-imperialist vitriol was primarily directed at Japanese or Western countries, chiefly the United States. The DPRK leadership could not afford to directly offend its Soviet patrons on most occasions. Thus, there were limits to North Korea's autonomous anti-colonialism.

In 1982 during a trip to Pyongyang, the North Korean leadership told Pakistani president Muhammad Zia-ul-Haq that it did not appreciate his anti-Soviet stance on Afghanistan. According to the Hungarian embassy in Pakistan, "They let President Zia know that good and close cooperation had been established between Afghanistan and the DPRK. [North] Korea highly appreciates the Afghan standpoint on the issue of South Korea." The Hungarian report added, "The DPRK would like to prevent the elevation of the level of the South Korean consulate-general in Islamabad [to the ambassadorial level]."[72] Thus, Pyongyang's decision to not criticize Soviet intervention or the DRA puppet government was extremely pragmatic and based on both international and inter-Korean conditions.

During the entire course of the Soviet-Afghan War, Pyongyang closely aligned itself with Moscow's position. When Mikhail Gorbachev announced plans to withdraw Soviet troops from Afghanistan in 1988, the *Rodong Sinmun* translated the Soviet leader's statement. A February 10, 1988, article in the *Rodong Sinmun* said, "Seeking to facilitate a rapid and successful conclusion of the Geneva talks between Afghanistan and Pakistan, the Government of the Soviet Union and the Republic of Afghanistan have agreed to set an exact date for beginning the withdrawal of Soviet troops—May 15, 1988—and to complete their withdrawal within ten months." The article added that Gorbachev "assured that the more rapidly peace gains ground in Afghanistan, the simpler it will be for Soviet troops to withdraw."[73] While North Korea's Third World policy was independently minded, it never strayed too far or defiantly from the Soviet line. The shrewd leadership in Pyongyang knew just how far it could push its anti-imperialist rhetoric.

The Declining Utility of the NAM and the Embarrassment of the Seoul Olympics

As early as 1979, members of the Non-Aligned Movement (NAM) started to complain that the DPRK government aggressively used the NAM as a forum for its sole political goals. Amid DPRK's support of the Pol Pot regime, the Vietnamese ambassador to Hungary complained in June 1979 that North Korea "does its best to isolate Vietnam and, if possible, achieve its expulsion from the Non-Aligned Movement."[74] In 1982, Vietnam warned, "Now the DPRK has launched a campaign to obtain the position of vice-chair in the [Non-Aligned] Movement as a representative of the Asian continent, after the summit to be held in New Delhi. Vietnam is of the opinion that if the Koreans [manage to obtain] this position, they will start undermining the Non-Aligned Movement from within, and this will endanger the unity of the movement."[75] At a 1983 NAM Conference for ministers of education and culture, which was held in Pyongyang, the North Koreans "forcefully pressured the guests to place the adulation of the 'all-encompassing wise leadership' of Comrades Kim Il Sung and Kim Jong Il, and the acceptance of the 'international applicability of the Juche [idea],' in the focus of their presentations and utterances." In the mid-1980s, North Korea's overly aggressive use of the NAM for its own political objectives irritated other members, which amplified the increasing isolation of the Kim family regime in the Third World.

Pyongyang primarily used the NAM as a way to undermine South Korean influence. The DPRK could not contend with the ROK's rising international status during the 1980s, as Seoul would host the 1986 Asian Games and 1988 Olympic Games. Nonetheless, the Kim family regime desperately lobbied to host NAM conferences in Pyongyang. The North Korean government lobbied unsuccessfully to host the Seventh and Eighth NAM summits of 1983 and 1986. Thus, Pyongyang resorted to hosting minor NAM conferences, such as a 1981 symposium of NAM countries on increasing food and agricultural production, the 1983 NAM Conference for Ministers of Education and Culture, and the 1987 Extraordinary Ministerial Conference of the NAM on South-South cooperation. At the 1987 NAM Extraordinary Ministerial Conference, Kim Il Sung gave a speech in which he said, "South-South cooperation is, in essence, an international movement of the peoples of the politically independent developing countries to win their economic emancipation and sovereignty."[76]

Privately, Kim Il Sung grew increasingly irritated with the NAM during the mid-1980s. In 1984, he told East German leader Honecker, "We had been members of the movement of nonaligned nations since 1975; most recently we no longer belong to the movement. . . . The movement set forth good solutions but is not in a position to resolve the basic issues."[77] In 1986, Kim Il Sung told Mongolian leader Batmunkh, "Recently the nonaligned movement has not been able to play a great role in international life. Because of the many difficult internal problems of the member states, and problems in relations between them, the unity of the movement has not reached such a [high] level."[78]

As China embraced market reforms and the Soviet Union's economy became increasingly stagnant in the 1980s, the seeds of capitalism started to creep into the

Third World. Thus, the NAM had decreasing utility as a viable international economic order. Kim Il Sung even admitted that some small market reforms might need to be tolerated in the Third World. He told Honecker in 1984, "[Third World] countries cannot be industrialized by cooperation within the nonaligned pact. The best solution for them would be close ties between the socialist market and the market of the developing lands. We must all think carefully about this. We also oppose the efforts of capitalism in the Third World."[79]

In the mid-1980s, the North Korean government began seeking ways to foment South-South economic cooperation outside the NAM framework. In 1986, the DPRK's foreign minister Kim Yong-nam visited Bulgaria and proposed organizing a large economic cooperation conference among heads of state from nearly fifty developing countries in the Third World and a select group of Eastern bloc countries, such as Bulgaria, East Germany, and Romania. According to a report from the Bulgarian Foreign Ministry on Kim Yong-nam's visit, the participation of these four Communist countries in this conference could "help to reduce the influence of the West in Africa and other regions, to oppose the machinations of imperialism and the South Korean regime, and to combine socialist countries' export opportunities with the market in developing countries." The report added, "DPRK is making efforts to stay active in the international arena; taking advantage of the interest of many developing countries [in] this conference and the slow ineffective mechanism of the Movement of Non-Aligned countries." The report continued, "Taking into account its own long-term economic and ideological interests in 'the third world,' specifically in Africa, DPRK is actively working to implement this initiative."[80] Despite the NAM's diminishing influence as an international body for developing countries, the North Korean government still considered the Third World an area of opportunity, both economically and ideologically.

As Kim's faith in the utility of the NAM as an anti-ROK political vehicle and as a powerful revolutionary force declined during the mid-1980s, the North Korean government focused on undermining South Korea's hosting of the 1988 Olympic Games. Seoul's successful bid to host the 1988 Olympics greatly embarrassed the DPRK. In response, Pyongyang proposed cohosting the Olympics with Seoul. Hwang Jang Yop, then the secretary of the Korean Workers' Party Central Committee, sent a letter to his Bulgarian comrades stating that the DPRK leaders "were not for canceling the 24th Olympics, [but] they wanted better organization." The letter said, "The Korean Workers' Party was against the vile intentions of the enemies who were trying to organize the Games in one of the two parts of a divided country, to abuse the Olympic movement, and to use it as an anti-communist and anti-socialist tool."[81] South Korea and the International Olympic Committee (IOC) declined this proposal to hold the games in both Koreas. Thus, the DPRK carried out an extremely active campaign calling for the boycott of the Olympics.

As most countries in the Eastern bloc, including the USSR, pledged to participate in the Seoul Olympics, the DPRK looked for allies in the Third World to follow its call for a boycott unless the games were cohosted by the two Koreas. Cuban leader Fidel Castro, a long-time friend of the Kim family regime, answered the DPRK's call and wrote a letter in 1984 to the president of the IOC in which he said, "With respect to the aforesaid, we estimate that when the XXIV Games were granted to Seoul, the best host was not chosen." Castro continued, "The South is practically occupied by troops and [military] bases of the United States. Its local government is not a precise example of respect of the liberties and the social and human rights of its people."[82]

Nicaragua, a close ally of Cuba, followed Castro's lead and also pledged to not participate in the 1988 Seoul Olympics unless it was cohosted between the two Koreas. On February 22, 1986, the *Pyongyang Times* reprinted Fidel Castro's report at the Cuban Communist Party's Third Congress, in which he said, "When the problem of cohosting the Olympic Games in the north and south of Korea is solved, Cuba will participate in it."[83] The *Pyongyang Times* also reprinted Nicaraguan president Daniel Ortega's message that "Nicaragua would not participate in the 24th Olympiad, if the DPRK's proposal for co-sponsorship was not realized."[84] During his first ever visit to the DPRK in March 1986, Castro renewed his pledge to not allow Cuban athletes to participate in the 1988 Seoul Olympics unless Pyongyang and Seoul shared the Games.[85] In addition to Cuba and Nicaragua, the leftist governments of Albania, Ethiopia, Madagascar, and the Seychelles joined the DPRK's boycott.[86]

As South Korea's reputation improved abroad during the mid-1980s, North Korean propaganda increasingly focused on the U.S. military presence in the ROK. An article in the February 10, 1988, issue of the *Rodong Sinmun* said, "The miserable schemes of the U.S. imperialists and its military officers who are trying to exploit the 24th Olympic Games for war purposes are becoming increasingly resisted" and added, "The U.S. invaders must remove their troops and withdraw all their military forces, including its nuclear weapons, from South Korea."[87]

North Korean propaganda also highlighted South Korean transgressions in the Third World. For example, in December 1984, the South Korean captain of the Panamanian cargo ship *Ange Atlantique* allegedly threw several African crewmembers overboard during an argument. North Korean propagandists used this incident as proof that South Korea was an enemy of the Third World. North Korea's state-run media said, "This murder shows that the South Korean puppets are expanding their human butchery even in newly emerging countries including those in Africa, not content with slaughtering their fellow countrymen with bayonets placed in their hands by the U.S. imperialists."[88] The Korea Central News Agency (KCNA) said that this incident shows that "the South Korean puppet clique can never become 'friends' of newly free Third World countries."[89] North Korean friendship societies in Africa also commented on the incident and added further hyperbolic comments in the North Korean state-run media. The spokesman for the Korea-Benin Friendship Society said, "This reminds us of the barbaric act committed by the medieval slave merchants against black African slaves." In addition, the Korea–Sierra Leone Friendship Society spokesman said, "It is ridiculous for [South Korea] to talk about 'friendship' and 'cooperation' with the Third World countries."[90]

South Korean fishermen illegally venturing into the territorial waters of African nations also grabbed the attention of North Korean propagandists. On October 20, 1984, Angolan authorities seized a South Korean boat illegally fishing off its coast. The KCNA said that this incident showed that the South Koreans "cry for 'promotion of relations' with the Third World but play dirty tricks on them to disguise themselves as their 'friends." The KCNA concluded, "The world's progressive people and the Third World people will never tolerate the [South Korean] puppets' shameless sophism and fraud."[91] The Central Committee of the Red Cross Society of the DPRK added, "The South Korean rulers humiliate and insult black Africans at will and do not treat them as human." The North Korean Red Cross continued, "This is why the pelagic fishing boats of South Korea wantonly intrude into the coastal waters of African countries and catch fish there, continuously violating their sovereignty, law, and order."[92]

Prior to the ROK's hosting of the 1988 Olympics, the DPRK's state-run media portrayed South Korea as a disease-ridden U.S. colony and the DPRK as clean and pure. North Korean propaganda claimed that U.S. soldiers initially brought the AIDS virus to ROK brothels and then spread it all over South Korea. According to a March 8, 1986, *Pyongyang Times* article, some South Korean construction workers contracted AIDS in the ROK and then spread the disease when they worked abroad in the Middle East. The *Pyongyang Times* said, "Last January, the authorities of Saudi Arabia went so far as to demand of the South Korean puppet authorities that a confirmation note on immunity from AIDS should be added to the entrance visa of South Koreans."[93] Meanwhile, the DPRK boasted that it was completely free from AIDS. Chang Byong Chol, the vice director of the DPRK's state hygienic inspection office, boasted in a 1992 *Korea Today* interview that North Korea's Ministry of Public Health conducted medical checkups of 50,000 North Korean officials who had traveled abroad from early 1986 to late 1991 and could not find a single case of AIDS. Chang added that a World Health Organization advisor conducted AIDS tests in 1989 on North Korean agricultural workers returning from Africa and found no positive results. Chang concluded, "Our socialist society has no room for immorality and depravity, unlike in the capitalist countries where money is everything and violates human ethics and morality."[94]

As North Korea's calls for a worldwide boycott of the 1988 Seoul Olympics failed, the Kim family regime looked for new and more violent ways to destabilize South Korea prior to the start of the games. Utilizing the DPRK's extensive international network of highly trained spies, Kim Jong Il personally ordered the bombing of a South Korean airliner in order to discourage countries from sending their athletes to the 1988 Seoul Olympics. On November 28, 1987, two North Korean agents, Kim Hyŏn-hŭi and Kim Seung Il, boarded Korean Air Flight 858 at Baghdad's international airport, which was bound for Seoul with layovers in Abu Dhabi and Bangkok. These two North Korean agents planted a bomb on the plane and deplaned at Abu Dhabi Airport. Korean Air Flight 858 blew up over the Andaman Sea in Southeast Asia. All 115 people on board, many of whom were South Korean laborers returning from construction work in Iraq, died in the crash.[95]

North Korea predictably denied any involvement in the crash. The KCNA released a statement on December 5, 1987, stating, "These facts clearly show that there is no elementary material evidence to clarify the cause of the incident of the South Korean air jetliner and it is, therefore, impossible to confirm who is responsible for it." The statement continued, "We can never overlook such anti-national acts of the South Korean puppets as conducting an anti-DPRK smear campaign, groundlessly carping about us."[96] The *People's Korea*, an English language publication of the pro-DPRK General Association of Korean Residents in Japan, stated on January 30, 1988, "The South Korean rulers must frankly admit even now, though belated, that the jetliner incident was their own fake-up, apologize for their insidious reckless attempts to besmirch the external authority of the DPRK through that incident and immediately stop their provocative anti-Communist smear campaign which pushes the situation on the Korean peninsula to a higher pitch of strain."[97]

The DPRK's use of the Third World as a space to carry out this terroristic act against their South Korean rivals echoed the actions of the 1983 Rangoon bombing and confirmed the increasing desperation of the Kim family regime to curb the growing international power of the ROK. Kim Jong Il's more violent nature decentered the inter-Korean conflict as he exported it beyond the geographical borders of the Korean peninsula. On January 20, 1988, in response to North Korea's bombing of KAL flight 858, the U.S. State Department proclaimed that the DPRK's actions "just don't live up to the standards of civilized behavior" and placed Pyongyang on the official U.S. list of state sponsors of terrorism.[98]

Despite the DPRK's violent provocations and subsequent denials, the Seoul 1988 Olympics was a success. In the late 1980s, South Korea's position as a rising economic power and new democracy worsened North Korea's already declining international status, even among socialist allies. After the conclusion of the Olympics, the Bulgarian embassy in Moscow noted, "South Korea is developing as one of the fastest progressing new industrial nations. The participation of a record number of countries, including USSR, China and other socialist countries in the Seoul Olympics, raised the international prestige of South Korea." The embassy's report continued, "North

Korean global prestige decreased to some extent due to the regime in the country, difficulties in economic development, improper behavior and pursue [*sic*] of selfish goals in relations with other countries. Some countries believe that DPRK participated in terrorist acts, etc." The report also criticized Pyongyang for refusing Seoul's offer to start duty-free trade between the two Koreas. The report concluded, "South Korea is far ahead of DPRK not only economically, but also initiating the dialogue for unification."[99]

In order to resurrect its crumbling image abroad and demonstrate its own ability to host a major international event, Pyongyang held the 13th World Festival of Youth and Students (WFYS) from July 1 to 8, 1989. In preparation for the festival, Pyongyang underwent a construction boom and invested heavily in improving its infrastructure. For example, the North Koreans built the massive 150,000-seat May Day stadium and 20,000 flats as the "festival village." DPRK propaganda stressed that the construction work for the WFYS was undertaken under the "wise guidance" of Kim Jong Il.[100]

This gathering of leftist youth from the Eastern bloc, the West, and the Third World was intended to boost the Kim family regime's international prestige. However, it backfired as pro-democracy protests dominated the opening ceremony. Two of the Scandinavian delegations protested the Chinese government's crackdown on pro-democracy demonstrators in Tiananmen Square at the opening ceremony of the festival. Another Scandinavian delegation denounced the DPRK's denial of visas to Amnesty International and unfurled a large banner at the opening ceremony asking, "Where's Amnesty?" After seeing the sign at the event, a North Korean minder asked the Swedish colonel from the Neutral Nations Commission at Panmunjom where the country of "Amnesty" was located. A British diplomat said that a video of the opening ceremony "was taken straight off North Korean TV but there was no attempt to hide or avoid the banners."[101]

Prior to the festival, the Danish Youth Council expressed reservations about North Korea's hosting of the event. In a summary packet found in the European Union archives, the Danish Youth Council explained, "The placement of the 13th WFYS in North Korea meant great political problems for many international and national westernly [*sic*] oriented and western youth organizations." The Danes felt Pyongyang's handling of the event was "far from satisfactory" as DPRK security personnel violently assaulted the Danish and Finnish delegations during the opening ceremonies after they presented banners promoting human rights in North Korea. The North Korean hosts "deliberately harassed" festival events on topics deemed sensitive to the DPRK government. For example, North Koreans harassed a joint solidarity meeting among Scandinavian students that discussed the Tiananmen Square massacre. Around 5,000 North Korean folk dancers loudly showed up outside the meeting room and the

FIGURE 6. Artist name: Ryu Hwan'gi. "Pyongyang Festival—the 13th World Festival of Youth and Students." Source: Leiden University Libraries, digital collection.

drivers who were to have driven other Scandinavian students to the meeting suddenly became sick. In a nod to global anti-colonialism, the North Korean government had also granted visas to participants from Greenland and the Faroe Islands as separate delegations apart from the Danish one. Since the government in Copenhagen claims these territories as their own, this move by the North Koreans naturally irritated the Danish delegation, which protested this arrangement.[102] The festival incidentally publicized the inherent conflict between North Korean political culture and Western sensibilities about human rights and state sovereignty.

At the opening ceremony, Kim Il Sung delivered a speech entitled "Youth and Students, Be Pioneers of the Times."[103] Kim Il Sung's personal friend Robert Mugabe came to Pyongyang to also give an address at the opening ceremony.[104] Touting the slogan, "For Anti-Imperialist Solidarity, Peace, and Friendship," the WFYS included sporting events, cultural exhibits, and activities such as a children's camp, a peace camp, a seminar on youth and student tourism, a forum on the Asian-Pacific region, regional solidarity rallies, and an "anti-imperialist tribunal." According to estimates from international news reports, the festival cost the Kim family regime over $4 billion.[105] According to Kong Dan Oh, Moscow provided Pyongyang with a grant of $33 million to help fund the festival, but upon seeing the lavish construction projects, the Soviets questioned whether the North Korean government was spending these funds wisely.[106]

Naturally, the North Koreans used the WFYS as a platform to push their political agenda and disseminate their propaganda. During the festival, North Koreans took participants on tours of Pyongyang and the countryside. On these tours, participants visited the Juche Tower, a showcase Korean home, Mangyongdae (Kim Il Sung's supposed birthplace), and the West Sea Barrage.[107] The North Koreans also tried to provide literature to participants. For example, the DPRK's Foreign Languages Publishing House translated two popular children's books as "told by the great leader Comrade Kim Il Sung," *A Winged Horse* and *A Tale of Two Generals*, into English for the WFYS. Both books tell the story of Koreans uniting together and successfully repelling aggressive foreign invaders against all odds.[108] The Foreign Languages Publishing House also published an informational booklet entitled "Do You Know about Korea?" in 1989. This booklet included information about the supposed greatness of the Kim family and the sole legitimacy of the DPRK on the Korean peninsula. The book starts with an outlandish propagandistic quote from Kim Il Sung stating, "Our socialist system is a genuinely democratic system which guarantees in practice the political rights and liberties of the workers, peasants and other working people."[109]

After the conclusion of the WFYS, North Korea's state-run media boasted that the event was "a pride of the 20th century." The *Pyongyang Times* published glowing remarks from attendees that the festival was a great success. Jose Antonio Moral

Santin, a Spanish Communist Party official and honorary guest at the WYFS, said, "The Workers' Party of Korea and the Korean people have won a big political victory through the Pyongyang festival." The paper also quoted an unnamed "Peruvian professor and writer who watched the opening ceremony through TV" as saying, "Perfect are the aesthetic sentiments of the Korean people who respect President Kim Il Sung as the sun of mankind." Meanwhile, Ecuador's vice general secretary of the Communist Youth League, who attended the festival, said that he saw "a true socialist society in Korea" and that "Korea today serves as a fine example for those who are aspiring after socialism."[110]

Despite the massive amounts of financial resources devoted to the WFYS by the Kim family regime, the event did not improve the DPRK's image abroad. The festival confirmed the West's idea of North Korea's system as anachronistic. As its largest patron, the Soviet Union, underwent political and economic reforms in the late 1980s, the Kim family regime clung to their cultish leader worship and centrally planned economy. Soviet leader Mikhail Gorbachev admitted in a 1988 Politburo meeting that all socialist countries "need changes" but that some, such as Romania and North Korea, "still do not admit its necessity . . . because their current political leadership does not want to change anything."[111] A year later, Gorbachev told West German chancellor Helmut Kohl that the "family clan[s]" of Romania and the DPRK are "such a primitive phenomenon."[112] The Soviet leadership's growing disdain for North Korea's political system mirrors the wider international community's view of the DPRK in the late 1980s. As global communism changed and later collapsed in the late 1980s and early 1990s, the Kim family gripped their absolute autocracy tighter. According to Pyongyang's worldview, the DPRK's continued persistence in a world of impure capitalism attested to the superiority of their socialist system. As a 2008 North Korean book explains, "Before and after the 1990s the renegades of socialism negated the revolutionary core of Marxist-Leninist theories, denied the class character of the political mode of socialism and advocated pure democracy, causing socialism to crumble in the long run in these countries."[113]

Although the utopian idea of a unified Third World anti-imperialist front came crashing down alongside the collapse of the Eastern bloc in the early 1990s, North Korea still remembers the not-so-distant past when it was a highly active player on the African continent. Amid the Trump administration's diplomatic pressure on African nations to cut ties with Pyongyang, the KCNA released a statement on November 26, 2017, claiming, "The DPRK is a country that has instilled those African countries which were moaning under the oppression of colonial rule by the imperialists with the rays of the Juche idea and rendered disinterested aid and assistance to those countries in their struggle for national liberation and building of [a] new society." The

KCNA continued, "Those African countries cannot harbor any feelings of hostility and grudge against the DPRK."[114] As evidenced by this statement, the DPRK has not forgotten its extensive solidarity with African nations during the Cold War era and believes African nations should continue their diplomatic ties with Pyongyang based on their history of anti-colonial solidarity.

While the rest of the Third World embraced capitalism in the early 1990s, North Korea neither reformed nor opened up. Instead, the North Korean government looked inwards and focused on military development, especially its nuclear weapons program. Many analysts predicted the DPRK would collapse soon after Kim Il Sung's death in 1994. The DPRK persisted, and Kim Jong Il continued the Kim family regime's long-standing tradition of autocracy. Amid natural disasters and economic mismanagement, North Korea suffered through a mass famine in the mid-1990s that killed more than 600,000 people.[115] On the other side of the DMZ, South Korea prospered and grew to be the world's thirteenth most powerful economy.[116]

These two divergent developmental paths affected the two Koreas' policies with African nations. On one hand, South Korea invested considerably in rural development programs and exported its "New Village Movement" model to African nations in the 1990s.[117] Meanwhile, the bankrupt Kim family regime ended most, if not all, of its aid programs in Africa during the 1990s. Instead, the cash-hungry North Korean government participated more widely in illicit activities on the world's largest continent. For example, North Korean diplomats became involved in ivory and rhino horn smuggling.[118] By the early 1990s, North Korea no longer saw itself as a developmental model and internationalist champion of the world's anti-colonial peoples. Instead, it became an ultranationalist monarchy intent on developing nuclear weapons as a means of survival.

Conclusion

IN THE EARLY 1980S, historian Jon Halliday asked Genaro Carnero Checa, a radical Peruvian writer and frequent traveler to the DPRK who published a book on the country in 1977 entitled *Korea: Rice and Steel*, his honest opinion of North Korea. Checa replied, "They fought the North Americans; they have done incredible things in the economy; it's the only Third World country where everyone has good health, good education and good housing." Halliday then asked Checa his view of North Korea as a poet. Checa said, "It is the saddest, most miserable country I've ever been in in my life. As a poet, it strikes bleakness into my heart."[1] Checa's statements reflect what many in the Third World thought of North Korea during the Cold War era.

On one hand, this small nation overcame Japanese imperialism, brought the mighty U.S. military to a standstill in a three-year war, and rapidly rebuilt itself into a modern socialist state. For many struggling peoples in the Third World that recently overcame decades of Western colonialism and imperialism, North Korea's economic recovery and military prowess were justifiably admirable. On the other hand, the oppressiveness and brutality of the North Korean political system undermined the appeal of the DPRK's developmental model to the Third World. The growing inefficiencies of North Korea's economic system also became too obvious to ignore. In fact, Kim Il Sung's Third World diplomacy may have furthered the DPRK's domestic economic troubles. A former member of the North Korean elite, Kang Myong-do, said after his defection to South Korea that "excessive aid to Third World countries had caused an actual worsening of North Korea's already serious economic problems."[2]

This book focused on the North Korean government's Third World policy and its highly active role in Africa, Asia, and Latin America during the Cold War era. While North Korea became increasingly isolated during the mid-1990s, North Korea during the Cold War era was very different as it routinely interacted with revolutionary governments, national liberation movements, and anti-colonial fighters around the world. According to some in the Third World, the DPRK was a model state. This is in stark contrast to the current view of North Korea as stuck in time and a Cold War relic—a modern day anachronism.

As part of its effort to gain recognition as the legitimate Korean state, the Kim family regime sent its people, its ideas, its values, its writings, and its arms to the Third World during the Cold War era. This history of North Korean internationalism gets lost in the West's historical prioritization of the industrialized Global North as the starting point of political, ideological, and cultural diffusion. Pyongyang forged a role in the Third World as a starting point of an alternative socialist system that stressed national autonomy and anti-colonialism. However, with the collapse of the Communist bloc and the DPRK's crumbling economy, the appeal of North Korean–style socialism naturally lost its luster.

The post–Cold War world necessitated a shift in North Korea's ideological orientation. In 1997, an editorial in the *Rodong Sinmun* introduced military-first politics, Songun, as the vanguard ideology of North Korea. The editorial explained, "Never before have the status and role of the People's Army been so extraordinarily elevated as today when it is being led energetically by the Respected and Beloved Comrade Supreme Commander." According to historian B. C. Koh, "The editorial added that in North Korea the People's Army was synonymous with the people, the state, and the party."[3]

As the Kim family regime transitioned to a post–Cold War world, militant nationalism became the dominant national identity of the DPRK. This ideological shift became glaringly obvious in 2009, when all references to communism were removed from the North Korean constitution. Three years later, the North Korean government removed portraits of Marx and Lenin in Pyongyang's Kim Il Sung Square.[4] As North Korea began to underemphasize its Communist legacy, the regime's internationalist commitment to the Third World also lessened. A large part of this more militant nationalistic identity of the North Korean leadership was its increased confidence in its nuclear development program.

Amid North Korea's recent missile tests and nuclear provocations, the U.S. government has encouraged foreign governments, especially those in Africa, Asia, and Latin America, to cut ties with Pyongyang.[5] Thus, the DPRK's few remaining ties with the Third World are more relevant than ever before. However, many of these Third World governments needed no urging from Washington to end diplomatic relations with Pyongyang after North Korea's assassination of Kim Jong Nam, the half brother of Kim Jong Un, in Malaysia's main international airport on February 13, 2017. Like the 1983 Rangoon bombing, the assassination of Kim Jong Nam in nonaligned Malaysia displayed the DPRK leadership's chauvinistic attitude towards Third World nations.

Since the early 1980s, the North Korean government has historically used the Third World as its own personal playground to wage violence against political enemies of the state and to gain hard currency for the regime. In 2016, North Korean hackers stole nearly US$1 billion from the Central Bank of Bangladesh. Exploiting the weaker online security and the outdated financial system of the developing country's central bank, North Korean hackers wreaked major havoc in Southeast Asia with this attack. A 2018 *New York Times* article explained, "North Korean hackers have become especially adept at targeting the weak links in the financial system: banks in developing nations, especially those in Southeast Asia."[6] For all the talk of defending territorial sovereignty in its propaganda, North Korea displayed little regard for the national sovereignty of many Third World governments.

The Third World responded and for the most part turned its back on North Korea. In the summer and fall of 2017, Mexico, Peru, and Kuwait expelled their North Korean ambassadors. The Qatari and Kuwaiti governments also decreased the number of North Korean guest workers working in their countries.[7] Despite the decreasing utility of the NAM after the collapse of the Eastern bloc in the early 1990s, the international body still organizes regular summits. A relic of the Cold War era when a "third way" of economic development and political orientation seemed possible, the NAM is now a movement devoid of any real prestige or power. Nonetheless, North Korea continues to send representatives to NAM summits and participate in this international organization that persists in its commitment to archaism and an outdated world order.

While many Third World governments have decreased or totally cut ties with Pyongyang, relics of North Korean internationalism remain in the developing world. For example, in the downtown center of Mozambique's capital city, Maputo, the U.S. cultural center currently sits at the corner of Kim Il Sung Avenue and Mao Zedong Avenue.[8] The existence of these two commemorative streets highlights how Kim Il Sung once rivaled the global popularity of China's "Great Helmsman."[9] Another relic of North Korean internationalism in the Third World is the Kim Il Sung Park in Syria's capital city of Damascus.[10] While the Western world now focuses on the Kim family regime's nuclear program, some in the Third World memorialize a bygone era when the DPRK was truly the Global Korea.

Notes

Abbreviations

AGN	Archivo General de la Nación, Mexico
AVPRF	Archive of Foreign Policy of the Russian Federation
CREST	CIA Records Research Tool
CWIHP	Cold War International History Project (Wilson Center)
FRUS	*Foreign Relations of the United States*, U.S. State Department
KCNA	Korea Central News Agency
MfAA	German Ministry of Foreign Affairs
MOL	National Archives of Hungary
NARA II	U.S. National Archives and Records Administration II
NKIDP	North Korean International Documentation Program (Wilson Center)
PolA AA	Political Archive of the Federal Foreign Office, Berlin
PRC FMA	Chinese Foreign Ministry Archives
RG	Record Group
RGANI	Russian State Archive of Contemporary History (Rossiiskii gosudarstvennyĭ arkhiv noveisheĭ istorii)
SAPMO-BA	Foundation Archives of the Political Parties and Mass Organizations of the GDR in the Federal Archives (Stiftung Archiv der Parteien und Massenorganisationen der DDR im Bundesarchiv)

SKDA	South Korea (ROK) Diplomatic Archives
UKNA	United Kingdom National Archives
WCDA	Wilson Center Digital Archive

Introduction

1. United Nations Panel of Experts, *Report of the Panel of Experts Established Pursuant to Resolution 1874 (2009)*, S/2017/150. https://digitallibrary.un.org/record/861367/files/S_2017_150-EN.pdf, 44.

2. *Mansudae Overseas Project Group of Companies Promotional Booklet,* 2014, found at University of North Korean Studies Library, Seoul, South Korea.

3. Alfred Sauvy, "Trois mondes, une planète," *L'Observateur*, August 14, 1952.

4. Amitav Acharya and See Seng Tan, eds., *Bandung Revisited: The Legacy of the 1955 Asian-African Conference for International Order* (Singapore: NUS Press, 2008); Naoko Shimazu, "Diplomacy as Theatre: Staging the Bandung Conference of 1955," *Modern Asian Studies* 48, no. 1 (2014), 225–52.

5. Frantz Fanon, *Les damnés de la terre* (Paris: François Maspero éditeur, 1961).

6. Vijay Prashad, *The Darker Nations: A People's History of the Third World* (New York: New Press, 2008).

7. In a 1999 journal article, Bruce Cumings went so far as to state, "I often take North Korea to be the vanguard of the Third World, anti-American rejectionist front." Bruce Cumings, "American Century and the Third World," *Diplomatic History*, 23, no. 2 (January 1999), 357.

8. The founder of the Soviet Union, Vladimir Lenin, defined *socialist internationalism* as "the amalgamation of all nations in the higher unity." See V. I. Lenin, "Critical Remarks on the National Question: 4. 'Cultural-National Autonomy,'" *Prosveshcheniye* (1913), https://www.marxists.org/archive/lenin/works/1913/crnq/4.htm#v20pp72–033.

9. Kim Il Sung, *Reminiscences: With the Century* (Pyongyang: Foreign Languages Publishing House, 1992), 4.

10. For more on the "guerilla state" thesis, see Wada Haruki, *Kim Il Sung gwa Manju Hangil Chŏnjaeng* (Seoul: Changbi, 1992); Adrian Buzo, *The Guerilla Dynasty: Politics and Leadership in North Korea*, 2nd ed. (New York: Routledge, 2018).

11. B. C. Koh, "North Korea and Its Quest for Autonomy," *Pacific Affairs* 38, no. 3/4 (Autumn-Winter 1965–1966), 294.

12. Jiyoung Song, *Human Rights Discourse in North Korea: Post-Colonial, Marxist, and Confucian Perspectives* (New York: Routledge, 2011), 123.

13. "Far East Department, Ministry of Foreign Affairs, 'The Domestic Situation and the Foreign Policy of the Korean People's Democratic Republic,'" March 28, 1969, WCDA, RGANI, fond 5, opis 61, delo 466, listy 71–81, obtained by Sergey Radchenko, trans. Gary Goldberg, https://digitalarchive.wilsoncenter.org/document/134226.

14. Hans J. Morgenthau, *Politics among Nations: The Struggle for Power and Peace* (New York: A. A. Knopf, 1948), 25.

15. Rudiger Frank, "North Korea's Autonomy 1965–2015," *Pacific Affairs* 87, no. 4 (December 2014), 792.

16. For more on China's presence in the Third World during the Cold War era, see Gregg Brazinsky, *Winning the Third World: Sino-American Rivalry during the Cold War* (Chapel Hill: University of North Carolina Press, 2017).

17. Francis Fukuyama, *Identity: The Demand for Dignity and the Politics of Resentment* (New York: Farrar, Straus and Giroux, 2018), 126.

18. Andre Schmid contends that too much scholarship on North Korea takes Kim Il Sung as the starting point. Domestically, that may be true but in terms of foreign policymaking decisions, Kim Il Sung was the central player. Andre Schmid, "Historicizing North Korea: State Socialism, Population Mobility, and Cold War Historiography," *American Historical Review* 123, no. 2 (April 2018), 439–62.

19. Kim Il Sung, *Let Us Intensify the Anti-Imperialist, Anti-U.S. Struggle* (Pyongyang: Foreign Languages Publishing House, 1968), 2.

20. Wada, *Kim Il Sung gwa Manju Hangil Chŏnjaeng*; Buzo, *The Guerilla Dynasty*, 2nd ed.

21. Harrison E. Salisbury, *To Peking and Beyond: A Report on the New Asia* (New York: New York Times Book Company, 1973), 199.

22. Jon Halliday, "North Korean Enigma," *New Left Review* 1, no. 127 (May-June 1981), 18.

23. Andrea Matles Savada, ed., "Economic Assistance," in *North Korea: A Country Study* (Washington, DC: GPO for the Library of Congress, 1993), http://countrystudies.us/north-korea/54.htm.

24. Liudmila Zakharova, "Economic Cooperation between Russia and North Korea: New Goals and New Approaches," *Journal of Eurasian Studies* 7, no. 2 (July 2016), 152.

25. Kim Il Sung, "On Socialist Construction and the South Korean Revolution in the Democratic People's Republic of Korea," April 1965, in Li Yuk-Sa, ed., *JUCHE!: The Speeches and Writings of Kim Il Sung* (New York: Grossman, 1972), 49.

26. Vladimir Ilyich Lenin, "What Is To Be Done?," in *Lenin's Selected Works*, vol. 5 (Moscow: Foreign Languages Publishing House, 1961), first published in March 1902, https://www.marxists.org/archive/lenin/works/1901/witbd/v.htm.

27. Robert Winstanley-Chesters, *Environment, Politics, and Ideology in North Korea: Landscape as Political Project* (Lanham, MD: Lexington Books, 2014), 5.

28. The phrase "speaking Juche" is derived from Stephen Kotkin's phraseology "speaking Bolshevik." For an explanation of "speaking Bolshevik" in Stalinist Russia, see Stephen Kotkin, *Magnetic Mountain: Stalinism as a Civilization* (Berkeley: University of California Press, 1995), 198–237.

29. Julia Lovell, *Maoism: A Global History* (London: Bodley Head, 2019).

30. For more on the Cultural Revolution, see Frank Dikotter, *The Cultural Revolution: A People's History, 1962–1976* (New York: Bloomsbury Publishing, 2016).

31. In July 1966, during the beginning of the Cultural Revolution, Mao Zedong infamously wrote in a letter to his wife, "Everything under heaven is in utter chaos; the situation is excellent." Quoted in Richard Javad Heydarian, "China: The Vanguard of Globalisation," *Al-Jazeera* (December 11, 2016), https://www.aljazeera.com/indepth/opinion/2016/12/china-vanguard-globalisation-161211080423735.html.

32. In calling the DPRK a Third World model of law and order, I do not discount the agency of the North Korean people and the ways in which they sometimes resisted official state mandates. For more on this, see Cheehyung Kim, *Heroes and Toilers: Work as Life in Postwar North Korea, 1953–1961* (New York: Columbia University Press, 2018).

33. For more on the Sovietization of nascent North Korea, see Fyodor Tertitskiy, *Kimilsŏng Ijŏnŭi Puk'an: 1945Nyŏn 8Wŏl 9Il Soryŏn-gun Ch'amjŏnbut'ŏ 10Wŏl 14Il P'yŏngyang Yŏnsŏlkkaji* (Seoul: Hanul Academy, 2018).

34. Stephen Kotkin, "Modern Times: The Soviet Union and the Interwar Conjuncture," *Kritika: Explorations in Russian and Eurasian History* 2, no. 1 (Winter 2001), 160.

35. "Report on Political Development in the DPRK," April 18, 1961, History and Public Policy Program Digital Archive, State Central Archive in Prague, trans. Adolf Kotlik, WCDA, https://digitalarchive.wilsoncenter.org/document/116752.

36. Joan Robinson, "Korean Miracle," *Monthly Review* 16, no. 8 (January 1965), 541.

37. Karrim Essack, *Juche-Korea*, vol. 2 (Dar es Salaam, Tanzania: Thakers Limited, 1983), ix.

38. A 2011 *American Historical Review* roundtable elucidates that modernity should be treated "not as something that spread like a virus from West to East, but rather as a global phenomenon created by the participation and, most importantly, the aspirations of people far and wide." AHR Roundtable, "Historians and the Question of 'Modernity': Introduction," *American Historical Review* 116, no. 3 (2011), 634.

39. "Report from East German Ambassador to North Korea, 'Some Aspects of the Political Line of the Korean Workers' Party after the January Events,'" February 15, 1968, WCDA, Archives of the Ministry of Foreign Affairs, trans. Vojtech Mastny, http://digitalarchive.wilsoncenter.org/document/113196.

40. Jeffrey Byrne, *Mecca of Revolution: Algeria, Decolonization, and the Third World Order* (New York: Oxford University Press, 2016), 9–10.

41. Kim Il Sung, "On Eliminating Dogmatism and Formalism and Establishing Juche in Ideological Work," December 28, 1955, in *Kim Il Sung: Selected Works*, vol. 1, 582–606, https://www.marxists.org/archive/kim-il-sung/1955/12/28.htm.

42. Balazs Szalontai, *Kim Il Sung in the Khrushchev Era: Soviet-DPRK Relations and the Roots of North Korean Despotism, 1953–1964* (Washington, DC: Woodrow Wilson Center Press; Stanford, CA: Stanford University Press, 2006); Zhihua Shen and Yafeng Xia, *A Misunderstood Friendship: Mao Zedong, Kim Il-sung, and Sino–North Korean Relations, 1949–1976* (New York: Columbia University Press, 2018); Zhihua Shen, *Mao, Stalin and the Korean War: Trilateral Communist Relations in the 1950s* (London: Routledge, 2013).

43. There has never been a comprehensive study of North Korea's Third World policy in English or Korean. However, there are a number of relevant scholarly articles on this subject. See Youn-soo Kim, "The Policies of Both Korean Governments towards the Third World 1945–1980: Nonaligned Nations as the Key Actor," *Koreanische Studien* 5 (1980), 32–57; S. Agbi Olu, "Africa and Korean Foreign Relations, 1948–84: A Historical Perspective," *Korean Journal of International Studies* 17, no. 1 (Winter 1985–1986), 37–74; Moe Taylor, "'Only a Disciplined People Can Build a Nation': North Korean Mass Games and Third Worldism in Guyana, 1980–1992," *Asia-Pacific Journal* 13, issue 4, no. 2, January 26, 2015, http://apjjf.org/2015/13/4/Moe-Taylor/4258.html; Moe Taylor, "'One Hand Can't Clap': Guyana and North Korea, 1974–1985," *Journal of Cold War Studies* 17, no. 1 (Winter 2015), 41–63.

44. Ji Hyung Kim, "1980 nyŏndae ch'o nambukhanŭi che3segye oegyogyŏngjaeng : konggae oegyomunsŏ(1979–1981)rŭl chungsimŭro," *Tongbugayŏn'gu* 28, no. 1 (2013), 5–35; Sangsook Lee, "1980nyŏndae ch'o oegyo hwan'gyŏng pyŏnhwawa pukhanŭi aungsan t'erŏ," *Tamnon 201* 19, no. 3 (2016), 83–110; Jean Do, "Pukhanŭi minjokhaebangjŏnjaeng kongsewa chunggugŭi haekpoyuguk pusang, 1962–1966," *Hyŏndaebukhanyŏn'gu* 19, no. 1 (2016), 136–86.

45. Tony Smith's trailblazing article on pericentrism highlights the role that junior actors played in the international system during the Cold War. Tony Smith, "New Bottles for New Wine: A Pericentric Framework for the Study of the Cold War," *Diplomatic History* 24, no. 4 (Fall 2000), 567–59. See also Piero Gleijeses, *Conflicting Missions: Havana, Washington, and Africa, 1959–1976* (Chapel Hill: University of North Carolina Press, 2003); Piero Gleijeses, *Visions of Freedom: Havana, Washington, Pretoria, and the Struggle for Southern Africa, 1976–1991* (Chapel Hill: University of North Carolina Press, 2013); Young-sun Hong, *Cold War Germany, the Third World, and the Global Humanitarian Regime* (New York: Cambridge University Press, 2015); Elidor Mehilli, *From Stalin to Mao: Albania in the Socialist World* (Ithaca, NY: Cornell University Press, 2017); Philip Muehlenbeck, *Czechoslovakia in Africa, 1945–1968* (New York: Palgrave Macmillan, 2016).

46. For two important works on the Sino-Soviet split in the Third World, see Jeremy Friedman, *Shadow Cold War: The Sino-Soviet Competition for the Third World* (Chapel Hill: University of North Carolina Press, 2015); Odd Arne Westad, *The Global Cold War: Third World Interventions and the Making of Our Times* (Cambridge: Cambridge University Press, 2007).

47. C. E Diggins, British Foreign Office, December 18, 1967, folder Cuba—Political Affairs Bilateral Relations with North Korea, Reference FCO 7/555, UKNA.

Chapter 1: Building a Reputation, 1956–1967

1. Bruce Cumings, *The Korean War: A History*, reprint ed. (New York: Penguin Modern Library, 2011).

2. Bruce Cumings, "Korea: Forgotten Nuclear Threats," *Le Monde Diplomatique*, December 2004, https://mondediplo.com/2004/12/08korea.

3. Shen Zhihua and Yafeng Xia, *China and the Post-War Reconstruction of North Korea, 1953–1961*, Wilson Center NKIDP Working Paper no. 4 (May 2012), 7.

4. Andrei Lankov, *From Stalin to Kim Il Sung: The Formation of North Korea, 1945–1960*. New Brunswick, NJ: Rutgers University Press, 2002.

5. In his article on East Germany's relations with SWAPO, Toni Weis said, "Solidarity discourse [with Africa] also became a means for GDR citizens to affirm their support for the political system." Toni Weis, "The Politics Machine: On the Concept of 'Solidarity' in East German Support for SWAPO," *Journal of Southern African Studies* 37, no. 2 (2011), 364.

6. For more on the international reaction to the 1956 Soviet invasion of Hungary, see Johanna Granville, *The First Domino: International Decision Making during the Hungarian Crisis of 1956* (College Station: Texas A&M University Press, 2004).

7. "Ap'ŭrik'aŭi sangawa shingminjuŭijadŭl," *Chollima* 4 (1964), 117.

8. "Chamŭl kkaera shinghal-ri ch'ŏngnyŏndŭriyŏ," *Chollima* 4 (1964), 118.

9. "T'ujaeng ŭi taeryuk—Ap'ŭrik'a," *Chollima* 11 (1963), 138–140.

10. Kyongsik Kim, "T'ujaengŭi pulgil t'aorŭnŭn p'odoaryŏng kinia," *Chollima* 4 (1964), 120.

11. "Chaju charip hanŭn T'anjania," *Chollima* 4 (1967), 122–123.

12. "Ap'ŭrik'aŭi ppullara somalli," *Chollima* 2 (1963), 116.

13. Airgram, from AmEmbassy, Aden, to Dept. of State, Subject: North Korean Activities in Southern Yemen, April 23, 1969, folder POL, KOR N-S AFR, 1/1/67, box 2263, RG 59, Central Foreign Policy Files 1967–1969, Political and Defense, POL KOR N-AFR to POL 31-1 KOR N-US, NARA II.

14. Airgram, from AmEmbassy, Gaborone, to Dept. of State, Subject: North Koreans Press Botswana for Diplomatic Relations and Support in UN, March 15, 1973, folder POL 7, KOR N, 7/17/72, box 2420, RG 59, Subject Numeric Files (SNF) 1970–73, Political and Defense, POL 32-4 KOR to POL 16 KOR N, NARA II.

15. "Journal of Soviet Ambassador to the DPRK A. M. Puzanov, May 16, 1957," WCDA, AVPRF, fond 0102, opis 13, P. 72, delo 5, listy 44–113, trans. Gary Goldberg, http://digitalarchive.wilsoncenter.org/document/115613.

16. "Note about a meeting on 29 November 1957 between Deputy Foreign Minister Pak Seong-cheol with GDR Ambassador Comrade Fischer and Comrade Behrens," December 10, 1957, WCDA, SAPMO-BA, trans. for NKIDP by Bernd Schaefer, http://digitalarchive.wilsoncenter.org/document/110011.

17. "Note about a meeting on 29 November 1957 between Deputy Foreign Minister Pak Seong-cheol with GDR Ambassador Comrade Fischer and Comrade Behrens."

18. "Journal of Soviet Ambassador to the DPRK A. M. Puzanov for March 15, 1958,"

WCDA, AVPRF, fond 0102, opis 14, delo 6, listy 61–70, trans. Gary Goldberg, http://digitalarchive.wilsoncenter.org/document/115973.

19. Airgram from SecState, Washington, to AmEmbassy, Jakarta, Subject: President Rhee's Statement of Support of Indonesia Rebels, March 9, 1962, folder 695.00/3–1361, box 1402, RG 59, Central Decimal File 1960–63, NARA II.

20. "Pak Jun Hi Serves U.S Imperialism in Its Aggression against A-A Nations, " *Pyongyang Times* (June 10, 1965).

21. "A Landmark in Friendship with Indonesia," *Korea Today* no. 32 (1959), 44–46.

22. "A Landmark in Friendship with Indonesia."

23. "Indonesian Art Troupe in Korea," *Korea Today* no. 42 (1959), 43–44.

24. Foreign Service Despatch, from AmEmbassy, Jakarta, to The Department of State, Washington, Subject: Indonesia-North Korea Joint Communique, July 3, 1961, folder 695.00/3–1361, box 1402, RG 59, Central Decimal File 1960–63, NARA II.

25. Airgram, from AmEmbassy, Jakarta, to SecState, Washington, no. A-368, February 6, 1962, folder 695.00/3–1361, box 1402, RG 59, Central Decimal File 1960–63, NARA II.

26. Hong Liu, "Constructing a China Metaphor: Sukarno's Perception of the PRC and Indonesia's Political Transformation," *Journal of Southeast Asian Studies* 28, no. 1 (1997), 28.

27. Ruth T. McVey, "Indonesian Communism and China," in *China in Crisis,* vol. 2: *China's Policies in Asia and America's Alternatives,* ed. Bingdi He, Tang Tsou, and Ping-ti Ho (Chicago: University of Chicago Press, 1968), 376.

28. *Banteng* is the Indonesian word for a wild bull. See D. N. Aidit, *Set Afire the Banteng Spirit! Ever Forward, No Retreat!* (Beijing: Foreign Languages Press, 1964), 8–9.

29. Airgram, from AmConsul, Lahore, to Dept. of State, Subject: North Korean Diplomat in Lahore, April 15, 1968, folder POL, KOR N-PAK, 1/1/1967, box 2263. RG 59, Central Foreign Policy Files 1967–1969, Political and Defense, POL KOR N-AFR to POL 31-1 KOR N-US, NARA II.

30. SJG Cambridge, British Embassy in Jakarta, "North Korean Diplomatic Activity," April 29, 1964, reference FO 371/176058, file 1022, UKNA.

31. "Two Divisions of Korean Volunteers Ready to Crush Malaysia," Antara Report, April 19, 1964, found in reference FO 371/176058, file 1022, UKNA.

32. British Embassy in Jakarta, "North Korean Diplomatic Activity," April 24, 1964, reference FO 371/176058, file 1022, UKNA.

33. British Embassy in Jakarta, "North Korean Diplomatic Activity."

34. British Embassy in Jakarta, "North Korean Diplomatic Activity."

35. "Indoneshia konghwagung suk'arŭno taet'ongnyŏnguŭl yŏllyŏrhi hwanyŏnghanda," *Rodong Sinmun*, November 1, 1964.

36. Jusuf Wanandi, *Shades of Grey: A Political Memoir of Modern Indonesia, 1965–1998* (Singapore: Equinox Publishing), 36.

37. Kim Il Sung, "On Socialist Construction and the South Korean Revolution in the Democratic People's Republic of Korea," lecture at the Ali Academy of Social Sciences of Indonesia, April 14, 1965 (Pyongyang: Foreign Languages Publishing House, 1968).

38. Heonik Kwon and Byung-Ho Chun, *North Korea: Beyond Charismatic Politics* (Plymouth, UK: Rowman & Littlefield), 139.

39. Kim Il Sung, "On Socialist Construction."

40. Kim Jong Il, "Kimilsungia Is an Immortal Flower That Has Bloomed in the Hearts of Mankind in the Era of Independence—Talk to the Senior Officials of the Information Department of the Central Committee of the Workers' Party of Korea," April 6, 2005, published in

Uriminzokkiri, June 20, 2007, https://web.archive.org/web/20110605190740/http://www.uriminzokkiri.com/Newspaper/english/2007/2007-06-20-r2.htm.

41. Kim Jong Il, "Kimilsungia Is an Immortal Flower."

42. J. D. Armstrong, *Revolutionary Diplomacy: Chinese Foreign Policy and the United Front Doctrine* (Berkeley: University of California Press, 1977), 133.

43. Dahlia Gratia Setiyawan, "The Cold War in the City of Heroes: U.S.-Indonesian Relations and Anti-Communist Operations in Surabaya, 1963–1965," PhD diss., UCLA, 2014, 57.

44. John Roosa, *Pretext for Mass Murder: The September 30th Movement and Suharto's Coup d'État in Indonesia* (Madison: University of Wisconsin Press, 2006).

45. "Record of conversation between Kim Il Sung and the Chinese delegation," October 29, 1965, WCDA, PRC FMA 106-01479-08, 85–88, obtained by Shen Zhihua, trans. Jeffrey Wang and Charles Kraus, https://digitalarchive.wilsoncenter.org/document/116553.

46. "Record of conversation between Kim Il Sung and the Chinese delegation."

47. "Record of second conversation of Premier Zhou Enlai and Vice Premier Chen Yi with Foreign Minister Pak Seong-cheol," November 11, 1965, WCDA, PRC FMA 106-01476-06, 70–117, trans. Stephen Mercado, http://digitalarchive.wilsoncenter.org/document/118693.

48. "Information report sent by István Garajszki to Deputy Foreign Minister Erdélyi, 'Hungarian-Korean Solidarity Meeting in Budapest and Salgótarján,' 14 November 1967," November 14, 1967, WCDA, MOL, XIX-J-1-j Korea, 1967, 60. doboz, 249, 003277/1/1967, trans. Balázs Szalontai, http://digitalarchive.wilsoncenter.org/document/116642.

49. "Puk'an—k'uba gwan'gye, 1960–1964," SKDA (1995), roll no. D-0002, file no. 15.

50. "Memorandum of conversation between Vice-Chairman Zhou Enlai, Party Secretary of the Cuban Popular Socialist Party Manuel Luzardo, and Member of National Directory Ernesto Che Guevara," November 21, 1960, WCDA, PRC FMA 204-00098-03, 1–19, trans. Zhang Qian, http://digitalarchive.wilsoncenter.org/document/115154.

51. I. F. Stone, "The Legacy of Che Guevara," *Ramparts*, December 1967, 21; Ernesto Che Guevara, *Guerrilla Warfare* (New York: Monthly Review Press, 1961).

52. "Warm Congratulations to Tenth Anniversary of Victorious Cuban Revolution," *Pyongyang Times*, January 6, 1969.

53. Howard Jones, *Bay of Pigs* (New York: Oxford University Press, 2008).

54. "K'ubae taehan mijeŭi mujang kansŏbŭl chŏjishik'ira," *Rodong Sinmun*, April 19, 1961.

55. "K'uba inminŭn sŭngnirŭl hwakshinhago chogung powiŭi ch'osorŭl kutkŏnhi chik'igo itta," *Rodong Sinmun*, April 19, 1961.

56. "Segyenŭn k'uba inminŭl ch'uk'ahago itta," *Rodong Sinmun*, April 22, 1961.

57. William M. Carey, "How Asian Schoolgirl, Tutored in Espionage, Became Bomber of Jet," *Wall Street Journal*, October 12, 1989.

58. "Record of a conversation with the Soviet Ambassador in the DPRK Comrade V.P. Moskovsky," February 16, 1965, WCDA, Central Committee of the Communist Party of Czechoslovakia, fund 02/1, folder 96/101, 1–26, trans. Adolf Kotlik, http://digitalarchive.wilsoncenter.org/document/114980.

59. "Report, Embassy of Hungary in North Korea to the Hungarian Foreign Ministry," January 8, 1965, WCDA, National Archives of Hungary (MOL), XIX-J-1-j Korea, 1965, 73. doboz, IV-100, 001819/1965, trans. Balázs Szalontai, http://digitalarchive.wilsoncenter.org/document/116488.

60. "Memorandum of a conversation with the USSR Ambassador, c. V. P. Moskovskyi," January 7, 1964, WCDA, State Central Archive in Prague, trans. Adolf Kotlik, http://digitalarchive.wilsoncenter.org/document/116747.

61. "From a 2 June 1967 memo of the Soviet Embassy in the DPRK (1st Secretary V. Nemchinov) about some new factors in Korean-Cuban relations," June 2, 1967, WCDA, AVPRF f. 0102, op. 23, p. 112, d. 24, pp. 53–57, obtained by Sergey Radchenko, trans. Gary Goldberg, http://digitalarchive.wilsoncenter.org/document/116706.

62. "Cuba's Red-Letter Day Feted," *Pyongyang Times*, July 29, 1965.

63. "Report on the incident involving the Cuban ambassador and the delegation of physicians from Cuba while in North Korea," April 2, 1965, WCDA, SAPMO-BA, DY 30, IV A2/20/251, trans. Grace Leonard, http://digitalarchive.wilsoncenter.org/document/112305.

64. "Report on the incident involving the Cuban ambassador."

65. "Report on the incident involving the Cuban ambassador."

66. "Report, Embassy of Hungary in North Korea to the Hungarian Foreign Ministry," March 9, 1967, WCDA, MOL, XIX-J-1-j Korea, 1967, 61. doboz, 1, 002130/1967, obtained by and trans. Balázs Szalontai, http://digitalarchive.wilsoncenter.org/document/114578.

67. "Kŭdaenŭn yŏngwŏnhi sŭngnihal kŏsida," *Rodong Sinmun*, January 1, 1963.

68. "Mijeŭi ch'imgongi swinbŏn, paek pŏn kŏdŭptoedŏrado k'uba inminŭn on'gat ch'imgongŭl chŭksŏgesŏ kyŏkp'ahal kŏsida," *Rodong Sinmun*, January 6, 1963.

69. "Premier Kim Il Sung Answers Questions Put by Cuban Journalists," *Pyongyang Times*, July 15, 1965.

70. "From a 2 June 1967 memo of the Soviet Embassy in the DPRK (1st Secretary V. Nemchinov) about some new factors in Korean-Cuban relations," June 2, 1967, WCDA, AVPRF, f. 0102, op. 23, p. 112, d. 24, pp. 53–57, obtained by Sergey Radchenko, trans. Gary Goldberg, https://digitalarchive.wilsoncenter.org/document/116706.

71. "Report, Hungarian Embassy in Cuba to the Hungarian Foreign Ministry, 25 January 1968," January 25, 1968, WCDA, MOL, XIX-J-1-j Cuba, 1968, 59. doboz, 1, 001121/1968, trans. Balázs Szalontai, https://digitalarchive.wilsoncenter.org/document/116665.

72. "Report, Hungarian Embassy in Cuba to Hungarian Foreign Ministry, 25 January 1968."

73. "Report, Embassy of Hungary in North Korea to the Hungarian Foreign Ministry," March 9, 1967, WCDA, MOL, XIX-J-1-j Korea, 1967, 61. doboz, 1, 002130/1967, obtained by and trans. Balázs Szalontai, http://digitalarchive.wilsoncenter.org/document/114578.

74. Sergey S. Radchenko, *The Soviet Union and the North Korean Seizure of the USS* Pueblo*: Evidence from Russian Archives*, Wilson Center Cold War International History Working Paper no. 47 (2011), 11, 16.

75. "First Secretary of the Soviet Embassy in North Korea, 'Korean-Chinese Relations in the Second Half of 1968,'" January 6, 1969, WCDA, RGANI, fond 5, opis 61, delo 466, listy 1–14, obtained by Sergey Radchenko, trans. Gary Goldberg, https://digitalarchive.wilsoncenter.org/document/134218.

76. "First Secretary of the Soviet Embassy, Korean-Chinese Relations."

77. "First Secretary of the Soviet Embassy, Korean-Chinese Relations."

78. "Report, Embassy of Hungary in Cuba to the Hungarian Foreign Ministry," April 2, 1967, WCDA, MOL, XIX-J-1-j Korea, 1967, 61. doboz, 1, 002397/1967, trans. Balázs Szalontai, http://digitalarchive.wilsoncenter.org/document/116649.

79. "Report from the Hungarian Embassy in Cuba to the Hungarian Foreign Ministry," January 25, 1968, MOL, XIX-J-1-j Cuba, Top Secret Documents, 1968, 59. doboz, 1, 001121/1968, in Balázs Szalontai, "In the Shadow of Vietnam: A New Look at North Korea's Militant Strategy, 1962–1970," *Journal of Cold War Studies* 14, no. 4 (Fall 2012), 133–34.

80. Tuong Vu, *Vietnam's Communist Revolution: The Power and Limits of Ideology* (Cambridge: Cambridge University Press, 2017), 18.

81. Kim Il Sung, "Asia, ap'ŭrik'a, rat'inamerik'a inmindŭrŭi widaehan panjehyŏngmyŏngwiŏbŭn p'ilssŭngbulp'aeida," *Rodong Sinmun*, October 10, 1968.

82. "Ch'e kebaraŭi hyŏngmyŏngjŏngsinŭn yŏngwŏnhi saraissŭlgŏsida," *Rodong Sinmun*, October 8, 1972.

83. "Ch'e kebara t'ansaeng 60tol," *Rodong Sinmun*, June 14, 1988.

84. Georgi D Boulychev, "Moscow and North Korea: The 1961 Treaty and After," in *Russia in the Far East and Pacific Region*, ed. Il Yung Chung and Eunsook Chung (Seoul: Sejong Institute, 1994); Adam Cathcart and Charles Kraus, "Peripheral Influence: The Sinuiju Student Incident of 1945 and the Impact of Soviet Occupation in North Korea," *Journal of Korean Studies* 13, no. 1 (Fall 2008), 1–28; Cathcart and Kraus, "The Bonds of Brotherhood: New Evidence on Sino-North Korean Exchanges, 1950–1954," *Journal of Cold War Studies* 13, no. 3 (Summer 2011), 27–51; Xiaohe Cheng, "The Evolution of the Lips and Teeth Relationship: China-North Korea Relations in the 1960s," in *China and North Korea: International Relations and Comparisons in Northeast Asia*, ed. C. P. Freeman (New York: Palgrave Macmillan, 2015); Chin-wee Chung, "North Korea's Relations with China," in *The Foreign Relations of North Korea: New Perspectives*, ed. Jae Kyu Park, Byung Chul Koh, and Tae-Hwan Kwak (Boulder, CO: Westview Press, 1987); Lankov, *From Stalin to Kim Il Sung*; Jae Kyu Park, "North Korea's Political and Economic Relations with China and the Soviet Union: From 1954 to 1980," *Comparative Strategy* 4, no. 3 (1984), 273–305; Szalontai, *Kim Il Sung in the Khrushchev Era*; Shen Zhihua, *Mao, Stalin and the Korean War;* Shen Zhihua and Yafeng Xia, *China and the Post-War Reconstruction of North Korea, 1953–1961*, Wilson Center NKIDP Working Paper no. 4 (May 2012).

85. "Journal of Soviet Ambassador to the DPRK A.M. Puzanov for 1 August 1957," August 1, 1957, WCDA, AVPRF, fond 0102, opis 13, p. 72, delo 5, listy 165–92, trans. for NKIDP by Gary Goldberg, http://digitalarchive.wilsoncenter.org/document/115641.

86. Szalontai, "In the Shadow of Vietnam," 122–66.

87. "Amid Warm Welcome of Chinese and Vietnamese Friends," *Korea Today* no. 33 (Pyongyang: DPRK Foreign Languages Publishing House, 1959).

88. "Chosŏn inminŭn hyŏngjejŏng wŏllam inminege mugirŭl modŭn p'ohamhan hyŏngt'aeŭi chiwŏnŭl tahal kŏshimyŏ yoch'ŏngi issŭl kyŏngue chiwŏn'gunŭl p'agyŏnhanŭn choch'irŭl ch'wihal kŏshida," *Rodong Sinmun*, March 27, 1965.

89. Jian Chen, *Mao's China and the Cold War* (Chapel Hill: University of North Carolina Press, 2001).

90. Merle Pribbenow, *North Korean Pilots in the Skies over Vietnam*, Wilson Center NKIDP e-Dossier no. 2 (November 2011), https://www.wilsoncenter.org/publication/north-korean-pilots-the-skies-over-vietnam.

91. "Wŏllam inminŭi t'ujaengŭl chŏkkŭng chiji sŏngwŏnhaja!" *Rodong Sinmun*, April 6, 1965.

92. "Chosŏn nyŏsŏngdŭrŭn namp'yŏn'gwa adŭlttaltŭrŭl nambu wŏllam inminŭl chijihanŭn chiwŏn'gunŭro ttŏna ponael kŏshida," April 7, 1965, *Rodong Sinmun.*

93. "Call for Resolute Action: Kim Ok Sun," *Pyongyang Times*, July 29, 1965.

94. Sonia Ryang explains, "An interesting point to note is that a revolutionized female figure is not depicted as a woman as such in North Korea's discourse, but as a mother." Sonia Ryang, "Gender in Oblivion: Women in the Democratic People's Republic of Korea (North Korea)," *Journal of Asian & African Studies* 35, no. 3 (2000), 336.

95. Suzy Kim, "Mothers and Maidens: Gendered Formation of Revolutionary Heroes in North Korea," *Journal of Korean Studies* vol. 19, no. 2 (Fall 2014), 275.

96. "Fighting Vietnam, Heroic People," *Pyongyang Times*, March 17, 1966.

97. "Greetings to South Vietnam Liberation Women's Union," *Pyongyang Times*, March 17, 1966.

98. "On the Development of Situation in DPRK in May 1965: Political Report No. 8 ," May 27, 1965, History and Public Policy Program Digital Archive, State Central Archive, Prague. Translated by Adolf Kotlik. https://digitalarchive.wilsoncenter.org/document/116743.

99. "S. Vietnamese People Are Powerful Enough to Prevail Over U.S Imperialism," *Pyongyang Times*, May 27, 1965.

100. "On the Development of Situation in DPRK in May 1965: Political Report No. 8," May 27, 1965, History and Public Policy Program Digital Archive, State Central Archive, Prague, trans. Adolf Kotlik, https://digitalarchive.wilsoncenter.org/document/116743.

101. "Report about Information on North Korea from 24 June 1965," June 28, 1965, WCDA, SAPMO, trans. Bernd Schaefer, http://digitalarchive.wilsoncenter.org/document/111821.

102. Lê Thanh Nghị, "Report on Meetings with Party Leaders of Eight Socialist Countries," 1965 (8058—"Báo cáo của Phó Thủ tướng Lê Thanh Nghị về việc gặp các đồng chí lãnh đạo của Đảng và Nhà nước 8 nước xã hội chủ nghĩa năm 1965," Phủ Thủ tướng, Vietnam National Archives Center 3, Hanoi), WCDA, obtained by Pierre Asselin, trans. Merle Pribbenow, http://digitalarchive.wilsoncenter.org/document/134601.

103. Report about Information on North Korea from 24 June 1965."

104. Lê Thanh Nghị, "Report on Meetings."

105. "Cable from the Chinese Embassy in North Korea to the Foreign Ministry, 'On the Transportation of North Korea's Material Aid for Vietnam,'" November 2, 1965, WCDA, PRC FMA 109-02845-03, 33, trans. Charles Kraus, http://digitalarchive.wilsoncenter.org/document/118696.

106. "Cable from the Chinese Embassy in North Korea, 'Supplement to the cable of 25 September 1965,'" September 26, 1965, WCDA, PRC FMA 109-02845-01, 4, trans. Charles Kraus, http://digitalarchive.wilsoncenter.org/document/118779.

107. "A 7 May 1967 DVO memo about intergovernmental relations between the DPRK and Romania, the DRV, and Cuba," May 7, 1967, WCDA, AVPRF, f. 0102, op. 23, p. 112, d. 24, pp. 39–42, obtained by Sergey Radchenko, trans. Gary Goldberg, http://digitalarchive.wilsoncenter.org/document/116701.

108. "Record of conversation between the Chinese Ambassador to the Soviet Union Pan Zili and the North Korean Ambassador to the Soviet Union Kim Byeong-jik," March 10, 1965, WCDA, PRC FMA 109-03628-01, 74–83, obtained by Shen Zhihua, trans. Jeffrey Wang and Charles Kraus, https://digitalarchive.wilsoncenter.org/document/116552.

109. "Record of conversation between the Chinese Ambassador to the Soviet Union," March 10, 1965.

110. Telegram, from AmEmbassy, Moscow to SecState, Subject: North Korea, November 14, 1967, folder POL 7, KOR N, 1/1/67, box 2262, RG 59, Central Foreign Policy Files 1967–1969, Political and Defense, POL 7 KOR N to POL 7 KOR N, NARA II.

111. "Letter to Wladyslaw Gomulka from Kim Il Sung," February 3, 1966, WCDA, Modern Records Archives, Warsaw, KC PZPR 2263/175–233, pp. 209–33, trans. Vojtech Mastny, http://digitalarchive.wilsoncenter.org/document/113390.

112. "Chajusŏngŭl onghohaja," *Rodong Sinmun*, August 12, 1966.

113. "Memorandum on the visit of the party and government delegation of the GDR, led by Comrade Prof. Dr. Kurt Hager, with the General Secretary of the KWP and Prime Minister of the DPRK, Comrade Kim Il Sung, on 16 April 1968, 5:00 p.m. until 6:50 p.m.," April 23,

1968, WCDA, MfAA, C 159/75, trans. Karen Riechert, http://digitalarchive.wilsoncenter.org/document/116731.

114. "General Vo Nguyen Giap's decision on North Korea's request to send a number of pilots to fight in Vietnam," September 21, 1966, History and Public Policy Program Digital Archive, excerpt from *The General Staff during the Resistance War against the United States, 1954–1975: Chronology of Events* (*Bien nien su kien BTTM trong KCCM 1954–1975*), official People's Army of Vietnam (PAVN) publication (accessed 30 November 2011 at http://www.vnmilitaryhistory.net/index.php/topic,5366.0.html), obtained by and trans. Merle Pribbenow, https://digitalarchive.wilsoncenter.org/document/113925.

115. "Signing of a protocol agreement for North Korea to send a number of pilots to fight the American Imperialists during the War of Destruction against North Vietnam," September 30, 1966, WCDA, Vietnam Ministry of Defense Central Archives, Central Military Party Committee Collection, file no. 433, obtained by and trans. Merle Pribbenow, http://digitalarchive.wilsoncenter.org/document/113926.

116. Pribbenow, "North Korean Pilots in the Skies over Vietnam."

117. Pribbenow, "North Korean Pilots in the Skies over Vietnam."

118. "Pyongyang's Attitudes towards the Conflict in Vietnam," June 7, 1967, Asie-Océanie, Corée du Nord Période 1956–1967, série 11, Politique étrangère, carton 11-23-1, vol. 4 (3), Politique étrangère: Fichier général—Conflit du Vietnam, French Ministry of Foreign Affairs, housed at National Institute of Korean History, Gwacheon, South Korea, box MU0000540.

119. Pribbenow, "North Korean Pilots in the Skies over Vietnam."

120. "Savingram no. 19, North Korea: Summary of Recent Developments, May 1967," Canadian Dept. of External Affairs, Political Affairs—Policy and Background, Foreign Policy Trends, North Korea, vol. 2, 1966/09 / 14–1969 / 06/31 (file: 20-N KOR-1–3), electronically housed at National Institute of Korean History, Gwacheon, South Korea.

121. "A 7 May 1967 DVO memo about intergovernmental relations between the DPRK and Romania, the DRV, and Cuba," May 7, 1967, WCDA, AVPRF, f. 0102, op. 23, p. 112, d. 24, pp. 39–42, obtained by Sergey Radchenko, trans. Gary Goldberg, https://digitalarchive.wilsoncenter.org/document/116701.

122. "A 7 May 1967 DVO memo."

123. "Pyongyang Students Support Vietnamese People's Struggle," March 17, 1966, *The Pyongyang Times*.

124. "A 7 May 1967 DVO memo."

125. "Record of conversation between Premier Kim and the Chinese friendship delegation," August 20, 1965, History and Public Policy Program Digital Archive, PRC FMA 106-01479-05, 46–51, trans. Charles Kraus, https://digitalarchive.wilsoncenter.org/document/118795.

126. Airgram, from AmEmbassy, Paris to DeptState, Subject: *Le Monde* series of articles on Korea, August 7, 1967, folder POL KOR N 1/1/67, box 2261, RG 59, Central Foreign Policy Files 1967–1969, Political and Defense, POL 32-4 KOR/UN to POL KOR N, NARA II.

127. "Telegram from Pyongyang to Bucharest, no. 76.247," July 6, 1967, WCDA, Romanian Foreign Ministry Archive, obtained by and trans. Eliza Gheorghe, http://digitalarchive.wilsoncenter.org/document/113927.

128. Colonel Nguyễn Văn Minh, ed., *Lịch Sử Kháng Chiến Chống Mỹ Cứu Nước,* Tập V, *Tổng Tiến Công và Nổi Dậy Năm 1968* (*History of the Resistance War against the Americans to Save the Nation, 1954–1975*, vol. 5: *The 1968 General Offensive and Uprisings*) (Hanoi: National Political Publishing House, 2001), 271, trans. Merle Pribbenow, quoted in Merle Pribbenow, "North Korean Psychological Warfare Operations in South Vietnam," Wilson

Center Sources and Methods blog, March 19, 2018, https://www.wilsoncenter.org/blog-post/north-korean-psychological-warfare-operations-south-vietnam.

129. Colonel Nguyen Trong Khue [Nguyễn Trọng Khuê], ed., *Công An Nhân Dân Việt Nam: Lịch Sử Biên Niên (1954–1975)*, Quyển II (*Vietnam's People's Public Security: Chronology of Events [1954–1975]*, vol. 2) (Hanoi: People's Public Security Publishing House, 2000), 288–89, trans. Merle Pribbenow, quoted in Pribbenow, "North Korean Psychological Warfare Operations in South Vietnam."

130. Sin Jae Lee, "Battle between the Two Koreas in Vietnam: An Analysis of Participation in the Vietnam War by the North Korean Psychological Warfare Unit and Propaganda Leaflets," *S/N Korean Humanities* 4, no. 1 (March 2018), 75–97.

131. Telegram from AmEmbassy, Abidjan, to SecState, Subject: None, May 31, 1967, folder POL 7, KOR N, 1/1/67, box 2262, RG 59, Central Foreign Policy Files 1967–1969, Political and Defense, POL 7 KOR N to POL 7 KOR N, NARA II.

132. "Telegram from Pyongyang to Bucharest, top secret, No. 76.040, Regular," February 12, 1968, WCDA, Political Affairs Fond, Telegrams from Pyongyang, top secret, 1968, Archive of the Romanian Ministry of Foreign Affairs, obtained by and trans. Eliza Gheorghe, http://digitalarchive.wilsoncenter.org/document/113955.

133. "Far East Department, Ministry of Foreign Affairs, 'The Domestic Situation and the Foreign Policy of the Korean People's Democratic Republic,'" March 28, 1969, WCDA, RGANI, fond 5, opis 61, delo 466, listy 71–81, obtained by Sergey Radchenko, trans. Gary Goldberg, http://digitalarchive.wilsoncenter.org/document/134226.

134. "Far East Department, Ministry of Foreign Affairs, 'The Domestic Situation.'"

135. "Soviet Embassy in North Korea, Concerning Changes in the Views of the Korean Leadership on Questions of the Unity of the Socialist Camp and the International Communist Movement," June 9, 1969, History and Public Policy Program Digital Archive, RGANI, fond 5, opis 61, delo 462, listy 79–94, obtained by Sergey Radchenko, trans. Gary Goldberg, https://digitalarchive.wilsoncenter.org/document/134242.

Chapter 2: Kimilsungism beyond North Korean Borders, 1968–1971

1. James F. Person, *The 1967 Purge of the Gapsan Faction and Establishment of the Monolithic Ideological System*, NKIDP e-Dossier no. 15 (December 14, 2013), https://www.wilsoncenter.org/publication/the-1967-purge-the-gapsan-faction-and-establishment-the-monolithic-ideological-system.

2. Fyodor Tertitskiy, "1967: Transition to Absolute Autocracy in North Korea," in *Change and Continuity in North Korean Politics*, ed. Adam Cathcart, Robert Winstanley-Chesters, Christopher K. Green (New York: Routledge, 2017), 82–94.

3. Aie-Rie Lee, Hyun-chool Lee, Ji-Yong Lee, and Il-Gi Kim, "The Paradox of North Korea's Ideological Radicalism: Shaky Social Basis of Strengthening Ideological Campaigns," *North Korean Review* vol. 5, no. 1 (Spring 2009), 50.

4. Robert A. Scalapino and Chong-sik Lee, *Communism in Korea* (Berkeley: University of California Press, 1972), 865.

5. Aie-Rie Lee, Hyun-chool Lee, Ji-Yong Lee, and Il-Gi Kim, "The Paradox of North Korea's Ideological Radicalism," 48.

6. "Information about the situation in Korea," February 4, 1968, WCDA, Czech Foreign Ministry Archives, trans. Adolf Kotlik, http://digitalarchive.wilsoncenter.org/document/114572.

7. Muhammad al Missuri, *Kimilsungism: Theory and Practice* (Pyongyang: Foreign Languages Publishing House, 1978), 35–36.

8. Schmid, "Historicizing North Korea," 439–62.

9. "North Korea," p. 52, Canadian Dept. of External Affairs, file no. dossier 20-N.KOR-1–3 C0713, May 16, 1973–December 31, 1976, Political Affairs—Policy and Background, Foreign Policy Trends, North Korea, electronically housed at National Institute of Korean History, Gwacheon, South Korea.

10. "Information about the situation in Korea," February 4, 1968, Czech Foreign Ministry Archives.

11. "North Korean Policy toward the Non-Communist World: Objectives, Results, and Prospects," CIA Office of National Estimates memorandum, December 16, 1971, 9, CIA-RDP85T00875R002000110036–4, CREST system, NARA II.

12. John F. Copper, *China's Foreign Aid and Investment Diplomacy*, vol. 3: *Strategy Beyond Asia and Challenges to the United States and the International Order* (New York: Springer, 2016), 32; "The Trade in Troublemaking," *Time* 97, no. 19 (May 10, 1971), 38.

13. "Revolution as Kim Does It," May 8, 1971, *The Economist*, found in Reference FCO 31/948, folder title: Political Relations between North Korea and Somali Democratic Republic, 1971, UKNA.

14. K. Q. F. Manning, "North Korean Activities in Somalia," June 16, 1971, Reference FCO 31/948, UKNA.

15. Renata Keller, *Mexico's Cold War: Cuba, the United States, and the Legacy of the Mexican Revolution* (New York: Cambridge University Press, 2015), 226–27.

16. "Memorandum from the director for Federal Security, Cap. Luis de la Barreda Moreno," March 1971, History and Public Policy Program Digital Archive, AGN, Instituciones Gubernamentales Siglo XX, Secretaría de Gobernación, Dirección Federal de Seguridad, Movimiento de Acción Revolucionaria version pública, expediente 1/14, fojas 111–114, obtained by Manuel Guerra de Luna, https://digitalarchive.wilsoncenter.org/document/134838.

17. "Press release," March 15, 1971, History and Public Policy Program Digital Archive, AGN, Instituciones Gubernamentales Siglo XX, Secretaría de Gobernación, Dirección de Investigaciones Políticas y Sociales, caja 2471, expediente único, obtained by Manuel Guerra de Luna, trans. Christopher Dunlap, https://digitalarchive.wilsoncenter.org/document/134859.

18. "The Trade in Troublemaking," *Time* 97, no. 19 (May 10, 1971), 38.

19. "Memorandum from the director for federal security, Cap. Luis de la Barreda Moreno," January 27, 1971, History and Public Policy Program Digital Archive, AGN, Instituciones Gubernamentales Siglo XX, Secretaría de Gobernación, Dirección Federal de Seguridad, Movimiento de Acción Revolucionaria versión pública, expediente 1/14, fojas 115–118, obtained by Manuel Guerra de Luna, trans. Christopher Dunlap, https://digitalarchive.wilsoncenter.org/document/134840.

20. "Press release," March 15, 1971.

21. "Memorandum from the director for federal security," January 27, 1971.

22. "Memorandum from federal director of security, Cap. Luís de la Barreda Moreno," February 28, 1971, History and Public Policy Program Digital Archive, AGN, Instituciones Gubernamentales Siglo XX, Secretaría de Gobernación, Dirección Federal de Seguridad, Movimiento de Acción Revolucionaria versión pública, expediente 1/14, fojas 113–132, obtained by Manuel Guerra de Luna, trans. Christopher Dunlap, https://digitalarchive.wilsoncenter.org/document/134856.

23. Keller, *Mexico's Cold War*, 226–27.

24. "Press release," March 15, 1971.

25. CIA Directorate of Intelligence, "North Korean Activities Overseas," August 1984, 5, CIA-RDP85T00310R000200050003–7, CIA Records Search Tool (CREST), NARA II.

26. "Press release from the Office of Los Angeles Mayor Sam Yorty," March 19, 1971,

History and Public Policy Program Digital Archive, AGN, Fondo Presidentes, Archivo Luis Echeverría Álvarez, caja 2196, sin números de fojas, obtained by Manuel Guerra de Luna, https://digitalarchive.wilsoncenter.org/document/134862.

27. "Puk'anŭi mekshik'ojŏngbu chŏnbok ŭmmosagŏn, 1971," SKDA (2002), roll no. D-0009, file no. 30.

28. "Sŭrirangk'a pallansat'ae min puk'an'gwaŭi kwan'gye, 1971," SKDA (2002), roll no. 0-0031, file no. 3.

29. "Ceylon Schools to Stay Closed," *Statesman*, April 17, 1971, found in "Sŭrirangk'a pallansat'ae min puk'an'gwaŭi kwan'gye, 1971."

30. ROK Ministry of Foreign Affairs Press Office, press release, April 16, 1971, found in "Sŭrirangk'a pallansat'ae min puk'an'gwaŭi kwan'gye, 1971."

31. Telegram, from AmEmbassy, Colombo, to AmEmbassy, New Delhi, Subject: North Korean/Sri Lanka relations, July 19, 1972, folder POL 7, KOR N, 7/17/72, box 2420, RG 59, NARA II.

32. Airgram, from AmEmbassy, Port Louis, to Dept. of State, Subject: Mauritanian/North Korean relations, March 23, 1971, folder POL, KOR N-KUW, 3/4/71, box 2422, RG 59, SNF 1970–73, Political and Defense, POL KOR N-KOR S to POL KOR N-Peru, NARA II.

33. Airgram, from AmEmbassy, La Paz, to Dept. of State, Subject: Visit of North Koreans to Bolivia, October 9, 1971, folder POL 7, KOR N, 1/1/71, box 2420, RG 59, SNF 1970–73, Political and Defense, POL 32-4 KOR to POL 16 KOR N, NARA II.

34. Minwoo Lee, "North Korea and Latin America," in *The Foreign Relations of North Korea: New Perspectives,* edited by Jae-Kyu Park, B. C. Koh, Tae-hwan Kwak (Boulder, CO: Westview Press, 1987), 422.

35. Patricia Steinhoff, "Kidnapped Japanese in North Korea: The New Left Connection," *Journal of Japanese Studies* 30, no. 1 (Winter, 2004), 123–42.

36. Ashish Kumar Sen, "U.S. Court Fines N. Korea for Terror Plot," *Washington Times*, July 19, 2010, http://www.washingtontimes.com/news/2010/jul/19/us-court-fines-n-korea-for-terror-plot.

37. al Missuri, *Kimilsungism*, 35.

38. "Information about the situation in Korea," February 4, 1968, WCDA, Czech Foreign Ministry Archives, trans. Adolf Kotlik, https://digitalarchive.wilsoncenter.org/document/114572.

39. Chi-kwan Mark, *The Everyday Cold War: Britain and China, 1950–1972* (Sydney, Australia: Bloomsbury Publishing, 2017); Çağdaş Üngör, "Reaching the Distant Comrade: Chinese Communist Propaganda Abroad (1949–1976)," PhD diss., SUNY Binghamton, 2009.

40. Patryk Babiracki, *Soviet Soft Power in Poland: Culture and the Making of Stalin's New Empire, 1943–1957* (Chapel Hill: University of North Carolina Press, 2015).

41. John Spicer Nichols, "Effects of International Propaganda on U.S-Cuba Relations," in *Communication in Latin America: Journalism, Mass Media, and Society*, ed. Richard R. Cole (Wilmington, DE: Scholarly Resources, 1996), 81.

42. "Hungarian Embassy in the DPRK, Report, 11 March 1982, Subject: North Korean activities in the Non-Aligned Movement," March 11, 1982, WCDA, MOL, XIX-J-1-j Korea, 1982, 80. doboz, 10, 002796/1982, obtained by and trans. Balazs Szalontai, http://digitalarchive.wilsoncenter.org/document/116016.

43. Airgram, from AmEmbassy, Aden, to Dept. of State, Subject: North Korean activities in Southern Yemen, April 23, 1969, folder POL, KOR N- S AFR, 1/1/67, box 2263, RG 59, Central Foreign Policy Files 1967–1969, Political and Defense, POL KOR N-AFR to POL 31-1 KOR N-US, NARA II.

44. From Australian High Commission in Dar es Salaam, Subject: DPRK—Their relations and influence in Tanzania, folder: Tanzania—Relations with North Korea, 1965–72, series number A1838, control symbol 154/11/91, National Archives of Australia Digital Archive, https://recordsearch.naa.gov.au/SearchNRetrieve/Interface/ViewImage.aspx?B=587947.

45. Telegram, from AmEmbassy, Dar es Salaam, to Dept. of State, Subject: Tanzania's relations with Communist countries, November 6, 1973, box 2616, RG 59, SNF 1970–73, NARA II.

46. C. T. Hart, "North Korean Activities in Somalia," May 25, 1971, reference FCO 31/948, folder title: Political Relations between North Korea and Somali Democratic Republic, 1971, UKNA.

47. Jim Bourn, "North Korean Activities in Somalia," May 25, 1971, reference FCO 31/948, folder title: Political Relations between North Korea and Somali Democratic Republic, 1971, UKNA.

48. Telegram, from AmEmbassy, Freetown, to SecState, Subject: None, May 4, 1971, folder POL 7, KOR N, 1/1/71, box 2420, RG 59, SNF 1970–73, Political and Defense, POL 32-4 KOR to POL 16 KOR N, NARA II.

49. Airgram, from AmEmbassy, Lagos, to Dept. of State, Subject: Kim Il Sung in Ibadan press, May 11, 1973, folder POL, KOR N-KUW, 3/4/71, box 2422, RG 59, SNF 1970–73, Political and Defense, POL KOR N-KOR S to POL KOR N-Peru, NARA II.

50. Airgram, from AmEmbassy, Lagos, to Dept. of State, Subject: North Korean activities in Nigeria, April 27, 1972, folder POL 7, KOR N, 1/1/71, box 2420, RG 59, SNF 1970–73, Political and Defense, POL 32-4 KOR to POL 16 KOR N, NARA II.

51. Airgram, from AmEmbassy, Lagos, to Dept. of State, Subject: Kim Il Sung in Ibadan press, May 11, 1973.

52. Airgram, from AmEmbassy, Monrovia, to Dept. of State, Subject: Activities of North Korean delegation, August 24, 1970, folder POL 7, KOR N, 1/1/70, box 2420, RG 59, SNF 1970–73, Political and Defense, POL 32-4 KOR to POL 16 KOR N, NARA II.

53. Airgram, from AmEmbassy, Yaounde, to Dept. of State, Subject: North Korean press insert, June 14, 1972, folder POL 7, KOR N, 1/1/71, box 2420, RG 59, SNF 1970–73, Political and Defense, POL 32-4 KOR to POL 16 KOR N, NARA II.

54. Telegram, from AmEmbassy, Jakarta, to SecState, Subject: DPRK embassy activity, October 14, 1971, folder POL, KOR N, 1/1/70, box 2420b RG 59, SNF 1970–73, Political and Defense, POL 32-4 KOR to POL 16 KOR N, NARA II.

55. Airgram, from AmEmbassy Office, Karachi, to Dept. of State, Subject: PAK-North Korean relations, April 17, 1968, folder POL, KOR N-PAK, 1/1/1967, box 2263, RG 59, Central Foreign Policy Files 1967–1969, Political and Defense, POL KOR N-AFR to POL 31-1 KOR N-US, NARA II.

56. "Puk'an P'ak'isŭt'an Kwan'gye, 1971," SKDA (2002), roll no. D-0009, file no. 34.

57. Airgram, from AmEmbassy, Kathmandu, to Dept. of State, Subject: North Korean propaganda in Nepal, September 18, 1970, folder POL, KOR N-KUW, 3/4/71, box 2422. RG 59, SNF 1970–73, Political and Defense, POL KOR N-KOR S to POL KOR N-Peru, NARA II.

58. Airgram, from AmEmbassy, Kuwait, to Dept. of State, Subject: North Korean activity in Kuwait, March 4, 1971, folder POL, KOR N-KUW, 3/4/71, box 2422, RG 59, SNF 1970–73, Political and Defense, POL KOR N-KOR S to POL KOR N-Peru, NARA II.

59. "Sŭrirangk'a pallansat'ae min puk'an'gwaŭi kwan'gye, 1971," SKDA (2002), roll no. 0-0031, file no. 3.

60. Bradley K. Martin, *Under the Loving Care of the Fatherly Leader* (New York: Thomas Dunne Books, 2004), 138.

61. "Kimilsŏngdongjiŭi hyŏngmyŏng hwaltong nyangnyŏk," *Rodong Sinmun*, October 19, 1973.

62. Suk-Young Kim, *Illusive Utopia: Theater, Film, and Everyday Performance in North Korea* (Ann Arbor: University of Michigan Press, 2010), 162–63.

63. Airgram, from AmEmbassy, Bujumbura, to Dept. of State, Subject: Evaluation of North Korean diplomatic representation in Burundi, February 7, 1970, folder POL, KOR N-A, 1/1/70, box 2421, RG 59, SNF 1970–73, Political and Defense, POL 16 KOR N to POL KOR N-KOR S, NARA II.

64. Aidan Foster-Carter, "Pyongyang Watch: Some of That Old-Time Religion," *Asia Times Online*, December 23, 2000, accessed July 25, 2016, http://www.atimes.com/koreas/BL23Dg02.html.

65. "North Korea Seeks Arab Support for Reunification," April 1973, reference FCO 95/2102, folder title: Middle East and Maghreb Topics, 1973, UKNA. Many thanks to Tycho Van Der Hoog for getting this file for me.

66. Airgram, from AmEmbassy, Rangoon, to Dept. of State, Subject: Arrival of new DPRK consul general in Rangoon, August 24, 1968, folder POL KOR N-AFR 1/1/1967, box 2263, RG 59, Central Foreign Policy Files 1967–1969, Political and Defense, POL KOR N-AFR to POL 31-1 KOR N-US, NARA II.

67. Telegram, from AmEmbassy, Freetown, to SecState, May 4, 1971.

68. Airgram, from AmEmbassy, Kathmandu, to Dept. of State, September 18, 1970.

69. "Puk'an P'ak'isŭt'an Kwan'gye, 1971," SKDA (2002), roll no. D-0009, file no. 34.

70. Martin, *Under the Loving Care of the Fatherly Leader*, 406.

71. Volumes of Kim Il Sung's works can still be found in some Third World libraries. During a research trip to Tanzania in summer 2015, British researcher George Roberts found more than thirty volumes of Kim Il Sung's works in the main library of the ruling party, the Chama Cha Mapinduzi (CCM; Party of the Revolution). George Roberts, personal communication with author, July 6, 2015.

72. "Puk'an-Morisyŏsŭ Kwan'gye, 1973," SKDA (2004), roll no. D-0014, file no. 12.

73. Duncan Money, personal communication, June 7, 2018.

74. Airgram, from AmEmbassy, Manama, to Dept. of State, Subject: North Korean request for support from Bahrain, May 9, 1973, folder POL 32-4, KOR, 5/3/1972, box 2420, RG 59, SNF 1970–73, Political and Defense, POL 32-4 KOR to POL 16 KOR N, NARA II.

75. Airgram, from AmEmbassy, Bamako, to Dept. of State, Subject: Communist propaganda—Happy Birthday Kim Il Sung, May 1, 1968, folder POL, KOR N-LA, 1/1/67, box 2263, RG 59, Central Foreign Policy Files 1967–1969, Political and Defense, POL KOR N-AFR to POL 31-1 KOR N-US, NARA II.

76. Airgram, from AmEmbassy, Dar es Salaam, to Dept. of State, Subject: Tanzania and North Korea, September 11, 1968, folder POL 17-4, KOR N, 1/1/67, box 2262, RG 59, Central Foreign Policy Files 1967–1969, Political and Defense, POL 7 KOR N to POL 7 KOR N, NARA II.

77. Airgram, from AmEmbassy, Bamako, to Dept. of State, May 1, 1968.

78. James Bourn, "North Korean Aid for Somalia," August 1, 1972, reference FCO 31/1271, folder title: Political Relations between North Korea and Somali Democratic Republic, 1972, UKNA.

79. U.S companies purchased roughly eighty percent of Burundi's coffee exports in 1972, which accounted for sixty-five percent of Burundi's foreign exchange earnings. See David Callahan, *Unwinnable Wars: American Power and Ethnic Conflict* (New York: Twentieth Century Fund, 1997), 94.

80. Telegram, From AmEmbassy, Bujumbura to SecState, Subject: None, July 22, 1968. Folder POL KOR N-AFR 1/1/1967. Box 2263. RG 59, Central Foreign Policy Files 1967–1969, Political and Defense, POL KOR N-AFR to POL 31-1 KOR N-US. NARA II.

81. For a fascinating study of the North Korean attack on the USS *Pueblo*, see Mitchell Lerner, *The* Pueblo *Incident: A Spy Ship and the Failure of American Foreign Policy* (Lawrence, KS: University Press of Kansas, 2002).

82. Airgram, from AmEmbassy, Rangoon, to State Dept., August 24, 1968.

83. Telegram, from AmEmbassy, Niamey, to SecState, Subject: North Korea, May 21, 1969, folder POL 7, KOR N, 1/1/69, box 2262, RG 59, Central Foreign Policy Files 1967–1969, Political and Defense, POL 7 KOR N to POL 7 KOR N, NARA II.

84. Telegram, from AmEmbassy, Niamey, to SecState, Subject: North Korea, May 24, 1969, folder POL 7, KOR N, 1/1/69, box 2262, RG 59, Central Foreign Policy Files 1967–1969, Political and Defense, POL 7 KOR N to POL 7 KOR N, NARA II.

85. "Hungarian Embassy in Guinea, Report, 19 May 1978, Subject: Guinean–South Korean relations," May 19, 1978, WCDA, MOL, XIX-J-1-j Guinea, 1978, 59. doboz, 54–1, 003757/1978, trans. Balazs Szalontai, https://digitalarchive.wilsoncenter.org/document/115821.

86. Airgram, from AmEmbassy, Bujumbura, to Dept. of State, Subject: Evaluation of North Korean diplomatic representation in Burundi, February 7, 1970, folder POL, KOR N-A, 1/1/70, box 2421, RG 59, NARA II.

87. C. T. Hart, "North Korean Visit to Tanzania," April 17, 1970, reference FCO 31/692, folder title: Relations between North Korea and Tanzania, 1970, UKNA.

88. Telegram, from AmEmbassy, Khartoum, to SecState, Subject: North Korean delegation visits Khartoum, May 17, 1971, folder POL 7, KOR N, 1/1/71, box 2420, RG 59, SNF 1970–73, Political and Defense, POL 32-4 KOR to POL 16 KOR N, NARA II.

89. "Activities of the Korean Embassy in the GDR among foreign students," July 4, 1979, WCDA, BStU, MfS, HA XX, Nr. 13507, 142–143, obtained by and trans. Thomas Stock, https://digitalarchive.wilsoncenter.org/document/208235.

90. "Great Victories of Korean People Are Brilliant Fruition of Idea of Juche," *Pyongyang Times*, January 6, 1969.

91. Joaquin Molano Campusano, "I Saw Excellent Progress of Korea," *Korea Today* 2, no. 209 (Pyongyang: Foreign Languages Publishing House, 1974), 55.

92. Airgram, from AmEmbassy, Gaborone, to Dept. of State, Subject: Botswana's "good will" mission to North Korea, September 6, 1973, folder POL 7, KOR N, 7/17/72, box 2420, RG 59, SNF 1970–73, Political and Defense, POL 32-4 KOR to POL 16 KOR N, NARA II.

93. Airgram, from AmEmbassy, Nouakchott, to Dept. of State, Subject: North Korean youth delegation visits Mauritania, March 6, 1972, folder POL 12, KOR N, 1/1/70, box 2420. RG 59, SNF 1970–73, Political and Defense, POL 32-4 KOR to POL 16 KOR N, NARA II.

94. Text, from AmEmbassy, Tegucigalpa, to AmEmbassy, Seoul, Subject: Honduran university rector talks with Kim Il Sung, November 30, 1978, NARA AAD, https://aad.archives.gov/aad/createpdf?rid=301064&dt=2694&dl=2009.

95. Telegram, from AmEmbassy, Freetown, to AmEmbassy, Seoul Subject: Sierra Leone visitors to North Korea, September 18, 1970, folder POL KOR N-PERU 1/18/1972, box 2422, RG 59, SNF 1970–73, Political and Defense, POL KOR N-KOR S to POL KOR N-Peru, NARA II.

96. Airgram, from AmEmbassy, Conakry, to Dept. of State, Subject: Activities of North Korean Embassy in Guinea, July 24, 1967, folder POL KOR N-AFR 1/1/1967, box 2263, RG 59, Central Foreign Policy Files 1967–1969, Political and Defense, POL KOR N-AFR to POL 31-1 KOR N-US, NARA II.

97. Airgram, from AmConGen, Hong Kong, to Dept. of State, Subject: Conditions in North Korea, March 28, 1969, folder POL 2, KOR N, 1/1/1967, box 2262, RG 59, Central Foreign Policy Files 1967–1969, Political and Defense, POL 7 KOR N to POL 7 KOR N, NARA II.

98. Telegram, from AmEmbassy, Moscow, to SecState, Subject: Sierra Leonean ambassador visits North Korea, November 9, 1967, folder POL, KOR N- S AFR, 1/1/67, box 2263, RG 59, Central Foreign Policy Files 1967–1969, Political and Defense, POL KOR N-AFR to POL 31-1 KOR N-US, NARA II.

99. Airgram, from AmEmbassy, Dar es Salaam, to Dept. of State, Subject: Tanzanians to observe "Socialist Villages" in North Korea, September 11, 1968, folder POL, KOR N- S AFR, 1/1/67, box 2263, RG 59, Central Foreign Policy Files 1967–1969, Political and Defense, POL KOR N-AFR to POL 31-1 KOR N-US, NARA II.

100. D. G. Barr, "Somalia/North Korea," April 20, 1971, reference FCO 31/948, folder title: Political Relations between North Korea and Somali Democratic Republic, 1971, UKNA.

101. RGANI, fond 5, opis 63, delo 590, listy 71–81, 87–96. Many thanks to Sergey Radchenko for sharing this document with me via email.

102. Airgram, from AmEmbassy, Mogadishu, to Dept. of State, Subject: Joint Somali-North Korean communiqué, March 19, 1972, folder POL 7, KOR N, 1/1/71, box 2420, RG 59, SNF 1970–73, Political and Defense, POL 32-4 KOR to POL 16 KOR N, NARA II.

103. Jim Bourn, "North Korean Activities in Somalia," May 25, 1971, reference FCO 31/948, folder title: Political Relations between North Korea and Somali Democratic Republic, 1971, UKNA.

104. Telegram, from AmEmbassy, Mogadishu, to SecState, Subject: Joint Somali-North Korean communiqué, March 1, 1972, folder POL 7, KOR N, 1/1/71, box 2420, RG 59, SNF 1970–73, Political and Defense, POL 32-4 KOR to POL 16 KOR N, NARA II.

105. P. B. Hall, "North Korean Activities in Somalia," June 29, 1971, reference FCO 31/948, folder title: Political Relations between North Korea and Somali Democratic Republic, 1971, UKNA.

106. "Praise for North Korea," March 25, 1972, reference FCO 31/1271, folder title: Political Relations between North Korea and Somali Democratic Republic, 1972, UKNA.

107. D. G. Barr, "Somalia/North Korea," April 20, 1971.

108. "Answers to the Questions Raised by Abdel Hamid Ahmed Hamrouche, General Manager of Dar-El-Tahrir of the United Arab Republic," July 1, 1969, in *Kim Il Sung Works*, vol. 24, *June-December 1969* (Pyongyang: Foreign Languages Publishing House, 1985), 91.

109. "Aptwi, anp⊠ak esŏ tŭsen t⊠agyŏk ŭl patko innŭn Mije," *Chollima* 11 (1963), 135–37.

110. For more on the Black Panther Party's relationship with North Korea, see Benjamin R. Young, "Juche in the United States: The Black Panther Party's Relations with North Korea, 1969–1971," *Asia-Pacific Journal* 13, issue 12, no. 2 (March 30, 2015), https://apjjf.org/2015/13/12/Benjamin-Young/4303.html.

111. FBI declassified file #100-HQ-447251, section 17. I would like to thank Sean Malloy for sending Cleaver's declassified FBI file to me.

112. Young, "Juche in the United States."

113. Benjamin R. Young, "North Korea's Unlikely History with Black Radicals," *Black Perspectives*, April 11, 2019, https://www.aaihs.org/north-koreas-unlikely-history-with-black-radicals.

114. Eldridge Cleaver, foreword to *JUCHE!: The Speeches and Writings of Kim Il Sung*, ed. Li Yuk-Sa (New York: Grossman Publishers, 1972), xii.

115. Rachel Applebaum, "The Friendship Project: Socialist Internationalism in the Soviet Union and Czechoslovakia in the 1950s and 1960s," *Slavic Review* 74, no. 3 (Fall 2015), 484–507; Maxim Matusevich, *No Easy Row for a Russian Hoe: Ideology and Pragmatism in*

Nigerian-Soviet Relations (Trenton, NJ: Africa World Press, 2003), 79–80, 115, 124; John McNair, "Winning Friends, Influencing People: Soviet Cultural Diplomacy in Australia, 1928–1968," *Australian Journal of Politics and History* 61, no. 4 (November 2015), 515–29.

116. Joshua Eisenman and David Shinn, *China and Africa: A Century of Engagement* (Philadelphia: University of Pennsylvania Press, 2012), 36, 60.

117. Louis Nemzer, "The Soviet Friendship Societies," *Public Opinion Quarterly* 13, no. 2 (Summer 1949), 283.

118. Airgram, from AmConsul, Lahore, to Dept. of State, Subject: North Korean diplomat in Lahore, April 15, 1968, folder POL, KOR N-PAK, 1/1/1967, box 2263, RG 59, Central Foreign Policy Files 1967–1969, Political and Defense, POL KOR N-AFR to POL 31-1 KOR N-US, NARA II.

119. From Office of the High Commission for Canada in Islamabad to Under-Secretary of State for External Affairs, Ottawa, Subject: Pakistan and Korea, March 10, 1970, Canadian Dept. of External Affairs, file no. 20-N KOR-1–3, vol. 3, June 1, 1969–May 15, 1972, Political Affairs—Policy and Background, Foreign Policy Trends, North Korea, electronically housed at National Institute of Korean History, Gwacheon, South Korea.

120. Telegram, from AmEmbassy, Islamabad, to SecState, Subject: Bhutto administration and Korean representation, December 22, 1971, folder POL, KOR N-KUW, 3/4/71, box 2422, RG 59, SNF 1970–73, Political and Defense, POL KOR N-KOR S to POL KOR N-Peru, NARA II.

121. Telegram, from AmEmbassy, Freetown, to SecState, May 4, 1971.

122. "Tanzania-North Korea Relations," September 29, 1970. FCO 95/860, Relations between North Korea and Tanzania 1970, UKNA. I would like to thank George Roberts for sending me documents on DPRK-Tanzania relations.

123. Airgram, from AmEmbassy, Kathmandu, to Dept. of State, Subject: North Korean propaganda in Nepal, September 18, 1970, folder POL, KOR N-KUW, 3/4/71, box 2422, RG 59, SNF 1970–73, Political and Defense, POL KOR N-KOR S to POL KOR N-Peru, NARA II.

124. Telegram, from AmEmbassy, Lagos, to SecState, Subject: ROK Ambassador Moon in Lagos, May 11, 1972, folder POL, KOR N-KUW, 3/4/71, box 2422, RG 59, SNF 1970–73, Political and Defense, POL KOR N-KOR S to POL KOR N-Peru, NARA II.

125. "North Korean Policy toward the Non-Communist World: Objectives, Results, and Prospects," CIA Office of National Estimates memorandum, December 16, 1971, 9.

126. Airgram, from AmEmbassy, Dar es Salaam, to State Dept, Subject: Conversation with Nyerere, September 16, 1970, folder 2315, box 2619, RG 59, SNF 1970–73, NARA II.

127. Airgram, from AmEmbassy, Kathmandu, to StateDept, Subject: Nepalese views on Korea, June 23, 1967, folder POL KOR N-LA 1/1/67, box 2263, RG 59, Central Foreign Policy Files 1967–1969, Political and Defense, POL 32-4 KOR/UN to POL KOR N, NARA II.

128. Airgram, from AmEmbassy to StateDept, Subject: North and South Korean activity in Lebanon, October 8, 1969, folder POL KOR N-LA 1/1/67, box 2263, RG 59, Central Foreign Policy Files 1967–1969, Political and Defense, POL 32-4 KOR/UN to POL KOR N, NARA II.

129. Tariq Ali, "Diary," *London Review of Books* 34, no. 2 (January 26, 2012), 34–35.

130. Joseph Nye, the Harvard political scientist who first coined the term *soft power* in the 1980s, states that a nation's soft power depends primarily on its resources of "culture (in places where it is attractive to others), its political values (when it lives up to them at home and abroad), and its foreign policies (when they are seen as legitimate and having moral authority)." Joseph S. Nye, Jr., "Public Diplomacy and Soft Power," *Annals of the American Academy of Political and Social Science* 616, no. 1, Public Diplomacy in a Changing World (March 2008), 94–109.

Chapter 3: Kim Il Sung's "Korea First" Policy, 1972–1979

1. Jung-en Woo, *Race to the Swift: State and Finance in Korean Industrialization* (New York: Columbia University Press, 1991).

2. "North Korea: Turnaround in Foreign Debt Management and Trade Patterns," February 1, 1985, CIA Directorate of Intelligence, CIA-RDP90T01298R000200160001–5, CREST.

3. Ali Lameda, *A Personal Account of the Experience of a Prisoner of Conscience in the Democratic People's Republic of Korea* (London: Amnesty International, 1979), 13.

4. "Venezuelan Ex-Prisoner Alleges Brutal Treatment in North Korea," *New York Times*, July 2, 1979.

5. Mitchell Lerner, "The Domestic Origins of the Second Korean War: New Evidence from Communist Bloc Archives," *Seoul Journal of Korean Studies* 31, no. 1 (June 2018), 75–98.

6. Lerner, *The* Pueblo *Incident*.

7. Buzo, *The Guerilla Dynasty*, 2nd ed., 81.

8. "Minutes of conversation taken on the occasion of the Romanian-Korean discussions from May 23, 1975," May 23, 1975, WCDA, Romanian National Central Historical Archives, Central Committee of the Romanian Communist Party—External Relations Department, 73/1975, obtained by and trans. Ioana M. Niculescu and Eliza Gheorghe, http://digitalarchive.wilsoncenter.org/document/116128.

9. "Summarized evaluation of Kim Il Sung's visit to the PR China (18 to 26 April 1975)," May 6, 1975, History and Public Policy Program Digital Archive, Political Archive of the Federal Foreign Office, Berlin (PolA AA), MfAA, C 6857, trans. Bernd Schaefer, https://digitalarchive.wilsoncenter.org/document/114125.

10. "Information on the situation in Korea," February 5, 1968, History and Public Policy Program Digital Archive, Archive of the Central Committee of the Communist Party of Czechoslovakia, fund 02/1, folder 68/61, trans. for NKIDP by Adolf Kotlik, http://digitalarchive.wilsoncenter.org/document/116724.

11. Buzo, *The Guerilla Dynasty*, 2nd ed., 81.

12. Wasilewski, "Urgent report regarding the current situation in the DPRK, on the Korean Peninsula," April 29, 1976, WCDA, AMSZ, Department II, 12/79, w. 1, obtained by Marek Hańderek, trans. Jerzy Giebułtowski, https://digitalarchive.wilsoncenter.org/document/208553.

13. Interview with Ambassador Donald P. Gregg, interviewed by Charles Stuart Kennedy, initial interview March 3, 2004, Foreign Affairs Oral History Project of the Association for Diplomatic Studies and Training, Library of Congress, https://cdn.loc.gov/service/mss/mfdip/2010/2010greo2/2010greo2.pdf.

14. Research Department note no. 16/83: North Korean objectives and activities in Sub-Saharan Africa, September 1983, reference FCO 31/3922, folder title: Political Relations between Ethiopia and North Korea, 1983, UKNA.

15. "Interview: Meet Ko Young-hwan, the First Diplomat Who Escaped North Korea," *New Focus International*, August 22, 2014, accessed July 5, 2015, http://newfocusintl.com/ko-young-hwan-unification-preparatory-committee- member/.

16. Telegram, from AmEmbassy, Mogadishu, to SecState, Subject: Somalia's relations with Communist countries, November 15, 1979, AAD, https://aad.archives.gov/aad/createpdf?rid=251510&dt=2776&dl=2169.

17. "Tanzania-North Korea," November 2, 1982, British High Commission, Dar es Salaam, Tanzania, reference FCO 31/3674, folder title: Tanzania-Korea Relations, 1982, UKNA.

18. Research Department note no. 16/8: North Korean objectives and activities in Sub-Saharan Africa, September 1983.

19. Juvénal Habyarimana, "Discours, messages et entretiens de Son Excellence le

général-major Habyarimana Juvénal, president de la République rwandaise," Service des affaires sociales, en collaboration avec l'Office rwandais d'information (1980), 387, 405–9. Many thanks to John Doldo for his help in translating this Rwandan government document.

20. "Telegram 066.793 from the Romanian Embassy in Pyongyang to the Romanian Ministry of Foreign Affairs," July 17, 1978, WCDA, AMAE, folder 784/1978, issue 220: January 7, 1978–September 23, 1978, obtained and trans. Eliza Gheorghe, http://digitalarchive.wilsoncenter.org/document/116497.

21. Telegram, from AmEmbassy, Bujumbura, to SecState, Subject: Relations with Communist countries, November 15, 1979, AAD Digital Archives, NARA, https://aad.archives.gov/aad/createpdf?rid=251156&dt=2776&dl=2169; Telegram, from AmEmbassy Antananarivo, to SecState, Subject: President Ratsiraka to build new presidential palace with North Korean assistance, August 17, 1979, AAD Digital Archives, NARA, https://aad.archives.gov/aad/createpdf?rid=32623&dt=2776&dl=2169.

22. From AmEmbassy, Kigali, to SecState, Subject: President Habyarimana returns from PRC, DPRK, June 20, 1978, AAD Archives, NARA, https://aad.archives.gov/aad/createpdf?rid=162685&dt=2694&dl=2009.

23. From AmEmbassy, Kigali, to SecState, Subject: Relations with Communist countries, November 6, 1979, AAD Archives, NARA, https://aad.archives.gov/aad/createpdf?rid=269924&dt=2776&dl=2169.

24. Telegram, from AmEmbassy, Bamako, to AmEmbassy, Abidjan, Subject: None, December 3, 1968, folder POL, KOR N-LA, 1/1/67, box 2263, RG 59, Central Foreign Policy Files 1967–1969, Political and Defense, POL KOR N-AFR to POL 31-1 KOR N-US, NARA II.

25. Robert Baker, "Vaccinating Mali: Posters, Pamphlets, One Slave, One Vampire Bat," *American Diplomacy: Foreign Service Dispatches and Periodic Reports on U.S Foreign Policy* (April 2013), accessed September 16, 2017, http://www.unc.edu/depts/diplomat/item/2013/0105/fsl/baker_vaccinating.html.

26. Telegram, from AmEmbassy, Bujumbura, to SecState, Subject: Relations with Communist countries, November 15, 1979.

27. "Hungarian Embassy in Guinea, Report, 19 May 1978, Subject: Guinean–South Korean relations," May 19, 1978, WCDA, MOL, XIX-J-1-j Guinea, 1978, 59. doboz, 54–1, 003757/1978, trans. Balazs Szalontai, http://digitalarchive.wilsoncenter.org/document/115821.

28. Interview with Onejoon Che, South Korean filmmaker and artist, who traveled to Gabon in December 2014 to research the history of North and South Korean architectural influence there; Seoul, South Korea, November 1, 2016.

29. "TELEGRAM 047.011 from the Romanian Embassy in Libreville to the Romanian Ministry of Foreign Affairs," January 6, 1978, History and Public Policy Program Digital Archive, AMAE, folder 784/1978, issue 220: Features of political-diplomatic relations between the Democratic People's Republic of Korea and some countries in Europe, Asia, Africa, America (Cyprus, Spain, USA, Bangladesh, Philippines, India, Indonesia, Japan, Pakistan, Sri Lanka, Central African Republic, Egypt, Gabon, Iraq, Iran, Libya, Nigeria, Mozambique, Syria), January 7, 1978–September 23, 1978, obtained and trans. for NKIDP by Eliza Gheorghe, https://digitalarchive.wilsoncenter.org/document/116427.

30. "TELEGRAM 047.011 from the Romanian Embassy in Libreville."

31. "TELEGRAM 047.011 from the Romanian Embassy in Libreville."

32. "Grand Ground-Breaking Ceremony Held for Construction of Matoto Porcelain Factory in Guinea by Aid of DPRK Government," *Pyongyang Times*, March 6, 1971.

33. "Our Construction Service Abroad," *Foreign Trade*, June 1978, 8–10.

34. "Developing Agricultural Science," *Pyongyang Times*, June 10, 1987.

35. *Bukhan beomnyeongjip*, vol. 5 (Seoul: Continental Research Institute, 1990), 26–40, quoted in Christopher Hale, "Multifunctional Juche: A Study of the Changing Dynamic between Juche and the State Constitution in North Korea," *Korea Journal* 42, no. 3 (Autumn 2002), 283–308.

36. Hale, "Multifunctional Juche," 296.

37. Bruce Cumings, *Korea's Place in the Sun: A Modern History* (New York: W.W. Norton, 1997), 414.

38. Kim Il Sung, "On Some Problems of Our Party's Juche Idea and the Government of the Republic's Internal and External Policies: Answers to the Questions Raised by Journalists of the Japanese Newspaper 'Mainichi Shimbun, 1972,'" reprinted in *For the Independent and Peaceful Reunification of Korea* (New York: Guardian, 1976), 118–44.

39. Yokoko Yamba, in *President Kim Il Sung Moves Asia and the World* (Pyongyang, DPRK: Foreign Languages Publishing House, 1976), 66.

40. Thomas Menyassan, in *President Kim Il Sung Moves Asia and the World*, 109.

41. Regina Kessy, personal communication with author, June 27, 2019.

42. Jiyoung Kim, "The Politics of Foreign Aid in North Korea," *Korean Journal of International Studies* 12, no. 2 (December 2014), 425–50.

43. "Note on a meeting in the Embassy of Czechoslovakia on 5 September 1973," September 13, 1973, WCDA, PolA AA, MfAA, C 295/78, obtained by and trans. Bernd Schaefer, https://digitalarchive.wilsoncenter.org/document/116674.

44. "On relations between DPRK and PRC," November 17, 1977, WCDA, Political Archive of the Federal Foreign Office, Berlin, PolA AA, MfAA C 6857, trans. Bernd Schaefer, http://digitalarchive.wilsoncenter.org/document/114128.

45. "Hungarian Embassy in the DPRK, Report, 28 April 1976, Subject: Visit of an Ethiopian government delegation in the DPRK," April 28, 1976, WCDA, MOL, XIX-J-1-j Ethiopia, 1976, 52. doboz, 41–1, 003195/1976, trans. Balazs Szalontai, http://digitalarchive.wilsoncenter.org/document/115818.

46. "Hungarian Embassy in the DPRK, Telegram, 2 June 1976. Subject: Visit of the president of Mali in the DPRK," June 2, 1976, WCDA, MOL, XIX-J-1-j Mali, 1976, 94. doboz, 97–1, 003704/1976, trans. Balazs Szalontai, http://digitalarchive.wilsoncenter.org/document/115819.

47. "Telegram 066.712 from the Romanian Embassy in Pyongyang to the Romanian Ministry of Foreign Affairs," June 3, 1978, WCDA, AMAE, folder 784/1978, issue 220: January 7, 1978–September 23, 1978, obtained by and trans. Eliza Gheorghe, http://digitalarchive.wilsoncenter.org/document/116500.

48. "Record of conversation between N. M. Shubnikov and Janos Lewandowski, the director of the 2nd Department of the Ministry of Foreign Affairs of Poland," August 28, 1969, WCDA, RGANI, fond 5, opis 61, delo 463, listy 206–14, obtained by Sergey Radchenko, trans. Gary Goldberg, https://digitalarchive.wilsoncenter.org/document/134251.

49. Wasilewski, "Urgent report regarding the current situation in the DPRK, on the Korean Peninsula," April 29, 1976.

50. *The International Seminar on the Juche Idea* (Pyongyang, DPRK: Foreign Languages Publishing House), 1977.

51. "We Must Rely on Ourselves," *The Black Panther* 4, no. 13 (February 28, 1970).

52. "Eldridge Cleaver's notes on Korea," September 28, 1969, WCDA, Texas A&M University, Cushing Memorial Library and Archives, Eldridge Cleaver Collection, 1959–1981, obtained by Charles Kraus, https://digitalarchive.wilsoncenter.org/document/114563.

53. "Korean Vice-President Arrives in Dar," *Daily News*, March 12, 1973. Many thanks to George Roberts for sending this excerpt to me.

54. "Speech of President Mobutu Sese Seko at the Pyongyang Mass Rally, December 15, 1974," *Korea Today* 4, no. 223 (Pyongyang, DPRK: Foreign Languages Publishing House, 1975), 15–17.

55. Cammie Ramsaroop, in discussion with Moe Taylor, Georgetown, December 17, 2010, found in Taylor, "One Hand Can't Clap," 48.

56. "Chuch'e Sasang Kukche Seminar, New Delhi, 1979, 4.14–16," SKDA (2015), roll no. 2014-0014, file no. 41.

57. "CIA, KGB and Now JUCHE!," *CURRENT*, May 12, 1979, found in SKDA (2015), roll no. 2014-0014, file no. 41.

58. "[Puk'an] Chuch'e Sasang Seminar, New Delhi (Indo) 1982, 4.9–11," SKDA (2013), roll no. 2012-0029, file no. 9.

59. Swedish State Department telegram, from Swedish Embassy, Pyongyang, to Swedish Ambassador in Beijing, Subject: Jucheideologien—en metmask ifrån Orienten, December 4, 1975, obtained from the Swedish Ministry of Foreign Affairs via email, trans. Benjamin Young.

60. Adrian Buzo, *The Guerilla Dynasty: Politics and Leadership in North Korea* (London: I. B. Tauris, 1999), 265.

61. Karrim Essack, *Juche-Korea*, vol. 2 (Dar es Salaam, Tanzania: Thakers Limited, 1983), viii.

62. Gerry MacLochlainn, *The Irish Republican and Juche Conception of National Self-Dignity Are One and the Same* (London: Mosquito Press, 1985).

63. Luise Rinser, *Nordkoreanisches Reisetagebuch* (A North Korean Travel Diary) (Frankfurt: Fischer, 1986). Rinser's travelogue was translated into Korean, as *Ruije Rinjŏ ŭi Puk'an iyagi* (Seoul: Hyŏngsŏngsa, 1988).

64. Joanne Miyang Cho, "Luise Rinser's Third World Politics: Isang Yun and North Korea," in *Transnational Encounters between Germany and Korea: Affinity in Culture and Politics since the 1880s*, ed. Joanne Miyang Cho and Lee M. Roberts (New York: Palgrave MacMillan, 2017), 161–62.

65. Miyang Cho, "Luise Rinser's Third World Politics," 166–69.

66. Jon Halliday, "The North Korean Model: Gaps and Questions," *World Development* 9, no. 9/10 (1981), 899.

67. Erik Cornell, *North Korea Under Communism: Report of an Envoy to Paradise* (London and New York: RoutledgeCurzon, 2002), 45.

68. Kim Il Sung, *Answers to the Questions Raised by the Iraqi Journalists' Delegation to Pyongyang, 1971* (Pyongyang: Foreign Languages Publishing House, 1971), https://www.marxists.org/archive/kim-il-sung/1971/x01/x01.htm.

69. Dario Leone, "An Unknown Story from the Yom Kippur War: Israeli F-4s vs. North Korean MiG-21s," *The Aviationist*, June 24, 2013, https://theaviationist.com/2013/06/24/iaf-f-4-vs-nk-mig21/#.UcmblT773kM.

70. Kim Il Sung, *Answers to the Questions Raised by Chief Editor of Al Sahafa, Organ of the Sudanese Government* (Pyongyang, DPRK: Foreign Languages Publishing House, 1974), 10.

71. "Minutes of conversation at the official meeting between the Romanian delegation and the Korean delegation," May 20, 1978, WCDA, National Central Historical Archives, Romanian Communist Party, Central Committee, Foreign Relations Section, obtained by and trans. Eliza Gheorghe, http://digitalarchive.wilsoncenter.org/document/114456.

72. From US Intel, Cairo, to SecState, Subject: Report of North Korean and North Vietnamese activity in Egypt, November 4, 1973, AAD Archives, NARA, https://aad.archives.gov/aad/createpdf?rid=98988&dt=2472&dl=1345.

73. "North Korean Arms Supplies to Developing Countries," June 1983, reference FCO 31/3922, folder title: Political Relations between Ethiopia and North Korea, 1983, UKNA.

74. Bruce E. Bechtol Jr., "North Korea and Syria: Partners in Destruction and Violence," *Korean Journal of Defense Analysis* 27, no. 3 (September 2015), 284.

75. Bechtol, "North Korea and Syria," 284.

76. "Suriainminŭi kudŭn ŭiji," *Rodong Sinmun*, April 17, 1984.

77. Joseph Bermudez, *Terrorism: The North Korean Connection* (New York: Taylor & Francis, 1990), 72.

78. "Letter of General Military Intelligence Directorate about Iranian use of chemical weapons on Iraqi troops," April 14, 1987, WCDA, Conflict Records Research Center, National Defense University, SH-GMID-D-001–125, https://digitalarchive.wilsoncenter.org/document/111667.

79. "Mieczysław Dedo, Polish Ambassador to the DPRK, untitled report concerning the results of Kim Jong Nam's visit to Iran," January 9, 1989, WCDA, AMSZ, Department II, 3/94, w. 3, obtained by Marek Hańderek, trans. Jerzy Giebułtowski, https://digitalarchive.wilsoncenter.org/document/208563.

80. "Arabinmine taehan mijegung chuŭijadŭrŭi saeroun tojŏn," *Rodong Sinmun*, October 23, 1976.

81. "Isŭraelch'imnyakchadŭrŭn arabinmindŭrŭi kŭgahan wŏnssu," *Rodong Sinmun*, November 22, 1976.

82. "Telegram 066.918 from the Romanian Embassy in Pyongyang to the Romanian Ministry of Foreign Affairs," September 22, 1978, WCDA, AMAE, folder 784/1978, issue 220: January 7, 1978–September 23, 1978, obtained by and trans. Eliza Gheorghe, http://digitalarchive.wilsoncenter.org/document/116426.

83. "Minutes of conversation at the official meeting between the Romanian delegation and the Korean delegation," May 20, 1978.

84. "Puk'an anggolla kwan'gye, 1975," SKDA (2006), roll no. D-0019, file no. 1

85. "Speech of President Mobutu Sese Seko at the Pyongyang Mass Rally, December 15, 1974."

86. Andrea Berger, *Target Markets: North Korea's Military Customers* (Milton Park, UK: Routledge, 2017).

87. Bruce Loudon, "N. Koreans Aid Mobutu in Angola War," *Daily Telegraph*, November 28, 1975, found in "Puk'an anggolla kwan'gye, 1975."

88. Swedish State Department telegram, from Swedish Embassy, Pyongyang, to Swedish Ambassador in Beijing, Subject: Nordkoreansk aktiv utrikespolitik i Afrika och gentemot östtimor, January 28, 1976, obtained from Swedish Ministry of Foreign Affairs via email.

89. Swedish State Department telegram, January 28, 1976.

90. Swedish State Department telegram, January 28, 1976.

91. Cornell, *North Korea under Communism*, 44.

92. "Sae anggollaŭi ttangue k'ŏdaran pyŏnhyŏgi iruktoegoitta," *Rodong Sinmun*, November 11, 1976.

93. "Minutes of conversation at the official meeting between the Romanian delegation and the Korean delegation," May 20, 1978.

94. Prashad, *The Darker Nations*.

95. Buzo, *The Guerilla Dynasty* (1999), 99.

96. "Journal of Soviet Ambassador in the DPRK A. M. Puzanov for 16 April 1960," April 16, 1960, WCDA, AVPRF, fond 0102, opis 16, delo 6, pp.147–163, trans. Gary Goldberg, http://digitalarchive.wilsoncenter.org/document/116162.

97. "Hungarian Embassy in the DPRK, Report, 27 September 1973. Subject: The DPRK and the Non-Aligned Summit in Algiers," September 27, 1973, WCDA, MOL, XIX-J-1-j

Non-Aligned Movement, 1973, 120. doboz, 209–10, 00614/49/1973, obtained by and trans. Balazs Szalontai, http://digitalarchive.wilsoncenter.org/document/116004.

98. "Correspondence from Kim Il Sung to Tito," May 23, 1974, APR-KPR I-1–648, Archive of Josip Broz Tito, courtesy of Christian Ostermann via email, obtained by and trans. Martin Coles.

99. "Memorandum of Conversation, Washington, March 28, 1975," *Foreign Relations of the United States, 1969–1976*, vol. E-12, *Documents on East and Southeast Asia, 1973–1976*, ed. Daniel J. Lawler and Erin R. Mahan (Washington, DC: Government Printing Office, 2010), https://history.state.gov/historicaldocuments/frus1969–76ve12/d266.

100. "Memorandum of Conversation, Washington, July 14, 1976," *Foreign Relations of the United States, 1969–1976*, vol. E–8, *Documents on South Asia, 1973–1976*, https://history.state.gov/historicaldocuments/frus1969–76ve08/d96.

101. Taehwan Kim, "North Korea's Independent Policy Line and Its Relationship with the Third World, Beijing, and Moscow," *East Asian Review* 1, no. 3 (1989), 52.

102. "Comment on the Entry of North Korea into the Nonalignment Conference," August 27, 1975, *Rodong Sinmun*, found in Kim, "North Korea's Independent Policy Line," 52.

103. "Memorandum of Conversation, New York, September 6, 1975," *Foreign Relations of the United States, 1969–1976*, vol. E–8, *Documents on South Asia, 1973–1976*, 1973–1976, https://history.state.gov/historicaldocuments/frus1969–76ve08/d18.

104. "Report from the GDR Embassy in the USSR, 'Note about a Conversation between Comrade Bauer and Comrade Basmanov, Deputy Head of the 1st Far Eastern Department of the USSR Foreign Ministry, on 10 May 1976,'" May 13, 1976, WCDA, PolA AA, MfAA, C 6857, trans. for NKIDP by Bernd Schaefer, http://digitalarchive.wilsoncenter.org/document/114288.

105. "Report from the GDR Embassy in the USSR," May 13, 1976.

106. Gregory Winger, "Prospect Theory and Civil-Military Conflict: The Case of the 1976 Korean Axe Murder Incident," *Armed Forces & Society* 43, no. 4 (October 2017), 734–57.

107. "The Bloody Axes of Kim," *Chicago Tribune*, August 20, 1976.

108. "Report from the GDR Embassy in the DPRK, 'Note concerning a Conversation in Moscow on 12 May, 1976, with the Head of the Far East Department, Comrade Kapitsa, and the Head of the Southeast Asia Department, Comrade Sudarikov,'" May 27, 1976, WCDA, PolA AA, MfAA, C 6857, trans. Bernd Schaefer, http://digitalarchive.wilsoncenter.org/document/114290.

109. Samuel S. Kim, "Pyongyang, the Third World, and Global Politics," in *The Two Koreas in World Politics*, ed. Tae-Hwan Kwak et al. (Boulder, CO: Westview Press, 1984), 453–54.

110. "Telegram 066567 from the Romanian Embassy in Pyongyang to the Romanian Ministry of Foreign Affairs," April 13, 1977, WCDA, Archive of the Romanian Ministry of Foreign Affairs, folder 929/1977, issue 220/E: April–December 1977, obtained by and trans. Eliza Gheorghe, http://digitalarchive.wilsoncenter.org/document/114849.

111. "Regarding President Tito's official visit to the DPRK," September 4, 1977, WCDA, Archive of the Romanian Ministry of Foreign Affairs, folder 929/1977, issue 220/E: April–December 1977, obtained by and trans. Eliza Gheorghe, http://digitalarchive.wilsoncenter.org/document/114857.

112. "Report on the official friendship visit to the DPRK by the party and state delegation of the GDR, led by Comrade Erich Honecker," December 13, 1977, WCDA, SAPMO-BA, DY 30, J IV 2/2A/2123, trans. Grace Leonard, http://digitalarchive.wilsoncenter.org/document/112308.

113. "Telegram to the Director of the Korean Central Intelligence Agency from the Minister of Foreign Affairs, 'Report on DPRK's Foreign Minister Heo Dam's Visit to Yugoslavia, etc.,'"

April 7, 1979, WCDA, roll 2007–25, file 8, frames 11–12, South Korean Foreign Ministry Archive, http://digitalarchive.wilsoncenter.org/document/118391.

114. "Strengthening Solidarity and Cooperation among Countries of New Emerging Forces—Trend of Our Time," *Pyongyang Times*, April 30, 1977.

115. "Active Nationalization Measures Adopted," *Pyongyang Times*, March 5, 1977.

116. "Hungarian Embassy in Canada, ciphered telegram, 8 June 1979, Subject: Vietnamese-DPRK relations," June 8, 1979, WCDA, MOL, XIX-J-1-j Korea, 1979, 80. doboz, 81–1, 001791/1/1979, trans. Balazs Szalontai, http://digitalarchive.wilsoncenter.org/document/115837.

117. "GDR Ambassador Pyongyang to Ministry for Foreign Affairs, Berlin," April 14, 1975, WCDA, PA AA, MfAA, C 6862, obtained by and trans. Bernd Schaefer, http://digitalarchive.wilsoncenter.org/document/113929.

118. "Telegram from the Hungarian Embassy in Pyongyang, 'The Korean Workers' Party's 6th Congress,'" September 10, 1980, WCDA, MNL OL XIV-J-1-j Korea 25–001140/1980, obtained by North Korean Materials Archive, IFES, Kyungnam University, trans. Imre Májer, http://digitalarchive.wilsoncenter.org/document/123734.

119. "Telegram from the Hungarian Embassy in Pyongyang, 'The KWP's 6th Congress,'" October 7, 1980, WCDA, MNL OL XIV-J-1-j Korea 25–001140/1980, obtained by North Korean Materials Archive, IFES, Kyungnam University, trans. Imre Májer, http://digitalarchive.wilsoncenter.org/document/123740.

120. "Report from East German Ambassador to North Korea, 'Some Aspects of the Political Line of the Korean Workers' Party after the January Events,'" February 15, 1968, WCDA, Archives of the Ministry of Foreign Affairs, trans. Vojtech Mastny, http://digitalarchive.wilsoncenter.org/document/113196.

121. Sung Chull Kim, *North Korea under Kim Jong Il: From Consolidation to Systemic Dissonance* (Albany: State University of New York Press, 2006).

Chapter 4: Kim Jong Il's World and Revolutionary Violence, 1980–1983

1. Namkoong Young, "A Comparative Study on North and South Korean Economic Capability," *Journal of East Asian Affairs* 9, no. 1 (1995), 1–43.

2. "Records of conversation between Congressman Stephen J. Solarz and Kim Il Sung and Kim Yong-nam," August 4, 1980, WCDA, Jimmy Carter Library, Carter White House Central Files, White House Central Files Subject File, CO-41, CO-82 Executive 12077–12081, obtained by Charles Kraus, http://digitalarchive.wilsoncenter.org/document/115254.

3. Gi-Wook Shin and Kyung Moon Hwang, eds., *Contentious Gwangju: The May 18th Uprising in Korea's Past and Present* (Oxford, UK: Rowman and Littlefield, 2003).

4. "Report, Embassy of Hungary in North Korea to the Hungarian Foreign Ministry," July 30, 1975, WCDA, MOL, XIX-J-1-j Korea, 1975, 83. doboz, 81–10, 002835/8/1975, obtained by and trans. Balazs Szalontai, http://digitalarchive.wilsoncenter.org/document/111468.

5. Buzo, *The Guerilla Dynasty* (1999), 112–13.

6. Wada, *Kim Il Sung gwa Manju Hangil Chŏnjaeng*.

7. Kim Jong Il, "On Giving Wide Publicity to the Leader's Greatness among the South Korean People," Talk to Officials of the Central Committee of the Workers' Party of Korea, April 27, 1965, in *Kim Jong Il: Selected Works*, vol. 1, *1964–1969* (Pyongyang: Foreign Languages Publishing House, 1992), 81.

8. Kim Jong Il, "Let Us Strengthen Friendship and Solidarity with the Newly-Emergent Countries," Talk to Officials in Charge of Foreign Affairs, May 9, 1965, in *Kim Jong Il: Selected Works*, vol. 1, 92.

9. "Telegram from the Hungarian Embassy in Pyongyang, 'Foreign Opinions regarding the KWP's 6th Congress,'" November 11, 1980, WCDA, MNL OL XIV-J-1-j Korea 25–001140/1980, obtained by North Korean Materials Archive, IFES, Kyungnam University, trans. Imre Májer, http://digitalarchive.wilsoncenter.org/document/123748.

10. "Telegram from the Hungarian Embassy in Pyongyang, 'The KWP's 6th Congress (Mongolian Evaluation),'" November 22, 1980, WCDA, MNL OL XIV-J-1-j Korea 25–001140/1980, obtained by North Korean Materials Archive, IFES, Kyungnam University, trans. Imre Májer, http://digitalarchive.wilsoncenter.org/document/123747.

11. "Report to the Political Bureau on the Korean Workers' Party's 6th Congress and on the celebrations of the 35th anniversary of the foundation of the KWP," October 16, 1980, WCDA, MNL OL XIV-J-1-j Korea 25–005249/1980, obtained by North Korean Materials Archive, IFES, Kyungnam University, trans. Imre Májer, https://digitalarchive.wilsoncenter.org/document/123775.

12. "A Brief Introduction and Assessment of the Juche Ideology," November 1980, WCDA, MNL OL XIV-J-1-j Korea 25–001140/1980, obtained by North Korean Materials Archive, IFES, Kyungnam University, trans. Imre Májer, http://digitalarchive.wilsoncenter.org/document/123762.

13. *Paektu* refers to Paektusan, a sacred Korean mountain that is mythologized in both Koreas as the birthplace of the Korean nation. According to DPRK propaganda, Kim Jong Il was supposedly born at the base of Mount Paektu. In reality, he was born in the Soviet Far East.

14. Jae Kyu Park, "A Critique on 'The Democratic Confederal Republic of Koryo,'" *Journal of East and West Studies* 12, no. 1 (1983), 13–25.

15. Lisa Burnett, "Let Morning Shine over Pyongyang: The Future-Oriented Nationalism of North Korea's Arirang Mass Games," *Asian Music* 44, no. 1 (Winter 2013), 3–32.

16. On North Korean Mass Games in Africa, see Benjamin R. Young, "Cultural Diplomacy with North Korean Characteristics: Pyongyang's Exportation of the Mass Games to the Third World, 1972–1996," *International History Review*, 42, no. 3 (2020), 543–55.

17. Kim Jong Il, *On Further Developing Mass Gymnastics in Korea: Speech to Mass Gymnastics Producers*, trans. Korea Friendship Association (Pyongyang: Foreign Languages Publishing House, [1987] 2006), https://www.korea-dpr.com/lib/Kim%20Jong%20Il%20-%205/ON%20FURTHER%20DEVELOPING%20MASS%20GYMNASTICS.pdf.

18. *Mass Gymnastics in Korea* (Pyongyang, DPRK: Foreign Languages Publishing House, 2002), 6, found in the British Library, London.

19. Kim Jong Il, *On Further Developing Mass Gymnastics in Korea.*

20. Kim Jong Il, *On Further Developing Mass Gymnastics in Korea.*

21. *Mass Gymnastics in Korea,* 42.

22. This concept was first promoted by Kim Il Sung in 1967 as a power consolidation measure. See Tertitskiy, "1967," 82–94.

23. Airgram, from AmEmbassy, Mogadishu, to Dept. of State, Subject: GSR recognition of DPRK, April 29, 1967, folder POL, KOR N-S AFR, 1/1/67, box 2263, RG 59, General Records of the Department of State, Central Foreign Policy Files 1967–1969, Political and Defense, POL KOR N-AFR to POL 31-1 KOR N-US, NARA II.

24. John Markakis, "Radical Military Regimes in the Horn of Africa," in *Military Marxist Regimes in Africa*, ed. John Markakis and Michael Waller (London: Routledge, 2013), 37.

25. Mohamed Haji Ingiriis, *The Suicidal State in Somalia: The Rise and Fall of the Siad Barre Regime* (Lanham, MD: University Press of America, 2016), 120, 121.

26. Airgram, from AmEmbassy, Mogadishu, to Dept. of State, Subject: Joint Somali-North

Korean Communiqué, March 19, 1972, folder POL 7, KOR N, 1/1/71, box 2420, RG 59, SNF 1970–73, Political and Defense, POL 32-4 KOR to POL 16 KOR N, NARA II.

27. I. M. Lewis, *Blood and Bone: The Call of Kinship in Somali Society* (Trenton, NJ: Red Sea Press, 1994), 152–53.

28. For a video of the Somali Mass Games event, see "Siad Barre Hosts Idi Amin of Uganda in Mogadishu 23.10.1972," YouTube, https://youtu.be/-Axpvvsm9lo.

29. Telegram, from AmEmbassy, Kigali, to SecState, Subject: Expected North Korean Visit, May 7, 1973, folder POL 7, KOR N, 7/17/72, box 2420, RG 59, SNF 1970–73, Political and Defense, POL 32-4 KOR to POL 16 KOR N, NARA II.

30. "Gymnastics Course Opened in E. Buganda," *Voice of Uganda*, November 24, 1973, found in "Puk'an t'm uganda kwan'gye, 1973," SKDA (2004), roll no. D-014, file no. 34.

31. Alicia Decker, *In Idi Amin's Shadow: Women, Gender, and Militarism in Uganda* (Athens: Ohio University Press, 2014).

32. Paul S. Nsereko, "The Great Juche Idea: A Phrase for Economic War," *Voice of Uganda*, November 15, 1973, found in "Puk'an t'm uganda kwan'gye, 1973," SKDA (2004), roll no. D-014, file no. 34.

33. "Full text of the joint press release of the visit to Uganda by Ho Dam, Foreign Minister of North Korea," found in "Puk'an t'm uganda kwan'gye, 1974," SKDA (2005), roll no. D-017, file no. 34.

34. "Advantages of Gymnastics," *Voice of Uganda* n.d., found in "Puk'an t'm uganda kwan'gye, 1973," SKDA (2004), roll no. D-014, file no. 34.

35. "Advantages of Gymnastics."

36. "Gymnastic Critics 'Ashamed,'" *AY*, February 8, 1974, found in "Puk'an t'm uganda kwan'gye, 1974," SKDA (2005), roll no. D-017, file no. 34.

37. "Peace Must Prevail in Korea, Says Gen," *Voice of Uganda*, May 16, 1974, found in "Puk'an t'm uganda kwan'gye, 1974," SKDA (2005), roll no. D-017, file no. 34.

38. "We Say: Do Not Interfere, Says President," *Voice of Uganda*, October 1974, found in "Puk'an t'm uganda kwan'gye, 1974," SKDA (2005), roll no. D-017, file no. 34.

39. "Gymnastic Critics 'Ashamed.'"

40. From AmEmbassy, Bujumbura, to SecState, Subject: Preparations for National Day November 28 Celebrations in Burundi, October 31, 1974, AAD Archives, NARA, https://aad.archives.gov/aad/createpdf?rid=221847&dt=2474&dl=1345.

41. From AmEmbassy, Bujumbura, to SecState, Subject: November 28 Revolution Day celebrations in Burundi, November 29, 1974, AAD Archives, NARA, https://aad.archives.gov/aad/createpdf?rid=253264&dt=2474&dl=1345.

42. "Purundi taet'ongnyŏngi uri nara chiptanch'ejo taep'yodanŭl mannatta," *Rodong Sinmun*, October 8, 1978.

43. From AmEmbassy, Kigali, to SecState, Subject: Second Republic launches new national movement," July 9, 1975, AAD Archives, NARA, https://aad.archives.gov/aad/createpdf?rid=154086&dt=2476&dl=1345.

44. From AmEmbassy, Conakry, to SecState, Subject: Guinean November 22 anniversary celebration, November 26, 1976, AAD Archives, NARA, https://aad.archives.gov/aad/createpdf?rid=276163&dt=2082&dl=1345.

45. From AmEmbassy, Lomé, to SecState, Subject: North Korean Vice-Premier visits Togo, January 24, 1977, AAD Archives, NARA, https://aad.archives.gov/aad/createpdf?rid=17122&dt=2532&dl=1629.

46. From AmEmbassy, Antananarivo, to SecState, Subject: National Day in Madagascar, June 27, 1977, AAD Archives, NARA, https://aad.archives.gov/aad/createpdf?rid=147133&dt=2532&dl=1629.

47. "Gymnasts in Madagascar," *Korea Central News Agency*, July 9, 1977.

48. From AmEmbassy, Bujumbura, to SecState, Subject: Seventeenth anniversary of Uprona victory, September 19, 1978, AAD Archives, NARA, https://aad.archives.gov/aad/createpdf?rid=232008&dt=2694&dl=2009.

49. From AmEmbassy, Kigali, to SecState, Subject: 'China Option' colors National Day celebrations, July 13, 1978, AAD Archives, NARA, https://aad.archives.gov/aad/createpdf?rid=175294&dt=2694&dl=2009.

50. From AmEmbassy, Kigali, to SecState, Subject: Rwanda celebrates 17th anniversary of independence, July 9, 1979, AAD Archives, NARA, https://aad.archives.gov/aad/createpdf?rid=131805&dt=2776&dl=2169.

51. Philip Gourevitch, *We Wish to Inform You That Tomorrow We Will Be Killed with Our Families: Stories From Rwanda* (New York: Farrar, Straus and Giroux, 1999), 75.

52. Taylor, "'One Hand Can't Clap,'" 41–63.

53. Janis Prince, author's interview via email, June 24, 2014.

54. Vibert C. Cambridge, *Musical Life in Guyana: History and Politics of Controlling Creativity* (Jackson: University Press of Mississippi, 2015), 238–39.

55. Letter to the editor, "Not Too Busy to Have a Good Time," *Guyana Chronicle*, January 29, 2017.

56. Browne, "Zimbabwe/North Korea," October 21, 1980, reference FCO 36/2764, UKNA.

57. R. W. Johnson, "Birds of a Feather," *Wall Street Journal*, August 8, 2007, https://www.wsj.com/articles/SB118651948756990787.

58. "Zimbabwean Prime Minister Meets DPRK Ambassador," Korean Central News Agency, January 9, 1987.

59. "So What Exactly Is a 'Mass Display' Exam, President Mugabe?" *News24*, January 23, 2017, https://www.news24.com/Africa/Zimbabwe/so-what-exactly-is-a-mass-display-exam-president-mugabe-20170123.

60. "Mouvement d'ensemble," *Sidawaya*, August 6, 1984, in SKDA (2015), roll no. 2014-0038, file no. 9.

61. "Puk'anŭi taegana masŭgeim min k'adŭseksyŏn chŏnmun'ga p'agyŏn, 1984–85," SKDA (2017), roll no. 2016-0036, file no. 5.

62. "Puk'an tongbuap'ŭrik'a kwan'gye, 1986," SKDA (2017), roll no. 2016-0037, file no. 20.

63. *Mass Gymnastics in Korea,* 42.

64. *Mass Gymnastics in Korea,* 42.

65. *Mass Gymnastics in Korea,* 42.

66. CIA Directorate of Intelligence, "Rangoon Bombing Incident: The Case against the North Koreans," October 19, 1983, CREST, https://www.cia.gov/library/readingroom/document/0000408056.

67. *International Renegades: North Korean Diplomacy through Terror* (Seoul: Korea Overseas Information Service, 1983).

68. *International Renegades.*

69. William Chapman, "North Korean Leader's Son Blamed for Rangoon Bombing," *Washington Post,* December 3, 1983.

70. Kong Dan Oh, "Leadership Change in North Korean Politics: The Succession to Kim Il Sung," *RAND,* October 1988, https://apps.dtic.mil/dtic/tr/fulltext/u2/a216962.pdf.

71. David W. Shin, *Rationality in the North Korean Regime: Understanding the Kims' Strategy of Provocation* (Lanham, MD: Rowman & Littlefield, 2018), 103.

72. Kim Tae Hong, "Kim Will Never Admit Terror Guilt," *Daily NK*, July 1, 2010, http://www.dailynk.com/english/read.php?cataId=nk02200&num=6554.

73. *International Renegades.*

74. Ra Jong-yil, *Aungsan t'erŏrisŭt'ŭ kangminch'ŏl* (Seoul: Changbi Publishers, 2013).

75. "Statement of Korean Central News Agency," *Pyongyang Times*, October 15, 1983.

76. "Resolutely Reject Burmese Govt's Measure as Unjustifiable Act Infringing upon the Dignity and Authority of Our Republic," *Pyongyang Times*, November 9, 1983.

77. "Ranggunp'okpal sagŏnŭl tullŏssan kongmogyŏlt'agŭi chinsangŭn pandŭshi tŭrŏnalgŏshida," *Rodong Sinmun*, November 9, 1983.

78. "Ranggunp'okpalsagŏnŭi ch'aegimŭl nŏmgyŏssŭiunŭn miillamjosŏn'goeroedodangŭi kukchejŏkkongmogyŏlt'akŭl kyut'anbaegyŏk'anda," *Rodong Sinmun*, November 5, 1983.

79. "Anti-DPRK Campaign to Tide Over Crisis of Fascist Rule," *Pyongyang Times*, November 5, 1983.

80. "Shidaeŭi yŏk'aengjadŭrŭn kŭ ŏttŏn moryakŭrossŏdo uri naraŭi chonŏminnŭn kukchejŏkkwŏnwirŭl chŏltaero hŏmulsu ŏpta," *Rodong Sinmun*, November 11, 1983.

81. "History Will Disclose Reactionaries' Criminal Compact," *Pyongyang Times*, November 16, 1983.

82. "Culprit of Rangoon Bomb Blast Is Puppet Traitor Himself, Says World Public," *Pyongyang Times*, November 26, 1983.

83. "What Does Japanese Reactionaries' 'Favour' to Burma Show?," *Pyongyang Times*, November 16, 1983.

84. For a sample of such articles in the U.S. press, see "U.S. Cites North Korea for Burma Bombing," *Daytona Beach Sunday News-Journal*, October 27, 1983; "1 Million at Funeral for 17 Koreans," *Toledo Blade*, October 12, 1983. For a sample of such articles in the South Korean press, see "Pŏma, [k'orian] t'erŏbunja 1myŏng kŏmgŏ," *Kyŏnghyang Sinmun*, October 12, 1983; "Pukkoeŭi pŏmhaenggŏjŏm noch'ul," *Tong-A Ilbo*, October 13, 1983.

85. "T'erŏjiptan tanjoerŭl," *Tong-A Ilbo*, November 5, 1983.

86. "T'ŭksubudaeŭi chŏnjaeng norŭm," *Kyŏnghyang Sinmun*, November 5, 1983.

87. *International Renegades*.

88. "Puk'an-k'omoro kwan'gye, 1983," SKDA (2014), roll no. 2013-0044, file no. 3.

89. "Puk'an-k'osŭt'arik'a kwan'gye, 1983," SKDA (2015), roll no. 2014-0036, file no. 1.

90. "Samoa(ku sŏsamoa)ŭi taebukhan oegyogwan'gye tanjŏl, 1983.12.22," SKDA (2014), roll no. 2013-0046, file no. 3.

91. "Pŏma aungsan amsalp'okpalsagŏn: kakkung panŭng min taebuk'an taeŭngjoch'i kyosŏm (aju chiyŏk) 1983–84, Vol. 4," SKDA (2014), roll no. 2013-0004, file no. 8.

92. "The Unyielding Fighting Spirit of Palestinian People Has Become an Example for Oppressed and Humiliated Peoples: Speech of President Kim Il Sung at Banquet," *Pyongyang Times*, October 18, 1981.

93. "Undeclared Wars on Israel: East Germany and the West German Far Left 1967–1981: An Interview with Jeffrey Herf," *Fathom*, http://fathomjournal.org/undeclared-wars-on-israel-east-germany-and-the-west-german-far-left-1967–1981-an-interview-with-jeffrey-herf/.

94. Jeffrey Herf, *Undeclared Wars with Israel: East Germany and the West German Far Left, 1967–1989* (Cambridge: Cambridge University Press, 2015).

95. "Isŭraerŭn chunggŭndomgp'yŏngwaŭi am," *Kulloja* no. 523 (November 1985), 92–96.

96. Bermudez, *Terrorism*, 74–77.

97. Kim Il Sung, "Answers to the Questions Raised by Correspondent of the Lebanese Newspaper, 'Al Anwar,'" November 22, 1969, in *Three Interviews with Kim Il Sung* (London, UK: Prinkipo Press, 1970), 80–85.

98. Kim Il Sung, *Answers to the Questions Raised by the Iraqi Journalists' Delegation to Pyongyang, 1971*.

99. "Isŭraerŭi chŏngch'ewa kŭ paeujojongjadŭl," *Chollima* no. 285 (February 1983), 115–17.

100. "Parakhanŭn isŭrael," *Chollima* no. 314 (July 1985), 68–69.

101. "Palestinian People Are Close Comrades-in-Arms of Korean People," *Pyongyang Times*, May 28, 1977.

102. "Just Cause of Palestinian People Sure to Win," *Pyongyang Times*, May 10, 1980.

103. "Day of World Solidarity with Palestinian People," *Pyongyang Times*, November 26, 1983.

104. Bermudez, *Terrorism*, 74–77.

105. "Untitled report from Mieczysław Dedo, Polish Ambassador to the DPRK, concerning the visit of Yasser Arafat in North Korea (25–26 June 1989)," June 27, 1989, WCDA, AMSZ, Department II, 3/94, w. 3, obtained by Marek Hańderek, trans. Jerzy Giebułtowski, https://digitalarchive.wilsoncenter.org/document/208561.

106. "Jamaica/North Korea Relations," August 14, 1980, reference FCO 21/1879, file title: North Korea Foreign Policy, 1980. UKNA.

107. "Puk'an chameik'a kwan'gye, 1983," SKDA (2014), role no. 2013–044, file no. 18.

108. "Puk'an chameik'a kwan'gye, 1984," SKDA (2015), role no. 2014–0037, file no. 8.

109. "Puk'an chameik'a kwan'gye, 1983."

110. "Puk'an chameik'a kwan'gye, 1983."

111. "Puk'an chameik'a kwan'gye, 1984."

112. George Dickson, British High Commission in Jamaica, "North Korea's Role in the Caribbean," February 28, 1985, reference FCO 21/3218, folder title: Korean Relations with the Caribbean, 1985, UKNA.

113. "Puk'an -chungmi kwan'gye, 1983–84," SKDA (2014), roll no. 2013-0046, file no. 9.

114. For more on this unique relationship, see Benjamin R. Young, "Not There for the Nutmeg: North Korean Advisors in Grenada and Pyongyang's Internationalism, 1979–1983," *Cross-Currents: East Asian History and Culture Review* No. 27, (June 2018), 113–35.

115. "St. Lucia/North Korea Relations," October 14, 1980, reference FCO 21/1879, file title: North Korea Foreign Policy, 1980, UKNA.

116. "Diplomatic Relations between St. Vincent and North Korea," May 7, 1981, reference FCO 21/1988, file title: North Korea Foreign Policy, 1981, UKNA.

117. "Himŭi Kwangshinjadŭrŭi P'ogŏn," *Rodong Sinmun*, August 10, 1983.

118. "Migukshik P'yŏnghwa," *Rodong Sinmun*, August 11, 1983.

119. Bermudez, *Terrorism*, 61–62.

120. "Communist Military Assistance to Nicaragua: Trends and Implications," CIA Declassified Online Library, https://www.cia.gov/library/readingroom/docs/CIA-RDP97R00694R000800340001–5.pdf.

121. G. J. A. Slater, British High Commission, Solomon Islands, "North Koreans' Visit to Solomon Islands," August 22, 1980, reference FCO 21/1879, file title: North Korea Foreign Policy, 1980, UKNA.

122. G. J. A. Slater, British High Commission, Solomon Islands, "North Korea, Australia, and the South Pacific," December 23, 1981, reference FCO 21/1988, folder title: North Korean Foreign Policy, 1981, UKNA.

123. Slater, "North Korea, Australia, and the South Pacific," December 23, 1981.

124. Philip C. Boobbyer, "Soviet Perceptions of the South Pacific in the 1980s," *Asian Survey* 28, no. 5 (May 1988), 573–93.

125. D. Makarov, "Micronesia Under the Pentagon's Boot," *Krasnaia Zvezda*, February 2, 1982, found in Boobbyer, "Soviet Perceptions of the South Pacific in the 1980s," 578.

126. B. England, British Foreign Office, "North Korea, Australia, and the South Pacific," November 20, 1981, reference FCO 21/1988, folder title: North Korean Foreign Policy, 1981, UKNA.

127. R. A. R. Barltrop, British High Commission, "Fiji and North Korea," April 30, 1985, reference FCO 21/3210 folder title: Korean Relations with Fiji, 1985, UKNA.

128. "League Trio to Visit North Korea," May 25, 1984, *Fiji Times*, found in "Puk'an-P'iji kwan'gye, 1984," SKDA (2015), roll no. 2014-0036, file no. 7.

129. "N. Korean Tour," May 30, 1984, *Fiji Times*; and "Soviet Society," June 6, 1984, *Fiji Times*, found in "Puk'an-P'iji kwan'gye, 1984," SKDA (2015), roll no. 2014-0036, file no. 7.

130. "Answers of Great Leader Comrade Kim Il Sung President of DPRK to Questions Raised by Yugoslav News Agency Tanjug Delegation," March 5, 1982, *Fiji Sun*, found in "Puk'an-P'iji kwan'gye, 1981–82," SKDA (2013), roll no. 2012-0026, file no. 10.

131. "Students in Bias Claim," March 30, 1984, *Fiji Times*, found in "Puk'an-P'iji kwan'gye, 1984," SKDA (2015), roll no. 2014-0036, file no. 7.

132. External Intelligence Bureau, New Zealand's Prime Minister's Department, "South Pacific: North Korean Approaches," May 25, 1984, reference FCO 21/1869, folder title: Korean Relations with the Pacific, 1984, UKNA.

133. "Puk'an-Nauru oegyogwan'gye surip, 1982.2.25," SKDA (2013), roll no. 2012-0026, file no. 19.

134. John Dunrossil, British High Commission in Fiji, "Nauru: Relations with North Korea," May 7, 1982, reference FCO 107/398, folder title: Relations between North Korea, Australia, and the South Pacific, 1982, UKNA.

135. Charles Thompson, British High Commission in Kiribati, "Visit to Tarawa by Korean Ambassador," July 17, 1984, reference FCO 21/2869, folder title: Korean Relations with the Pacific, 1984, UKNA.

136. Barltrop, "Fiji and North Korea," April 30, 1985.

137. I. C. Orr, British Foreign and Commonwealth Office in London, "Visit to Tarawa by Korean Ambassador," August 3, 1984, reference FCO 21/2869, folder title: Korean Relations with the Pacific, 1984, UKNA.

138. Sang-Hwan Seong, "Korean-German Relations from the 1950s to the 1980s: Archive-Based Approach to Cold War–Era History," in Cho and Roberts, *Transnational Encounters between Germany and Korea,* 154.

139. Benjamin R. Young, "North Korea's Unlikely Alliance with German Environmentalists," *NK News*, June 12, 2015, https://www.nknews.org/2015/06/north-koreas-unlikely-alliance-with-german-environmentalists/.

140. Young, "Not There for the Nutmeg."

141. Balazs Szalontai and Sergey Radchenko, *North Korea's Efforts to Acquire Nuclear Technology and Nuclear Weapons: Evidence from Russian and Hungarian Archives*, Wilson Center Cold War International History Project Working Paper no. 53 (August 2006).

Chapter 5: Survival By Any Means Necessary, 1984–1989

1. "Pŏma aungsan amsalp'okpalsagŏn: pŏma chŏngbuŭi choch'i min sagŏn susa, 1983–84, Chon 5 kwŏn," SKDA (2014), roll no. 2013-0006, file no. 6.

2. For more on North Korea's relations with Zimbabwe, see Benjamin R. Young, "An Emotional Relationship: Trust, Admiration, and Fear in North Korea–Zimbabwe Relations, 1976–1988," *S/N Korean Humanities* 4, no. 2 (September 2018), 129–49.

3. Catholic Commission for Justice and Peace in Zimbabwe, *Report on the 1980s Disturbances*

in Matabeleland and the Midlands (March 1997), http://www.rhodesia.nl/Matabeleland%20 Report.pdf.

4. British High Commission in Addis Ababa, "Ethiopia: Relations with North Korea," January 4, 1984, reference FCO 31/3922, folder title: Political Relations between Ethiopia and North Korea, 1983, UKNA.

5. "Puk'an-et'iop'ia kwan'gye, 1983," SKDA (2014), roll no. 2013-0044, file no. 6.

6. Personal interview with Dr. Min Chul Yoo, February 18, 2017. Many thanks to Jun Yoo for his help.

7. "Hungarian Embassy in Ethiopia, ciphered telegram, 2 November 1983. Subject: Mengistu's visit in the DPRK," November 2, 1983, WCDA, MOL, XIX-J-1-j Ethiopia, 1983, 51. doboz, 41-103, 005863/1983, trans. Balazs Szalontai, http://digitalarchive.wilsoncenter.org/document/115833.

8. "Mengistu, Haile Mariam, Idiop'ia kunsawiwŏnhoe ŭijang puk'an pangmun, November 10–17, 1985," SKDA (2016), roll no. 2015-0035, file no. 2.

9. "Memorandum of conversation between Erich Honecker and Kim Il Sung," June 1, 1984, WCDA, SAPMO-BA, DY 30, 2460, trans. Grace Leonard, http://digitalarchive.wilsoncenter.org/document/113199.

10. "Puk'an-et'iop'ia kwan'gye, 1984," SKDA (2015), roll no. 2014-0036, file no. 6.

11. "Chosŏnnongŏpkisuljadŭri kŏnsŏrhan pat'kaesisŏrŭn et'iop'iaŭi nongŏppaljŏne k'ŭge kiyŏhalgŏsida. Sahoejuŭiet'iop'ia rimsigunsahaengjŏngnisahoe wiwŏnjangi amigŭnahoronon gŏpsaengsanhyŏptongjohabŭl ch'amgwan," *Rodong Sinmun*, July 5, 1985.

12. "Hungarian Embassy in Ethiopia, ciphered telegram, 26 September 1985, Subject: Ethiopia's relations with the DPRK," September 26, 1985, WCDA, MOL, XIX-J-1-j Ethiopia, 1985, 56. doboz, 41–10, 004776/1985, trans. Balazs Szalontai, http://digitalarchive.wilsoncenter.org/document/115834.

13. "Hungarian Embassy in Ethiopia, ciphered telegram, 26 November 1985, Subject: Ethiopian-DPRK relations," November 26, 1985, WCDA, MOL, XIX-J-1-j Ethiopia, 1985, 56. doboz, 41–10, 004776/2/1985, trans. Balazs Szalontai, http://digitalarchive.wilsoncenter.org/document/115835.

14. "Puk'an-et'iop'ia kwan'gye, 1985," SKDA (2016), roll no. 2015-0032, file no. 12.

15. "Hungarian Embassy in Ethiopia, ciphered telegram, 26 November 1985."

16. "Hungarian Embassy in Ethiopia, ciphered telegram, 27 November 1985, Subject: Ethiopia's relations with the DPRK," November 27, 1985, WCDA, MOL, XIX-J-1-j Ethiopia, 1985, 56. doboz, 41–10, 004776/3/1985, trans. Balazs Szalontai, http://digitalarchive.wilsoncenter.org/document/115836.

17. "Memorandum of conversation between Erich Honecker and Kim Il Sung," June 1, 1984, WCDA, SAPMO-BA, DY 30, 2460, trans. Grace Leonard, http://digitalarchive.wilsoncenter.org/document/113199.

18. "Record of conversation between Comrade J. Batmunkh and Kim Il Sung," November 20, 1986, WCDA, Mongolian Foreign Ministry Archive, fond 3, dans 1, kh/n 173, khuu 123–164, obtained by and trans. Sergey Radchenko and Onon Perenlei, https://digitalarchive.wilsoncenter.org/document/116671.

19. "Puk'an-ap'ŭrik'ajiyŏk kwan'gye, 1983–84," SKDA (2015), roll no. 2014-0038, file no. 12.

20. "Puk'an-ap'ŭrik'ajiyŏk kwan'gye, 1983–84."

21. "Puk'an-tongbu ap'ŭrik'a kwan'gye, 1984," SKDA (2015), roll no. 2014-0038, file no. 22.

22. Kim Il Sung, "For the Development of the Non-Aligned Movement," June 20, 1986,

concluding speech at a joint meeting of the Political Bureau of the Central Committee of the Workers' Party of Korea and the Central People's Committee of the Democratic People's Republic of Korea, https://www.marxistsfr.org/archive/kim-il-sung/1986/06/20.htm.

23. Bruce E. Bechtol, Jr., *The Last Days of Kim Jong-Il: The North Korean Threat in a Changing Era* (Dulles, VA: Potomac Books, 2013), 115.

24. "North Korea's Military Involvement in Africa," *Vantage Point*, March 1986, 16–19.

25. "Ch'uak'an chŏngch'ijŏkkiman'gŭk," *Rodong Sinmun*, June 20, 1985.

26. "Namap'ŭrik'ainjongjuŭijadŭrŭn namibiae chojak'an rimshijŏngburŭl haech'ehago iunnaradŭre taehan ch'imnyakch'aektongŭl chungjihayŏya handa," *Rodong Sinmun*, July 4, 1984.

27. Meghan Laurel Elizabeth Kirkwood, "Postcolonial Architecture through North Korean Modes: Namibian Commissions of the Mansudae Overseas Project," MA thesis in art history, University of Kansas 2011, https://kuscholarworks.ku.edu/bitstream/handle/1808/10702/Kirkwood_ku_0099M_11463_DATA_1.pdf;sequence=1.

28. Personal interview with Mahmood Mamdani, March 1, 2016.

29. D. J. Young, British High Commission in Kampala, "Uganda/North Korea," January 8, 1982, reference FCO 31/3709, folder title: Uganda/Korea Relations, 1982, UKNA.

30. B. Hopkinson, British High Commission in Kampala, "Uganda-North Korea Relations," September 13, 1982, reference FCO 31/3709, folder title: Uganda/Korea Relations, 1982, UKNA.

31. D. J. Young, British High Commission in Kampala, "Uganda/Korean Relations," February 24, 1984, reference FCO 31/4455, folder title: Uganda—Relations with North Korea, 1984, UKNA

32. W. N. Wenban-Smith, East African Department of the British Foreign and Commonwealth Office, "Uganda/South Korea Relations," September 25, 1984, reference FCO 31/4455, folder title: Uganda- Relations with North Korea, 1984, UKNA.

33. "Pŏnyŏnghanŭn sae ugandarŭl wihayŏ," *Rodong Sinmun*, October 9, 1984.

34. "Cadre School in Uganda," KCNA, September 26, 1984.

35. P. A. Penfold, British High Commission in Kampala, "Ugandan/Korean Relations," October 26, 1984, reference FCO 31/4455, folder title: Uganda—Relations with North Korea, 1984, UKNA.

36. Mclean, British High Commission in Kampala, "North Koreans in Uganda," October 26, 1984, Reference FCO 31/4455, Folder title: Uganda—Relations with North Korea, 1984. UKNA.

37. "Uganda konghwagung kukkyŏngjŏl 22tolse chŭŭmhayŏ kinyŏmjip'oewa sajinjŏnshihoe chinhaeng," *Rodong Sinmun*, October 9, 1984.

38. "Pŏnyŏnghanŭn sae ugandarŭl wihayŏ," *Rodong Sinmun*, October 9, 1984.

39. P. A. Penfold, British High Commission in Kampala, "Ugandan/Korean Relations," October 26, 1984.

40. P. A. Penfold, British High Commission in Kampala, "Korean/Ugandan Relations," November 28, 1984, reference FCO 31/4455, folder title: Uganda—Relations with North Korea, 1984, UKNA.

41. D. J. Kerr, British High Commission in Kampala, "Press cuttings on Obote denying foreign involvement," December 4, 1984, reference FCO 31/4455, folder title: Uganda—Relations with North Korea, 1984, UKNA.

42. "North Koreans Train Uganda Terror Squads," *Observer*, June 23, 1985.

43. "British Paper Report on Murder in Uganda Scored," KCNA, June 24, 1985.

44. Mclean, British High Commission in Kampala, "North Koreans in Uganda," October

26, 1984. reference FCO 31/4455, folder title: Uganda—Relations with North Korea, 1984, UKNA.

45. D. J. Young, British High Commission in Kampala, "Uganda/North Korea," January 8, 1982.

46. P. A. Penfold, British High Commission in Kampala, "Ugandan/North Korean Relations," July 9, 1984, reference FCO 31/4455, folder title: Uganda—Relations with North Korea, 1984, UKNA.

47. Henry Louis Gates, Jr., "Interview with Eldridge Cleaver," *PBS Frontline*, 1997, https://www.pbs.org/wgbh/pages/frontline/shows/race/interviews/ecleaver.html.

48. W. N. Wenban-Smith, British Foreign and Commonwealth Office, "South Korea, North Korea, and Uganda," October 5, 1984, reference FCO 31/4455, folder title: Uganda—Relations with North Korea, 1984, UKNA.

49. "Puk'an uganda kwan'gye, 1985," SKDA (2016), roll no. 2015-0033, file no. 16.

50. McLean, British High Commission in Kampala, "North Koreans," September 3, 1985, reference FCO 31/4736, folder title: Uganda—Relations with North Korea, UKNA.

51. "Sycophantic Political Line Distorts Development," *Weekly Topic* (Ugandan newspaper), week ending May 13, 1987, found in reference FCO 31/5248, folder title: Uganda—Relations with North Korea, 1987, UKNA.

52. March, British High Commission in Kampala, "Uganda and North Korea," May 14, 1987, reference FCO 31/5248, folder title: Uganda—Relations with North Korea, 1987, UKNA.

53. Berger, *Target Markets*, 80–81.

54. "Museveni Praises North Korea Security Training," *East African*, April 17, 2014, http://www.theeastafrican.co.ke/news/Uganda-President-Museveni-praises-North-Korea-security-training/2558-2283098-utyqj6z/index.html.

55. "North Korea: Turnaround in Foreign Debt Management and Trade Patterns," February 1, 1985, CIA Directorate of Intelligence, CIA-RDP90T01298R000200160001-5, CREST.

56. Namdech Sihanouk, "Admirable Successes of the Democratic People's Republic of Korea in All Respects Fill Us, Asian Friends, with Enthusiastic Pride," *Pyongyang Times*, July 31, 1971.

57. John F. Burns, "Sihanouk Finds Caviar and Kim Il Sung Mix Well," *New York Times*, June 22, 1985.

58. Andrew Mertha, *Brothers in Arms: Chinese Aid to the Khmer Rouge, 1975–1979* (Ithaca, NY: Cornell University Press, 2014), 65, 122.

59. "Telegram 066764 from the Romanian Embassy in Pyongyang to the Romanian Ministry of Foreign Affairs, 'Pol Pot's Visit to the DPRK,'" October 10, 1977, WCDA, Archive of the Romanian Ministry of Foreign Affairs, folder 931/1977, issue 220/E, February–October 1977, obtained by and trans. Eliza Gheorghe, http://digitalarchive.wilsoncenter.org/document/114866.

60. David P. Chandler, *The Tragedy of Cambodian History: Politics, War, and Revolution since 1945* (New Haven, CT: Yale University Press, 1991), 276.

61. "Untitled report from Wolt, Polish Intelligence Station Beijing, concerning the mutual visit of Cambodian and North Korean delegations in China," August 12, 1978, WCDA, AIPN, 02011/600/D, obtained by Marek Hańderek, trans. Jerzy Giebułtowski, https://digitalarchive.wilsoncenter.org/document/208555.

62. Norodom Sihanouk, *The DPR of Korea (1980–82): Seen by Norodom Sihanouk* (Pyongyang: DPRK Foreign Languages Publishing House, 1983), 1.

63. Norodom Sihanouk, *Shadow over Angkor: Memoirs of His Majesty King Norodom Sihanouk of Cambodia* (Phnom Penh: Monument Books, 2005).

64. Kim Jun Hak, "Maehok," *Choson Munhak*, September 1998, found in Meredith Shaw,

"'Maehok'—Rosalynn Carter Encounters the Great Leader," *North Korean Literature in English*, September 20, 2016, http://dprklit.blogspot.com/2016/09/maehok-rosalynn-carter-encounters-great.html.

65. Leo Dobbs, "Sihanouk's Strongarm Bodyguards from N. Korea Bully Peace in Cambodia," *Seattle Times*, July 12, 1992.

66. "King Backs N. Korea Guard," *Phnom Penh Post*, May 6, 1994, http://www.phnompenhpost.com/national/king-backs-n-korea-guard.

67. "83. Memorandum of Conversation," *Foreign Relations of the United States, 1977–1980*, vol. 22, *Southeast Asia and the Pacific*, 283, https://history.state.gov/historicaldocuments/frus1977–80v22/d83.

68. The term *non-colonial colonialism* comes from Kotkin, "Modern Times," 160.

69. Messages exchanged between Kim Il Sung and Babrak Karmal, in *Rodong Sinmun*, August 19, 1980.

70. "Hungarian Embassy in Pakistan, ciphered telegram, 8 September 1980, Subject: Pakistani-DPRK and Pakistani-Japanese relations," September 8, 1980, WCDA, MOL, XIX-J-1-j Asia, 1980, 140. doboz, 203–10, 005421/1980, trans. Balazs Szalontai, http://digitalarchive.wilsoncenter.org/document/115822.

71. "Widaehan suryŏng kimilsŏngdongjikkesŏ ap'ŭganisŭt'anminjujuŭigonghwagung taep'yodanŭl chŏpkyŏnhashiyŏtta," *Rodong Sinmun*, September 1, 1981; "Ap'ŭganisŭt'anminju ch'ŏngnyŏnjojing taep'yodanŭrhwanyŏnghanŭn chip'oe chinhaeng," *Rodong Sinmun*, October 22, 1981.

72. "Hungarian Embassy in Pakistan, ciphered telegram, 29 October 1982, Subject: Pakistani-DPRK relations," October 29, 1982, WCDA, MOL, XIX-J-1-j Pakistan, 1982, 113. doboz, 119–103, 005589/2/1982, trans. Balazs Szalontai, http://digitalarchive.wilsoncenter.org/document/115828.

73. "Mihail korŭbach'yobŭdongjiga ap'ŭganisŭt'anmunjewa kwallyŏnhan sŏngmyŏngŭl palp'yo," *Rodong Sinmun*, February 10, 1988.

74. "Hungarian Embassy in Canada, ciphered telegram, 8 June 1979, Subject: Vietnamese-DPRK relations."

75. "Hungarian Embassy in Mongolia, report, 2 March 1983, Subject: Vietnamese views about North Korean policies," March 2, 1983, WCDA, MOL, XIX-J-1-j Vietnam, 1983, 125. doboz, 162–10, 002530/1983, trans. Balazs Szalontai, http://digitalarchive.wilsoncenter.org/document/115830.

76. "Let Us Develop South-South Cooperation: Congratulatory Speech Delivered by President Kim Il Sung," *Pyongyang Times*, June 10, 1987.

77. "Memorandum of conversation between Erich Honecker and Kim Il Sung," June 1, 1984, WCDA, SAPMO-BA, DY 30, 2460, trans. Grace Leonard, http://digitalarchive.wilsoncenter.org/document/113199.

78. "Record of conversation between Comrade J. Batmunkh and Kim Il Sung," November 20, 1986, WCDA, Mongolian Foreign Ministry Archive, fond 3, dans 1, kh/n 173, khuu 123–164, obtained by and trans. Sergey Radchenko and Onon Perenlei, http://digitalarchive.wilsoncenter.org/document/116671.

79. "Memorandum of conversation between Erich Honecker and Kim Il Sung," June 1, 1984.

80. "Information from Bulgarian Minister of Foreign Affairs, Peter Mladenov to the Central Committee of the Bulgarian Communist Party," January 4, 1985, WCDA, Central State Archive, Sofia, fond 1-B, opis 101, A.E. 1204, p. 1–7, obtained by Jordan Baev, trans. Greta Keremidchieva, http://digitalarchive.wilsoncenter.org/document/165347.

81. "Letter to the Central Committee of the Bulgarian Communist Party, from the Secretary of the Korean Workers' Party, Hwang Jang-yeop," July 3, 1985, WCDA, Central State Archive, Sofia, fond 1-B, opis 81, A.E. 14, p. 14–16, obtained by Jordan Baev, trans. Greta Keremidchieva, http://digitalarchive.wilsoncenter.org/document/165256.

82. "Letter from Fidel Castro to the President of the International Olympic Committee Juan Antonio Samaranch," November 29, 1984, WCDA, International Olympic Committee Archives (Switzerland), Seoul '88 / Political Matters de 1982 à mai 1986, obtained by Sergey Radchenko, trans. Sebastian Naranjo Rodriguez, http://digitalarchive.wilsoncenter.org/document/113916.

83. "If Co-Hosting Proposal Is Not Realized, We'll Not Participate in 24th Olympic Games," *Pyongyang Times,* February 22, 1986.

84. "If Co-Hosting Is Not Realized, We'll Not Participate in 24th Olympic Games," *Pyongyang Times,* February 22, 1986.

85. P. R. Fearn, British Embassy in Havana, "President Castro's Visit to North Korea," March 21, 1986, reference FCO 99/2303, folder title: Cuba/North Korea Relations, 1986, UKNA.

86. John Horne and Garry Whannel, *Understanding the Olympics* (New York and London: Routledge, 2016), 200.

87. "Ollimp'igŭi nŏurŭl ssŭn muryŏkchŭnggang," *Rodong Sinmun,* February 10, 1988.

88. "Daily Hits South Crew's Murder of Africans," KCNA, December 14, 1984.

89. "South Cannot Be Friends," KCNA, December 15, 1984.

90. "More Groups Comment," KCNA, December 18, 1984.

91. "KCNA Flays Illegal Fishing in Angola by South's Boat," KCNA, December 5, 1984.

92. "Groups Hit South," KCNA, December 17, 1984.

93. "AIDS Diffused," *Pyongyang Times* March 8, 1986.

94. "No AIDS in the DPRK," *Korea Today* 5, no. 428 (1992).

95. Kim Hyŏn-hŭi, *The Tears of My Soul* (New York: William Morrow, 1993); Dan Oberdorfer and Robert Carlin, *The Two Koreas: A Contemporary History* (New York: Basic Books, 2014), 144–46.

96. "Statement by the Spokesman for the Korean Central News Agency," KCNA, December 5, 1987.

97. "Pyongyang Will Never Overlook Seoul's Provocative Moves," *People's Korea,* January 30, 1988.

98. Daryl Plunk, "North Korea: Exporting Terrorism," Heritage Foundation's Asian Studies Center's Backgrounder no. 74 (February 25, 1988), http://www.heritage.org/node/21848/print-display.

99. "Report on North Korea's international situation under the new realities in the world," October 21, 1988, WCDA, Central State Archive, Sofia, fond 1-B, opis 81, A.E. 27, p. 5, obtained by Jordan Baev, trans. Greta Keremidchieva, http://digitalarchive.wilsoncenter.org/document/165257.

100. "The 1989 World Youth Festival," September 1988, reference FCO 21/4436, folder title: The 1989 World Youth Festival in Pyongyang, 1989, UKNA.

101. Warwick Morris and J. Ingamells, British Embassy in Seoul, "Pyongyang Youth Festival," October 5, 1989, reference FCO 21/4436, folder title: The 1989 World Youth Festival in Pyongyang, 1989, UKNA.

102. "13th World Festival of Youth and Students, July 1989 in Pyongyang, Danish Youth Council," Portfolio: Central European National Youth Committee and the 1989 World Festival of Youth and Students, Historical Archives of the European Union. Many thanks to Doug Gabriel for sharing these files with me.

103. "Voices of Anti-Imperialist Solidarity, Peace and Friendship Spread Far," *Pyongyang Times* July 15, 1989.

104. British Foreign and Commonwealth Office, "World Youth Festival: Retrospect and Prospect," August 1989, reference FCO 21/4436, folder title: The 1989 World Youth Festival in Pyongyang, 1989, UKNA.

105. British Foreign and Commonwealth Office, "World Youth Festival: Retrospect and Prospect," August 1989.

106. Kong Dan Oh, "North Korea in 1989: Touched by Winds of Change?," *Asian Survey* 30, no. 1 (January 1990), 74–80.

107. "The Juche Idea Is the Greatest Idea," *Pyongyang Times* July 9, 1989.

108. *A Winged Horse* (Pyongyang: Foreign Languages Publishing House, 1989); *A Tale of Two Generals* (Pyongyang: Foreign Languages Publishing House, 1989).

109. *Do You Know about Korea? Questions and Answers* (Pyongyang: Foreign Languages Publishing House, 1989).

110. "Pyongyang Festival a Pride of 20th Century," *Pyongyang Times* September 2, 1989.

111. "Georgy Shakhnazarov's preparatory notes for Mikhail Gorbachev for the meeting of the Politburo," October 6, 1988, WCDA, published in G. Kh. Zhakhnazarov, *Tsena prozreniia* (The Price of Enlightenment), trans. Vladislav Zubok, http://digitalarchive.wilsoncenter.org/document/112474.

112. "Conversation between M. S. Gorbachev and FRG Chancellor Helmut Kohl," June 14, 1989, WCDA, Archive of the Gorbachev Foundation, Notes of A. S. Chernyaev, trans. Svetlana Savranskaya, http://digitalarchive.wilsoncenter.org/document/120811.

113. *Songun Politics and Peace on the Korean Peninsula* (Pyongyang: Foreign Languages Publishing House, 2008)

114. "U.S. Gangster-like Threatening Diplomacy Rejected," KCNA, November 26, 2017.

115. Stephan Haggard and Marcus Noland, *Famine in North Korea: Markets, Aid, and Reform* (New York: Columbia University Press, 2007).

116. Uk Heo and Terence Roehrig, *South Korea's Rise: Economic Development, Power, and Foreign Relations* (New York: Cambridge University Press, 2014).

117. Edward P. Reed, "Is Saemaul Undong a Model for Developing Countries Today?," paper prepared for International Symposium in Commemoration of the 40th Anniversary of Saemaul Undong, hosted by the Korea Saemaul Undong Center, 2010, https://asiafoundation.org/resources/pdfs/SaemaulUndongReedSept2010FINAL.pdf.

118. Sheena Chestnut Greitens, *Illicit: North Korea's Evolving Operations to Earn Hard Currency* (Washington, DC: Committee for Human Rights in North Korea, 2014), 31–32.

Conclusion

1. Halliday, "The North Korean Enigma," 52.

2. Martin, *Under the Loving Care of the Fatherly Leader*, 137.

3. B. C. Koh, "'Military-First Politics' and Building a 'Powerful And Prosperous Nation' in North Korea," NAPSNet Policy Forum, April 14, 2005, https://nautilus.org/napsnet/napsnet-policy-forum/military-first-politics-and-building-a-powerful-and-prosperous-nation-in-north-korea/.

4. John Hudson, "North Korea Loses Its Communist Décor," October 9, 2012, *Atlantic*, https://www.theatlantic.com/international/archive/2012/10/north-korea-loses-its-communist-decor/322728/.

5. Paul Sonne and Felicia Schwartz, "U.S. Pressure on North Korea's Global Ties Bears Fruit," *Wall Street Journal*, October 8, 2017, https://www.wsj.com/articles/state-department-pressure-on-north-koreas-global-ties-bears-fruit-1507492004.

6. Joshua Hammer, "The Billion-Dollar Bank Job," *New York Times*, May 3, 2018, https://www.nytimes.com/interactive/2018/05/03/magazine/money-issue-bangladesh-billion-dollar-bank-heist.html.

7. Paul Sonne and Felicia Schwartz, "U.S. Pressure on North Korea's Global Ties Bears Fruit," *Wall Street Journal*, October 8, 2017, https://www.wsj.com/articles/state-department-pressure-on-north-koreas-global-ties-bears-fruit-1507492004.

8. Personal communications with Mozambique anthropologist M. Dores Cruz.

9. M. Dores Cruz, "Toponymy of the City and the Theater of Memory: Commemorative Street Names in Maputo during the Colonial and Socialist Periods," paper presented at the 2017 European Conference of African Studies. Thank you to the author for sharing his paper with me.

10. "Syria Names Park in Capital after N Korea Founder," Al Jazeera, August 31, 2015, http://www.aljazeera.com/news/2015/08/syria-names-park-capital-korea-founder-150831194857490.html.

Bibliography

Archives/Libraries

British National Library, London
Duke University Rubenstein Library, Durham, North Carolina
Georgetown University's Special Collections Center, Washington, DC
Harvard University Yenching Library, Cambridge, Massachusetts
Library of Congress, Washington, DC
Marxists.org (Digital Archive)
National Archives of Australia Digital Archive
National Archives of South Korea, Seongnam
National Assembly Library of Korea, Seoul
National Institute of Korean History, Gwacheon, South Korea (Housed materials from the Canadian Department of External Affairs and French Foreign Ministry)
National Library of South Korea, Seoul, South Korea
National Security Archive, Washington, DC
ROK Diplomatic Archives (SKDA), Seoul
Swedish Ministry of Foreign Affairs, Stockholm
UK National Archives (UKNA), London
University of North Korean Studies Library, Seoul
U.S. National Archives II, College Park, Maryland, U.S. (NARA II)
U.S. National Archives, Access to Archival Databases (AAD) System and CIA Records Search Tool (CREST)
Woodrow Wilson Center History and Public Policy Program Digital Archive (WCDA) and North Korea International Documentation Project Digital Archive (NKIDP)

Films

The Game of Their Lives (2002)
A State of Mind (2004)

Periodicals/News Sources

Al Jazeera
The Atlantic
The Black Panther
Chicago Tribune
Chollima
Daily NK
The East African
The Economist
Foreign Trade (DPRK)
Guyana Chronicle
The Herald (Zimbabwe)
Korea Central News Agency (KCNA)
Korea Today
Kulloja
Kyŏnghyang Sinmun
New Focus International
News24 (Zimbabwe)
The New York Times
People's Korea
The Phnom Penh Post
The Pyongyang Times
Ramparts
Rodong Sinmun
The Seattle Times
TIME
Tong-A Ilbo
Uriminzokkiri
The Wall Street Journal
Washington Post
The Washington Times
Vantage Point
Yonhap News

Published Primary Sources

Aidit, D. N. *Set Afire the Banteng Spirit! Ever Forward, No Retreat!* Beijing: Foreign Languages Press, 1964.

al Missuri, Muhammad. *Kimilsungism: Theory and Practice*. Pyongyang: Foreign Languages Publishing House, 1978.

Ali, Tariq. "Diary." *London Review of Books* 34, no. 2 (January 26, 2012).

A Tale of Two Generals. Pyongyang: Foreign Languages Publishing House, 1989.

A Winged Horse. Pyongyang: Foreign Languages Publishing House, 1989.

Catholic Commission for Justice and Peace in Zimbabwe. *Breaking the Silence: Building True Peace—A Report on the Disturbances in Matabeleland and the Midlands, 1980 to 1988*. Harare: Africa Synod House, February 1997. http://davidcoltart.com/wp-content/uploads/2006/10/breakingthesilence.pdf.

———. *Report on the 1980s Disturbances in Matabeleland and the Midlands*. March 1997. http://www.rhodesia.nl/Matabeleland%20Report.pdf.

Do You Know About Korea? Questions and Answers. Pyongyang: DPRK Foreign Languages Publishing House, 1989.

Essack, Karrim. *Juche-Korea*, vol. 2. Dar es Salaam, Tanzania: Thakers Limited, 1983.

Guevara, Ernesto Che. *Guerilla Warfare*. New York: Monthly Review Press, 1961.

Habyarimana, Juvénal. *Discours, messages et entretiens de Son Excellence le général-major Habyarimana Juvénal, president de la République rwandaise*. Kigali: Service des affaires sociales, en collaboration avec l'Office rwandais d'information, 1980.

International Renegades: North Korean Diplomacy through Terror. Seoul: Korea Overseas Information Service, 1983.

The International Seminar on the Juche Idea. Pyongyang, DPRK: Foreign Languages Publishing House, 1977.

Kim, Hyŏn-hŭi. *The Tears of My Soul*. New York: William Morrow, 1993.

Kim, Ji Ho, *Human Rights: Understanding Korea Series*, #9. Pyongyang: Foreign Languages Publishing House, 2017.

Kim Il Sung. *Answers to the Questions Raised by Chief Editor of Al Sahafa, Organ of the Sudanese Government*. Pyongyang: Foreign Languages Publishing House, 1974.

———. *Answers to the Questions Raised by the Iraqi Journalists' Delegation to Pyongyang, 1971*. Pyongyang: Foreign Languages Publishing House, 1971. https://www.marxists.org/archive/kim-il-sung/1971/x01/x01.htm.

———. "For the Development of the Non-Aligned Movement." Concluding speech at a joint meeting of the Political Bureau of the Central Committee of the Workers' Party of Korea and the Central People's Committee of the Democratic People's Republic of Korea, June 20, 1986. https://www.marxistsfr.org/archive/kim-il-sung/1986/06/20.htm.

———. *For the Independent and Peaceful Reunification of Korea*. New York: Guardian, 1976.

———. *Kim Il Sung Works*. Vol. 24, *June–December 1969*. Pyongyang: Foreign Languages Publishing House, 1985.

———. *Let Us Intensify the Anti-Imperialist, Anti-U.S. Struggle*. Pyongyang: Foreign Languages Publishing House, 1968.

———. "On Eliminating Dogmatism and Formalism and Establishing Juche in Ideological Work," December 28, 1955. In *Kim Il Sung: Selected Works*, vol. 1, 582–606. https://www.marxists.org/archive/kim-il-sung/1955/12/28.htm.

———. "On Socialist Construction and the South Korean Revolution in the Democratic People's Republic of Korea." Lecture at the Ali Archam Academy of Social Sciences of Indonesia, April 14, 1965. Pyongyang: Foreign Languages Publishing House, 1968.

———. *Reminiscences: With the Century*. Pyongyang: Foreign Languages Publishing House, 1992.

———. *The Non-Alignment Movement Is a Mighty Anti-Imperialist Revolutionary Force of Our Times*. Pyongyang: DPRK Foreign Languages Publishing House, 1976.

Kim Jong Il. *Kim Jong Il: Selected Works*. Vol. 1, *1964–1969*. Pyongyang: Foreign Languages Publishing House, 1992.

———. *On Further Developing Mass Gymnastics in Korea: Speech to Mass Gymnastics Producers*. Pyongyang: Foreign Languages Publishing House, 1987.

Lameda, Ali. *A Personal Account of the Experience of a Prisoner of Conscience in the Democratic People's Republic of Korea*. London: Amnesty International, 1979.

Lenin, Vladimir Ilyich. "What Is To Be Done?" *Lenin's Selected Works*, vol. 1. First published as a separate work in March 1902. https://www.marxists.org/archive/lenin/works/1901/witbd/v.htm.

MacLochlainn, Gerry. *The Irish Republican and Juche Conception of National Self-Dignity Are One and the Same*. London: Mosquito Press, 1985.

President Kim Il Sung Moves Asia and the World. Pyongyang: Foreign Languages Publishing House, 1976.

Rinser, Luise. *Nordkoreanisches Reisetagebuch*. Frankfurt: Fischer, 1986.

Sihanouk, Norodom. *The DPR of Korea (1980–82): Seen by Norodom Sihanouk*. Pyongyang: DPRK Foreign Languages Publishing House, 1983.

———. *Shadow over Angkor: Memoirs of His Majesty King Norodom Sihanouk of Cambodia*. Phnom Penh: Monument Books, 2005.

Socialist Constitution of the Democratic People's Republic of Korea.

Songun Politics and Peace on the Korean Peninsula. Pyongyang: Foreign Languages Publishing House, 2008.

The Tricontinental Conference of African, Asian, and Latin American Peoples: A Staff Study. Washington, DC: U.S. Government Printing Office, 1966.

Three Interviews with Kim Il Sung. London, UK: Prinkipo Press, 1970.

United Nations Panel of Experts. *Report of the Panel of Experts Established Pursuant to Resolution 1874 (2009)*, S/2017/150. https://digitallibrary.un.org/record/861367/files/S_2017_150-EN.pdf.

U.S. State Department. *Foreign Relations of the United States* (*FRUS*). Washington, DC: Government Printing Office, 1862-.

Secondary Sources

Acharya, Amitav, and See Seng Tan, eds. *Bandung Revisited: The Legacy of the 1955 Asian-African Conference for International Order*. Singapore: NUS Press, 2008.

AHR Roundtable. "Historians and the Question of 'Modernity': Introduction," *American Historical Review* 116, no. 3 (2011): 631–37.

Applebaum, Rachel. "The Friendship Project: Socialist Internationalism in the Soviet Union and Czechoslovakia in the 1950s and 1960s." *Slavic Review* 74, no. 3 (Fall 2015): 484–507.

Armstrong, J. D. *Revolutionary Diplomacy: Chinese Foreign Policy and the United Front Doctrine*. Berkeley: University of California Press, 1977.

Babiracki, Patryk. *Soviet Soft Power in Poland: Culture and the Making of Stalin's New Empire, 1943–1957*. Chapel Hill: University of North Carolina Press, 2015.

Baker, Robert. "Vaccinating Mali: Posters, Pamphlets, One Slave, One Vampire Bat." *American Diplomacy: Foreign Service Dispatches and Periodic Reports on U.S. Foreign Policy*, April 2013. http://www.unc.edu/depts/diplomat/item/2013/0105/fsl/baker_vaccinating.html.

Bechtol, Bruce E., Jr. *The Last Days of Kim Jong-Il: The North Korean Threat in a Changing Era*. Dulles, VA: Potomac Books, 2013.

———. "North Korea and Syria: Partners in Destruction and Violence." *Korean Journal of Defense Analysis* 27, no. 3 (September 2015): 277–92.

Berger, Andrea. *Target Markets: North Korea's Military Customers*. Milton Park, UK: Routledge, 2017.

Bermudez, Joseph. *Terrorism: The North Korean Connection*. New York: Taylor & Francis, 1990.

Boobbyer, Philip C. "Soviet Perceptions of the South Pacific in the 1980s." *Asian Survey* 28, no. 5 (May 1988): 573–93.

Boulychev, Georgi D. "Moscow and North Korea: The 1961 Treaty and After." In *Russia in the Far East and Pacific Region*, edited by Yung Chung and Eunsook Chung. Seoul: Sejong Institute, 1994.

Brazinsky, Gregg. *Winning the Third World: Sino-American Rivalry during the Cold War.* Chapel Hill: University of North Carolina Press, 2017.

Burnett, Lisa. "Let Morning Shine over Pyongyang: The Future-Oriented Nationalism of North Korea's Arirang Mass Games." *Asian Music* 44, no. 1 (Winter 2013): 3–32.

Buzo, Adrian. *The Guerilla Dynasty: Politics and Leadership in North Korea*. London: I. B. Tauris, 1999.

———. *The Guerilla Dynasty: Politics and Leadership in North Korea*. 2nd ed. New York: Routledge, 2018.

Byrne, Jeffrey. *Mecca of Revolution: Algeria, Decolonization, and the Third World Order*. New York: Oxford University Press, 2016.

Callahan, David. *Unwinnable Wars: American Power and Ethnic Conflict*. New York: Twentieth Century Fund, 1997.

Cambridge, Vibert C. *Musical Life in Guyana: History and Politics of Controlling Creativity.* Jackson: University Press of Mississippi, 2015.

Cathcart, Adam, and Charles Kraus. "The Bonds of Brotherhood: New Evidence on Sino-North Korean Exchanges, 1950–1954." *Journal of Cold War Studies* 13, no. 3 (Summer 2011): 27–51.

———. "Peripheral Influence: The Sinuiju Student Incident of 1945 and the Impact of Soviet Occupation in North Korea." *Journal of Korean Studies* 13, no. 1 (Fall 2008): 1–28.

Chandler, David P. *The Tragedy of Cambodian History: Politics, War, and Revolution since 1945.* New Haven, CT: Yale University Press, 1991.

Chen, Jian. *Mao's China and the Cold War*. Chapel Hill: University of North Carolina Press, 2001.

Cheng, Xiaohe. "The Evolution of the Lips and Teeth Relationship: China–North Korea Relations in the 1960s." In *China and North Korea: International Relations and Comparisons in Northeast Asia*, edited by C. P. Freeman. New York: Palgrave Macmillan, 2015.

Cho, Joanne Miyang. "Luise Rinser's Third World Politics: Isang Yun and North Korea." In *Encounters between Germany and Korea: Affinity in Culture and Politics since the 1880s*, edited by Joanne Miyang Cho and Lee M. Roberts. New York: Palgrave MacMillan, 2017.

Chung, Chin-wee. "North Korea's Relations with China." In *The Foreign Relations of North Korea: New Perspectives*, edited by Jae Kyu Park, Byung Chul Koh, and Tae-Hwan Kwak. Boulder, CO: Westview Press, 1987.

Copper, John F. *China's Foreign Aid and Investment Diplomacy*, Vol. 3: *Strategy Beyond Asia and Challenges to the United States and the International Order.* New York: Springer, 2016.

Cornell, Erik. *North Korea under Communism: Report of an Envoy to Paradise*. London and New York: RoutledgeCurzon, 2002.

Cruz, M. Dores. "Toponymy of the City and the Theater of Memory: Commemorative Street Names in Maputo during the Colonial and Socialist Periods." Paper presented at the 2017 European Conference of African Studies.

Cumings, Bruce. "American Century and the Third World." *Diplomatic History* 23, no. 2 (January 1999): 355–70.

———. "Korea: Forgotten Nuclear Threats." *Le Monde Diplomatique* (December 2004). https://mondediplo.com/2004/12/08korea.

———. *The Korean War: A History*. New York: Penguin Modern Library; reprint ed., 2011.

———. *Korea's Place in the Sun: A Modern History*. New York: W. W. Norton, 1997.

Decker, Alicia. *In Idi Amin's Shadow: Women, Gender, and Militarism in Uganda.* Athens: Ohio University Press, 2014.

Dikotter, Frank. *The Cultural Revolution: A People's History, 1962–1976.* New York: Bloomsbury Publishing, 2016.

Do, Jean. "Pukhanŭi minjokhaebangjŏnjaeng kongsewa chunggugŭi haekpoyuguk pusang, 1962-1966." *Hyŏndaebukhanyŏn'gu* 19, no. 1 (2016): 136–86.

Eisenman, Joshua, and David Shinn. *China and Africa: A Century of Engagement.* Philadelphia: University of Pennsylvania Press, 2012.

Fanon, Frantz. *Les damnés de la terre.* Paris: François Maspero éditeur, 1961.

Foster-Carter, Aidan. "Pyongyang Watch: Some of that Old-Time Religion." *Asia Times Online,* December 23, 2000. Accessed November 8, 2016. http://www.atimes.com/koreas/BL23Dg02.html.

Frank, Rudiger. "North Korea's Autonomy 1965–2015." *Pacific Affairs* 87, no. 4 (December 2014): 791–99.

Friedman, Jeremy. *Shadow Cold War: The Sino-Soviet Competition for the Third World.* Chapel Hill: University of North Carolina Press, 2015.

Fukuyama, Francis. *Identity: The Demand for Dignity and the Politics of Resentment.* New York: Farrar, Straus and Giroux, 2018.

Gates, Henry Louis Jr. "Interview with Eldridge Cleaver." *PBS Frontline,* 1997. https://www.pbs.org/wgbh/pages/frontline/shows/race/interviews/ecleaver.html.

Gleijeses, Piero. *Conflicting Missions: Havana, Washington, and Africa, 1959–1976.* Chapel Hill: University of North Carolina Press, 2003.

———. *Visions of Freedom: Havana, Washington, Pretoria, and the Struggle for Southern Africa, 1976–1991.* Chapel Hill: University of North Carolina Press, 2013.

Gourevitch, Philip. *We Wish to Inform You That Tomorrow We Will Be Killed with Our Families: Stories From Rwanda.* New York: Farrar, Straus and Giroux, 1999.

Granville, Johanna. *The First Domino: International Decision Making during the Hungarian Crisis of 1956.* College Station: Texas A&M University Press, 2004.

Greitens, Sheena Chestnut. *Illicit: North Korea's Evolving Operations to Earn Hard Currency.* Washington, DC: Committee for Human Rights in North Korea, 2014.

Haggard, Stephan, and Marcus Noland. *Famine in North Korea: Markets, Aid, and Reform.* New York: Columbia University Press, 2007.

Hale, Christopher. "Multifunctional Juche: A Study of the Changing Dynamic between Juche and the State Constitution in North Korea." *Korea Journal* 42, no. 3 (Autumn 2002): 283–308.

Halliday, Jon. "North Korean Enigma." *New Left Review* 1, no. 127 (May–June 1981).

———. "The North Korean Model: Gaps and Questions." *World Development* 9, no. 9/10 (1981): 889–905.

Heo, Uk, and Terence Roehrig. *South Korea's Rise: Economic Development, Power, and Foreign Relations.* New York: Cambridge University Press, 2014.

Herf, Jeffrey. "Undeclared Wars on Israel: East Germany and the West German Far Left 1967–1981: An Interview with Jeffrey Herf." *Fathom,* Spring 2017. http://fathomjournal.org/undeclared-wars-on-israel-east-germany-and-the-west-german-far-left-1967–1981-an-interview-with-jeffrey-herf/.

———. *Undeclared Wars with Israel: East Germany and the West German Far Left, 1967–1989.* Cambridge: Cambridge University Press, 2015.

Hong, Young-sun. *Cold War Germany, the Third World, and the Global Humanitarian Regime.* New York: Cambridge University Press, 2015.

Horne, John, and Garry Whannel. *Understanding the Olympics.* New York and London: Routledge, 2016.

Ingiriis, Mohamed Haji. *The Suicidal State in Somalia: The Rise and Fall of the Siad Barre Regime.* Lanham, MD: University Press of America, 2016.

Jones, Howard. *Bay of Pigs.* New York: Oxford University Press, 2008.

Keller, Renata. *Mexico's Cold War: Cuba, the United States, and the Legacy of the Mexican Revolution.* New York: Cambridge University Press, 2015.

Kim, Cheehyung. *Heroes and Toilers: Work as Life in Postwar North Korea, 1953–1961.* New York: Columbia University Press, 2018.

Kim, Ji Hyung. "1980 nyŏndae ch'o nambukhanŭi che3segye oegyogyŏngjaeng: konggae oegyomunsŏ(1979–1981)rŭl chungsimŭro." *Tongbugayŏn'gu* 28, no. 1 (2013): 5–35.

Kim, Jiyoung. "The Politics of Foreign Aid in North Korea." *Korean Journal of International Studies* 12, no. 2 (December 2014): 425–50.

Kim, Samuel S. "Pyongyang, the Third World, and Global Politics." In *The Two Koreas in World Politics,* edited by Jae-Kyu Park, B. C. Koh, and Tae-hwan Kwak. Boulder, CO: Westview Press, 1987.

Kim, Suk-Young. *Illusive Utopia: Theater, Film, and Everyday Performance in North Korea.* Ann Arbor: University of Michigan Press, 2010.

Kim, Sung Chull. *North Korea under Kim Jong Il: From Consolidation to Systemic Dissonance.* Albany: State University of New York Press, 2006.

Kim, Suzy. "Mothers and Maidens: Gendered Formation of Revolutionary Heroes in North Korea." *Journal of Korean Studies* 19, no. 2 (Fall 2014): 257–89.

Kim, Taehwan. "North Korea's Independent Policy Line and Its Relationship with the Third World, Beijing, and Moscow." *East Asian Review* 1, no. 3 (1989).

Kim, Youn-soo. "The Policies of Both Korean Governments towards the Third World 1945–1980: Nonaligned Nations as the Key Actor." *Koreanische Studien* 5 (1980): 32–57.

Kirkwood, Meghan Laurel Elizabeth. "Postcolonial Architecture through North Korean Modes: Namibian Commissions of the Mansudae Overseas Project." MA thesis in Art History, University of Kansas, 2011. https://kuscholarworks.ku.edu/bitstream/handle/1808/10702/Kirkwood_ku_0099M_11463_DATA_1.pdf;sequence=1.

Koh, B. C. "'Military-First Politics' and Building a 'Powerful and Prosperous Nation' in North Korea." NAPSNet Policy Forum, April 14, 2005. https://nautilus.org/napsnet/napsnet-policy-forum/military-first-politics-and-building-a-powerful-and-prosperous-nation-in-north-korea/.

———. "North Korea and Its Quest for Autonomy." *Pacific Affairs* 38, no. 3/4 (Autumn-Winter, 1965–1966): 294–306.

Kotkin, Stephen. *Magnetic Mountain: Stalinism as a Civilization.* Berkeley: University of California Press, 1995.

———. "Modern Times: The Soviet Union and the Interwar Conjuncture." *Kritika: Explorations in Russian and Eurasian History* 2, no. 1 (Winter 2001), New Series: 111–64.

Kwon, Heonik, and Byung-Ho Chun. *North Korea: Beyond Charismatic Politics.* Plymouth, UK: Rowman & Littlefield, 2012.

Lankov, Andrei. *From Stalin to Kim Il Sung: The Formation of North Korea, 1945–1960.* New Brunswick, NJ: Rutgers University Press, 2002.

Lee, Aie-Rie, Hyun-chool Lee, Ji-Yong Lee, and Il-Gi Kim. "The Paradox of North Korea's Ideological Radicalism: Shaky Social Basis of Strengthening Ideological Campaigns." *North Korean Review* 5, no. 1 (Spring 2009): 46–61.

Lee, Manwoo. "North Korea and Latin America." In *The Foreign Relations of North Korea: New Perspectives,* edited by Jae-Kyu Park, B. C. Koh, and Tae-hwan Kwak. Boulder, CO: Westview Press, 1987.

Lee, Sangsook. "1980nyŏndae ch'o oegyo hwan'gyŏng pyŏnhwawa pukhanŭi aungsan t'erŏ." *Tamnon 201* 19, no. 3 (2016): 83–110.

Lee, Sin Jae. "Battle between the Two Koreas in Vietnam: An Analysis of Participation in the Vietnam War by the North Korean Psychological Warfare Unit and Propaganda Leaflets." *S/N Korean Humanities* 4, no. 1 (March 2018): 75–97.

Leone, Dario. "An Unknown Story from the Yom Kippur War: Israeli F-4s vs. North Korean MiG-21s." *The Aviationist*, June 24, 2013. https://theaviationist.com/2013/06/24/iaf-f-4-vs-nk-mig21/#.UcmblT773kM.

Lerner, Mitchell. "The Domestic Origins of the Second Korean War: New Evidence from Communist Bloc Archives." *Seoul Journal of Korean Studies* 31, no. 1 (June 2018): 75–98.

———. *The* Pueblo *Incident: A Spy Ship and the Failure of American Foreign Policy.* Lawrence, KS: University Press of Kansas, 2002.

Lewis, I. M. *Blood and Bone: The Call of Kinship in Somali Society*. Trenton, NJ: Red Sea Press, 1994.

Li, Yuk-Sa, ed. *JUCHE!: The Speeches and Writings of Kim Il Sung*. New York: Grossman Publishers, 1972.

Liu, Hong. "Constructing a China Metaphor: Sukarno's Perception of the PRC and Indonesia's Political Transformation." *Journal of Southeast Asian Studies* 28, no. 1 (1997): 27–46.

Lovell, Julia. *Maoism: A Global History*. London: Bodley Head, 2019.

Mark, Chi-kwan. *The Everyday Cold War: Britain and China, 1950–1972*. Sydney, Australia: Bloomsbury Publishing, 2017.

Markakis, John. "Radical Military Regimes in the Horn of Africa." In *Military Marxist Regimes in Africa,* edited by John Markakis and Michael Waller. London: Routledge, 2013.

Martin, Bradley K. *Under the Loving Care of the Fatherly Leader.* New York: Thomas Dunne Books, 2004.

Matusevich, Maxim. *No Easy Row for a Russian Hoe: Ideology and Pragmatism in Nigerian-Soviet Relations.* Trenton, NJ: Africa World Press, 2003.

McNair, John. "Winning Friends, Influencing People: Soviet Cultural Diplomacy in Australia, 1928–1968." *Australian Journal of Politics and History* 61, no. 4 (November 2015): 515–29.

McVey, Ruth T. "Indonesian Communism and China." In *China in Crisis, Volume 2: China's Policies in Asia and America's Alternatives*, edited by Bingdi He, Tang Tsou, and Ping-ti Ho. Chicago: University of Chicago Press, 1968.

Mehilli, Elidor. *From Stalin to Mao: Albania in the Socialist World.* Ithaca: Cornell University Press, 2017.

Mertha, Andrew. *Brothers in Arms: Chinese Aid to the Khmer Rouge, 1975–1979.* Ithaca: Cornell University Press, 2014.

Morgenthau, Hans J. *Politics among Nations: The Struggle for Power and Peace.* New York: A. A. Knopf, 1948.

Muehlenbeck, Philip. *Czechoslovakia in Africa, 1945–1968.* New York: Palgrave Macmillan, 2016.

Nemzer, Louis. "The Soviet Friendship Societies." *Public Opinion Quarterly* 13, No. 2 (Summer 1949): 265–84.

Nichols, John Spicer. "Effects of International Propaganda on U.S.-Cuba Relations." In *Communication in Latin America: Journalism, Mass Media, and Society*, edited by Richard R. Cole. Wilmington, DE: Scholarly Resources, 1996.

Nye, Joseph S., Jr. "Public Diplomacy and Soft Power." *Annals of the American Academy of Political and Social Science* 616 (March 2008): 94–109.

Oberdorfer, Dan, and Robert Carlin. *The Two Koreas: A Contemporary History.* New York: Basic Books, 2014.

Oh, Kong Dan. "Leadership Change in North Korean Politics: The Succession to Kim Il Sung." *RAND*, October 1988. https://apps.dtic.mil/dtic/tr/fulltext/u2/a216962.pdf.

———. "North Korea in 1989: Touched by Winds of Change?" *Asian Survey* 30, no. 1 (January 1990): 74–80.

Olu, S. Agbi. "Africa and Korean Foreign Relations, 1948–84: A Historical Perspective." *Korean Journal of International Studies* 17, no. 1 (Winter 1985–1986): 37–74.

Park, Jae Kyu. "A Critique on 'The Democratic Confederal Republic of Koryo.'" *Journal of East and West Studies* 12, no. 1 (1983): 13–25.

———. "North Korea's Political and Economic Relations with China and the Soviet Union: From 1954 to 1980." *Comparative Strategy* 4, no. 3 (1984): 273–305.

Park, Jae-kyu, Byung Chul Koh, and Tae-Hwan Kwak, eds. *The Foreign Relations of North Korea: New Perspectives.* Boulder, CO: Westview Press, 1987.

Person, James F. "The 1967 Purge of the Gapsan Faction and Establishment of the Monolithic Ideological System." NKIDP e-Dossier no. 15, December 14, 2013. https://www.wilsoncenter.org/publication/the-1967-purge-the-gapsan-faction-and-establishment-the-monolithic-ideological-system.

Plunk, Daryl. "North Korea: Exporting Terrorism." Heritage Foundation's Asian Studies Center's Backgrounder no. 74 (February 25, 1988). http://www.heritage.org/node/21848/print-display.

Prashad, Vijay. *The Darker Nations: A People's History of the Third World.* New York: New Press, 2008.

Pribbenow, Merle. *North Korean Pilots in the Skies over Vietnam.* Wilson Center NKIDP e-Dossier no. 2, November 2011. https://www.wilsoncenter.org/publication/north-korean-pilots-the-skies-over-vietnam.

———. "North Korean Psychological Warfare Operations in South Vietnam." In *"A New Chapter" on North Korea.* Wilson Center Sources and Methods blog, March 19, 2018. https://www.wilsoncenter.org/blog-post/north-korean-psychological-warfare-operations-south-vietnam#_ftn1.

Ra, Jong-yil. *Aungsan t'erŏrisŭt'ŭ kangminch'ŏl.* Seoul: Changbi Publishers, 2013.

Radchenko, Sergey S. *The Soviet Union and the North Korean Seizure of the USS* Pueblo*: Evidence from Russian Archives.* Wilson Center Cold War International History Working Paper no. 47 (2011). https://www.wilsoncenter.org/publication/the-soviet-union-and-the-north-korean-seizure-the-uss-pueblo-evidence-russian-archives.

Reed, Edward P. "Is Saemaul Undong a Model for Developing Countries Today?" Paper prepared for International Symposium in Commemoration of the 40th Anniversary of Saemaul Undong, hosted by the Korea Saemaul Undong Center, 2010. https://asiafoundation.org/resources/pdfs/SaemaulUndongReedSept2010FINAL.pdf .

Robinson, Joan. "Korean Miracle." *Monthly Review* 16, no. 8 (January 1965), 541–49.

Roosa, John. *Pretext for Mass Murder: The September 30th Movement and Suharto's Coup d'État in Indonesia.* Madison: University of Wisconsin Press, 2006.

Ryang, Sonia. "Gender in Oblivion: Women in the Democratic People's Republic of Korea (North Korea)." *Journal of Asian & African Studies* 35, no. 3 (2000): 323–49.

Salisbury, Harrison E. *To Peking and Beyond: A Report on the New Asia.* New York: New York Times Book Company, 1973.

Sauvy, Alfred. "Trois mondes, une planète." *L'Observateur*, August 14, 1952.

Savada, Andrea Matles, ed. *North Korea: A Country Study.* Washington, DC: GPO for the Library of Congress, 1993. http://countrystudies.us/north-korea/.

Scalapino, Robert A., and Chong-sik Lee. *Communism in Korea.* Berkeley: University of California Press, 1972.

Schmid, Andre. "Historicizing North Korea: State Socialism, Population Mobility, and Cold War Historiography." *American Historical Review* 123, no. 2 (April 2018): 439–62.

Seong, Sang-Hwan. "Korean-German Relations from the 1950s to the 1980s: Archive-Based Approach to Cold War–Era History." In *Encounters between Germany and Korea: Affinity in Culture and Politics since the 1880s,* edited by Joanne Miyang Cho and Lee M. Roberts. New York: Palgrave MacMillan, 2017.

Setiyawan, Dahlia Gratia. *The Cold War in the City of Heroes: U.S.-Indonesian Relations and Anti-Communist Operations in Surabaya, 1963–1965*. PhD diss., UCLA, 2014.

Shaw, Meredith. " 'Maehok'—Rosalynn Carter Encounters the Great Leader." North Korean Literature in English, blog, September 20, 2016. http://dprklit.blogspot.com/2016/09/maehok-rosalynn-carter-encounters-great.html.

Shimazu, Naoko. "Diplomacy as Theatre: Staging the Bandung Conference of 1955." *Modern Asian Studies* 48, no. 1 (2014): 225–52.

Shin, David W. *Rationality in the North Korean Regime: Understanding the Kims' Strategy of Provocation*. Lanham, MD: Rowman & Littlefield, 2018.

Shin, Gi-Wook, and Kyung Moon Hwang, eds. *Contentious Gwangju: The May 18th Uprising in Korea's Past and Present.* Oxford, UK: Rowman and Littlefield, 2003.

Smith, Tony. "New Bottles for New Wine: A Pericentric Framework for the Study of the Cold War." *Diplomatic History* 24, no. 4 (Fall 2000): 567–91.

Song, Jiyoung. *Human Rights Discourse in North Korea: Post-Colonial, Marxist, and Confucian Perspectives*. New York: Routledge, 2011.

Steinhoff, Patricia. "Kidnapped Japanese in North Korea: The New Left Connection." *Journal of Japanese Studies* 30, no. 1 (Winter, 2004): 123–42.

Szalontai, Balazs. "In the Shadow of Vietnam: A New Look at North Korea's Militant Strategy, 1962–1970." *Journal of Cold War Studies* 14, no. 4 (Fall 2012): 122–66.

———. *Kim Il Sung in the Khrushchev Era: Soviet-DPRK Relations and the Roots of North Korean Despotism, 1953–1964*. Washington, DC: Woodrow Wilson Center Press; Stanford, CA: Stanford University Press, 2006.

Szalontai, Balazs, and Sergey Radchenko. *North Korea's Efforts to Acquire Nuclear Technology and Nuclear Weapons: Evidence from Russian and Hungarian Archives*. Wilson Center Cold War International History Project Working Paper no. 53 (August 2006). https://www.wilsoncenter.org/publication/north-koreas-efforts-to-acquire-nuclear-technology-and-nuclear-weapons-evidence-russian.

Taylor, Moe. " 'One Hand Can't Clap': Guyana and North Korea, 1974–1985." *Journal of Cold War Studies* 17, no. 1 (Winter 2015): 41–63.

———. " 'Only a Disciplined People Can Build a Nation': North Korean Mass Games and Third Worldism in Guyana, 1980–1992." *Asia-Pacific Journal* 13, issue 4, no.2 (January 26, 2015). https://apjjf.org/2015/13/4/Moe-Taylor/4258.html.

Tertitskiy, Fyodor. *Kimilsŏng Ijŏnŭi Puk'an: 1945Nyŏn 8Wŏl 9Il Soryŏn-gun Ch'amjŏnbut'ŏ 10Wŏl 14Il P'yŏngyang Yŏnsŏlkkaji.* Seoul: Hanul Academy, 2018.

———. "1967: Transition to Absolute Autocracy in North Korea." In *Change and Continuity in North Korean Politics*, edited by Adam Cathcart, Robert Winstanley-Chesters, and Christopher K. Green. New York: Routledge, 2017.

"Tyranny of the Weak: Part of a Decade Long Pattern?" *DailyNK.com,* February 20, 2017. https://www.dailynk.com/english/tyranny-of-the-weak-part-of-a-deca/.

Üngör, Çağdaş. "Reaching the Distant Comrade: Chinese Communist Propaganda Abroad (1949–1976)." PhD diss., SUNY Binghamton, 2009.

Vu, Tuong. *Vietnam's Communist Revolution: The Power and Limits of Ideology*. Cambridge: Cambridge University Press, 2017.

Wada Haruki. *Kim Il Sung gwa Manju Hangil Chŏnjaeng*. Seoul: Changbi, 1992.

Wanandi, Jusuf. *Shades of Grey: A Political Memoir of Modern Indonesia, 1965–1998*. Singapore: Equinox Publishing, 2012.

Weis, Toni. "The Politics Machine: On the Concept of 'Solidarity' in East German Support for SWAPO." *Journal of Southern African Studies* 37, no. 2 (2011).

Westad, Odd Arne. *The Global Cold War: Third World Interventions and the Making of Our Times*. Cambridge, New York: Cambridge University Press, 2007.

Winger, Gregory. "Prospect Theory and Civil–Military Conflict: The Case of the 1976 Korean Axe Murder Incident." *Armed Forces & Society* 43, no. 4 (October 2017): 734–57.

Winstanley-Chesters, Robert. *Environment, Politics, and Ideology in North Korea: Landscape as Political Project*. Lanham, MD: Lexington Books, 2014.

Woo, Jung-en. *Race to the Swift: State and Finance in Korean Industrialization*. New York: Columbia University Press, 1991.

Young, Benjamin R. "Cultural Diplomacy with North Korean Characteristics: Pyongyang's Exportation of the Mass Games to the Third World, 1972–1996." *International History Review* 42, no. 3 (2020): 543–55.

———. "An Emotional Relationship: Trust, Admiration, and Fear in North Korea–Zimbabwe Relations, 1976–1988." *S/N Korean Humanities* 4, no. 2 (September 2018): 129–49.

———."How North Korean Ads in Western Newspapers Backfired." *NK News*, September 27, 2013. http://www.nknews.org/2013/09/how-north-koreans-ads-in-western-newspapers-backfired/.

———. "Juche in the United States: The Black Panther Party's Relations with North Korea, 1969–1971." *Asia-Pacific Journal* 13, issue 12, no. 2 (March 30, 2015). http:// japanfocus.org/-Benjamin-Young/4303.

———. "North Korea's Unlikely Alliance with German Environmentalists." *NK News*, June 12, 2015. https://www.nknews.org/2015/06/north-koreas-unlikely-alliance-with-german-environmentalists/.

———. "North Korea's Unlikely History with Black Radicals." *Black Perspectives*. April 11, 2019. https://www.aaihs.org/north-koreas-unlikely-history-with-black-radicals/.

———. "Not There for the Nutmeg: North Korean Advisors in Grenada and Pyongyang's Internationalism, 1979–1983." *Cross-Currents: East Asian History and Culture Review* no. 27 (June 2018): 113–35.

Young, Namkoong. "A Comparative Study on North and South Korean Economic Capability." *Journal of East Asian Affairs* 9, no. 1 (1995): 1–43.

Zakharova, Liudmila. "Economic Cooperation between Russia and North Korea: New Goals and New Approaches." *Journal of Eurasian Studies* 7, no. 2 (July 2016): 151–61.

Zhihua, Shen. *Mao, Stalin and the Korean War: Trilateral Communist Relations in the 1950s*. London: Routledge, 2013.

Zhihua, Shen, and Yafeng Xia. *China and the Post-War Reconstruction of North Korea, 1953–1961*. Wilson Center NKIDP Working Paper no. 4 (May 2012). https://www.wilsoncenter.org/publication/china-and-the-post-war-reconstruction-north-korea-1953-1961.

———. *A Misunderstood Friendship: Mao Zedong, Kim Il-sung, and Sino–North Korean Relations, 1949–1976*. New York: Columbia University Press, 2018.

Index

COLD WAR
INTERNATIONAL HISTORY
PROJECT SERIES

Edited by James G. Hershberg

Between Containment and Rollback: The United States and the Cold War in Germany
Christian F. Ostermann
2021

The Whole World Was Watching: Sport in the Cold War
Edited by Robert Edelman and Christopher Young
2019

Trust, but Verify: The Politics of Uncertainty and the Transformation of the Cold War Order, 1969–1991
Edited by Martin Klimke, Reinhild Kreis, and Christian F. Ostermann
2016

Jimmy Carter in Africa: Race and the Cold War
Nancy Mitchell
2016

The Euromissile Crisis and the End of the Cold War
Edited by Leopoldo Nuti, Frédéric Bozo, Marie-Pierre Rey, and Bernd Rother
2015

The Regional Cold Wars in Europe, East Asia, and the Middle East: Crucial Periods and Turning Points
Edited by Lorenz Lüthi
2015

Poland's War on Radio Free Europe, 1950–1989
Paweł Machcewicz, translated by Maya Latynski
2015

Divided Together: The United States and the Soviet Union in the United Nations, 1945–1965
Ilya V. Gaiduk
2013

Battleground Africa: Cold War in the Congo, 1960–1965
Lise Namikas
2013

A full list of titles in the Cold War International History Project series is available online at www.sup.org/cwihp.